W9-AYZ-514

The Government and Politics of Postcommunist Europe

THE Government AND Politics OF Postcommunist Europe

ANDREW A. MICHTA

PRAEGER

Westport, Connecticut
London

Library of Congress Cataloging-in-Publication Data

Michta, Andrew A.
    The government and politics of postcommunist Europe / Andrew A.
Michta.
        p.   cm.
    Includes bibliographical references and index.
    ISBN 0–275–94406–9 (hard : alk. paper) — ISBN 0–275–94866–8
(pbk.)
        1. Europe, Eastern—Politics and government—1989– 2. Post-
communism—Europe, Eastern. 3. Europe, Eastern—Politics and
government—1945–1989. I. Title.
JN96.A2M53 1994
320.947—dc20   93–43073

British Library Cataloguing in Publication Data is available.

Copyright © 1994 by Andrew A. Michta

All rights reserved. No portion of this book may
be reproduced, by any process or technique, without
the express written consent of the publisher.

Library of Congress Catalog Card Number: 93–43073
ISBN: 0–275–94406–9
        0–275–94866–8 (pbk.)

First published in 1994

Praeger Publishers, 88 Post Road West, Westport, CT 06881
An imprint of Greenwood Publishing Group, Inc.

Printed in the United States of America

∞™

The paper used in this book complies with the
Permanent Paper Standard issued by the National
Information Standards Organization (Z39.48–1984).

10 9 8 7 6 5 4 3 2 1

For Cristina and Chelsea

CONTENTS

ACKNOWLEDGMENTS

I wish to thank the United States Department of State for its research support under the Title VIII Grant Program. Special thanks go to Professor George Schwab of the CUNY Graduate Center, Dr. Richard F. Staar of the Hoover Institution, Professor Ilya Prizel of the Paul Nitze School of Advanced International Studies, and Professor Vojtech Mastny of the Johns Hopkins University Bologna Center for their encouragement throughout the project. I am very much indebted to Tadeusz K. Zachurski of the Radio Free Europe/Radio Liberty Polish Section in Washington, D.C., for his advice and assistance, and to Deborah Ross of Greenwood Publishing Group whose expertise once again made the production process simple and efficient.

I wish to extend special gratitude to Mertie and Robert Buckman of Memphis for their support of my research. I am grateful to Deborah Ventura of the Hoover Institution for her help during my stay at the Hoover Institution. My student assistants at Rhodes College, Laura Lindley, Jason Githens, Katherine Federline, and Caroline Lenac, are owed a special word of thanks, as is Brenda Somes, whose help in organizing my work at Rhodes College was invaluable.

Most of all, I want to thank my wife, Cristina, and my daughter, Chelsea, for their support and patience throughout this project.

The Government
and Politics
of Postcommunist Europe

INTRODUCTION

The idea of writing this book developed during my last six years of teaching an Eastern and Central European Politics course at Rhodes College. As the events of the post-1989 transformation in the former Soviet bloc accelerated, I was confronted with the dearth of up-to-date teaching material comprehensive enough to meet the course needs of an upper-level undergraduate international studies curriculum. Few of the studies now available on the market venture beyond the familiar retelling of the post–World War II communist takeovers in the region, their failure to transform the societies in light of powerful domestic resistance, and finally the spectacular collapse of communism throughout the Soviet bloc.

Although the process of change is still very fluid, sufficient time has passed to review the direction of political reform in the postcommunist states. This book charts the changes in postcommunist Europe. It offers an overview of the history and the communist legacy of each country while focusing on the new constitutional framework (where available), the principal political parties, and the economic, foreign, and security policies. Former Yugoslavia is treated differently because the ongoing war makes a systematic review impossible.

This book surveys political change in postcommunist Europe along the western periphery of the former Soviet empire. It covers four distinct regions: (1) East Central Europe (Poland, the Czech Republic, Slovakia, and Hungary), (2) the Balkans (Bulgaria, Romania, Slovenia, Croatia, "Third Yugoslavia," Macedonia, and Albania), (3) the Baltic Rim (Lithuania, Latvia, and Estonia), and (4) Eastern Europe (Belarus and Ukraine). This nomenclature departs from the political concept of Eastern Europe used during the half-century of Soviet ascendancy on the Continent by including in the discussion the newly restored Baltic states as well as Belarus and Ukraine as Europe's new eastern periphery. Even though the long-term viability of independent Belarus and Ukraine remains uncertain in light of the unpredictable outcome of the current crisis in Russia, their domestic and foreign policies are important enough factors in the region's postcommunist transformation to merit their inclusion.

The collapse of communism in the aftermath of the 1989 revolutions in Eastern Europe and the December 1991 demise of the Soviet Union has remade the international system. The end of bipolarity has brought forth the hitherto suppressed nationalism as a defining element of European politics. The violent implosion of Yugoslavia and the peaceful division of Czechoslovakia are two poignant reminders of nationalism's recrudescence on the Continent.

The resurgence of nationalism has not been confined to the former Soviet bloc. National divisions, albeit attenuated by the legacy of cooperation during the Cold War and the remaining economic and security structures, have reemerged in Western Europe as historical cleavages, casting a long shadow over the near-term prospects for the Continent's supranational integration. The 1993 demise of the European Exchange Rate Mechanism and the widespread popular resistance in Western Europe to the Maastricht Treaty are but the most visible symptoms of the terrific problems lying in the path of the pan-European vision. Nationalism has become anew an increasingly important issue in European politics, replacing the great ideological contest between liberal democracy and communism that had defined Europe's geopolitics for over fifty years.

In the newly independent postcommunist states, nationalism has proven especially powerful, for it has been nurtured by the collectivist ideology of communism. Although communist theory has claimed to be governed by an internationalist perspective, its residual impact on communist states in Europe has been to reaffirm the primacy of the group over the individual and group allegiance over individual rights, contributing to the ease with which nationalism replaced communism. Other factors, such as the historical predominance of the German concept of the state as the formula for national self-realization (with its emphasis on the mythological *Volk*), have also contributed to the strength of resurgent nationalism in postcommunist states. The ethnic heterogeneity of the newly independent states (Poland, Czech Republic, Hungary, and Slovenia are the only ethnically homogeneous postcommunist nation-states today) has fueled ethnic strife as national groups interspersed across the region strive to reconnect with their ethnic core. Under these formidable pressures attendant to nation building, the postcommunist states have undertaken to make the radical transformation from totalitarianism and command economy to democracy and capitalism. It is not surprising, therefore, that reform in postcommunist Europe has suffered reversals or, in some cases, has failed outright. The diverse region is composed of nations with different cultures and histories that are today confronted by the common intractable task of overcoming the legacy of half a century of communism.

Western scholarship has little experience with the politics of postcommunist transition, for the very swiftness of the Soviet empire's collapse caught the academic community unprepared. We learn as we observe the growing pains of Europe's new democracies that the past axioms, such as the unremitting Polish-German hostility or the alleged unacceptability of armed conflict in Europe, are discounted by new cooperation in Central Europe and the most vicious fighting the Balkans have seen in half a century. Old animosities, irredentist claims, and ethnic feuds are played out against the background of a qualitatively new and uneven integrationist current, most readily apparent in the northern part of the region but reaching as far south as the newly independent Slovenian state.

The experience of postcommunist Europe must be set against its broader continental context. Freed from its Cold War divisions Europe is now reverting to its historical pattern of power distribution, as old alliances devolve away from the previously shared common purpose. Reunified Germany, albeit still tied down by the process of rebuilding its five eastern *Länder*, is poised to emerge eventually as the leader of the new *Mitteleuropa*. Concurrently, the relative influence of the United States has diminished, as the need for American security guarantees to Western Europe against Soviet aggression evaporated with the implosion and decomposition of Soviet power. The growing confusion within the ranks of the North Atlantic Treaty Organization (NATO) over the alliance's new mission is but the most apparent indication of how profoundly the end of the Cold War has transformed Europe's security framework. The manifest consensus among key Western European democracies that the Balkan wars ought to be contained, rather than brought to an end through direct allied intervention on the ground, may have foreshadowed the new European order.

Europe's geopolitical divisions since 1991 have shifted in two directions: (1) the East-West division of the Cold War era has been replaced by a new fault line that now separates the developed northwestern core of Europe from its southeastern periphery, and (2) Central Europe has reemerged as a distinct region combining both developed Western democracies and some postcommunist states. The Western policy of containment against the threat of possible greater instability generated by the Balkan war, pursued by the European Community (EC) and NATO since 1990, has raised questions about the eventual integration of East Central European postcommunist states with the West. Moscow's steadfast objection to expanding NATO eastward and the West's apparent willingness to abide by Russian wishes have become key political obstacles to extending membership in the alliance to selected postcommunist states. The West's steadfast refusal to intervene decisively in the Balkans has defined in practical terms the scope of its strategic interests. As in 1918 and 1945, the new geopolitical divides in Europe are drawn not by idealistic enlightened diplomacy but by the actions of states based on the perception of national interest and on the overall power distribution on the Continent.

In postcommunist Europe cultural and historical factors, rather than the existing state boundaries, define regional divisions and national identities. These countries evolved in the context of multinational empires, the former Soviet Union being the last. The distinct political cultures inherited from the imperial past are again important factors in the reconstitution of postcommunist Europe. Religion is one category that has historically formed the identity of peoples in central, eastern, and southeastern Europe. Today this old fault line has again separated Europe's historically Catholic people from the Greek Orthodox and the nations where Islam was for centuries the dominant faith. The division reflects the heritage of nations that were dominated in the past by (1) Poland-Lithuania and the Habsburg empire, (2) the Romanov empire, and (3) the Ottoman empire. In the case of Latvia and Estonia, the impact of Protestant Germany and Sweden is also visible.

Postcommunist Europe is a collection of very different states, which nevertheless share broad patterns of common historical experience. Historically often at odds with each other, these nations have borrowed from each other even as they fought. For example, the early Ukrainian Cossack state, although at war with the Commonwealth of Poland-Lithuania, borrowed heavily from the Commonwealth's institutional model to build its own administration. Between the fourteenth and eighteenth centuries Silesia was nominally part of the Crown of St. Wenceslaus, and hence Czech territory, even though it was being administered by the Habsburgs. The beginning of Christianity in Poland, Hungary, and the Czech Lands was similar, as was the adoption of Christianity by Croatia. The language and culture of Belorussia, while rooted in the indigenous tradition, owes as much to Polish culture as it does to Russian and Ukrainian influences. Lithuanians and Latvians share past influences of Polish, German, and Swedish cultures, and so forth. These shared historical experiences are highlighted not to imply that the postcommunist nations lack distinct national heritage; far from it, as the region is defined by diversity par excellence, both ethnically and culturally. However, the four regions that serve as a grid for this book, while sharing a broad commonality of experience, have each their own heritage to differentiate among them. One can speak of areas of postcommunist Europe where Turkish influences historically dominated the process of nation formation, those where Russian autocracy was a defining element, or those where Western heritage was the strongest. The distinctions are not always precise, for one could argue for example that the Belorussians have been influenced equally by the Grand Duchy of Lithuania and by the Romanov empire.

The rigorous adoption of the cultural-historical criteria, however, raises a number of issues relevant to the discipline of international studies. First, the cultural-historical perspective often cuts across the commonly accepted geopolitical regions of Europe. For example, it makes Lithuania clearly a significant part of East Central Europe, as the Lithuanians share their Catholic heritage with the Poles, Czechs, Slovaks, Hungarians, Slovenes, and Croats. However, it leaves the Baltic states of Latvia and Estonia on the periphery where Scandinavia, Eastern Europe, and East Central Europe meet. Likewise, in the Balkans, the "Habsburg states" of Slovenia and Croatia fall outside the Turkish Europe of rump Yugoslavia, Macedonia, Bulgaria, and Romania. Finally, Eastern Europe is now expanded to include Belarus and Ukraine, with the admittedly controversial exclusion of Russia, which is treated here as a Eurasian rather than a strictly European power. Therefore, for the purpose of structural clarity, in this book geographic considerations have been given coequal weight with historical and cultural factors.

The criteria for determining the geopolitics of postcommunist Europe must also include the speed of political and economic change since 1990. The divergent paths of reform constitute additional differences within the new subregions. Since 1990 the East Central European states of Poland, the Czech Republic, Slovakia, and Hungary (the so-called Visegrad Group) as well as Slovenia and possibly Croatia have made the greatest progress toward market capitalism. These states stand first in line for possible future membership in the European Union and NATO if these open up to new states. Among the northeastern and eastern Europeans, Estonia and Latvia have undergone a substantial transformation, with Lithuania lagging behind. On the other hand, Belarus and Ukraine have continued to decline economically, with political reform very much in its initial stages. In the Balkans, Bulgaria has shown signs of progress toward democracy and a market economy, while Romania, rump Yugoslavia, Macedonia, and Albania have stagnated.

The outside influence of great powers on postcommunist Europe must also be considered. Historically, Germany and Russia have dominated its politics. Since 1990 the Federal Republic of Germany has played an important role as a unifying force and the principal source of capital for investment and economic restructuring in the region, especially in its strong relations to the Visegrad Group. Beginning in early 1992 Russia has increasingly reasserted itself along its western periphery. Since then Belarus has concluded a new defense treaty with Russia, as well as a number of cooperative economic agreements, including the agreement to bring Belarus into the Russian ruble zone. Moscow has also put considerable pressure on Kiev, demanding concessions on security and territorial issues, including the transfer of all Ukrainian nuclear weapons to Russia and the lease of Ukraine's naval facilities in Sevastopol. In 1993 the Russian government used very effectively the threat of an energy embargo against Ukraine to drive its demands home. The relationship between Russia and Ukraine remains precarious, with Moscow visibly determined to maintain influence in Ukraine on account of the 300-year-long history of common statehood and the eleven-million-strong ethnic Russian minority living in the Donets (Donbas) Basin in eastern Ukraine.

The once grey and predictable communist Eastern Europe has been swept aside by its resurgent nationalism and by the efforts of the postcommunist successor states to define their political systems, to revive their moribund economies, and to provide for the security of their people. Ethnic wars, labor strife, irredentism, and confusion have become the hallmark of the emerging new order in postcommunist Europe. Much progress has been made toward stability in places where governments managed to push ethnonationalism to the back room of their agenda, but even the ethnically homogeneous states have suffered reversals in their reform effort, as evidenced by the fall 1993 communist electoral victory in Poland.

Postcommunist Europe is in the midst of a profound political and economic transformation. As if determined to make up for the half-century lost to the totalitarian bolshevik experiment, the societies of what once was the Soviet bloc strive to redefine themselves as (1) viable polities, (2) sustainable communities, (3) market economies, and (4) modern-day nation-states. These four directions of the current restructuring in former communist Eastern Europe, as well as their impact on Europe as a whole, constitute the guiding theme of this book.

I

EAST CENTRAL EUROPE

1

POLAND

THE COMMONWEALTH OF POLAND-LITHUANIA AND THE SECOND REPUBLIC

The historical Polish state, the largest of the Western Slavic kingdoms, dates back to A.D. 966 when Christianity was brought to the country through the marriage of Polish Duke Mieszko I to Czech Princess Dobrava. The millennium of the Polish state witnessed the country's rise to the pinnacle of power in Central Europe in the late fifteenth century, after its union with Lithuania established the multinational Commonwealth of Poland-Lithuania, including the territories of Poland proper (the so-called Crown) and the Grand Duchy of Lithuania, encompassing also present-day Ukraine, Belorussia, and the southern parts of Latvia. Nurtured by grain exports from its vast estates worked by enserfed peasants, the Polish nobility prided itself on the country's administrative decentralization and the "golden freedoms" that severely circumscribed the executive powers of the king.[1]

By the Middle Ages the country had created a unique parliamentary system, whereby the nobility enjoyed a wide range of civil rights, including the right to elect the king. The parliament (*Sejm*) was the principal institution of the country's government. The nobles (*szlachta*) elected their sovereign and voted on taxes in peacetime and in war according to the precept of "nothing about us without us." The "golden freedoms" of the Polish nobility were ultimately guaranteed by the right of *liberum veto*, by which each citizen could stop legislation deemed detrimental to his rights. Increasingly an anachronism in European politics at a time when centralized state power and absolute monarchy prevailed, the Commonwealth of Poland-Lithuania declined in the seventeenth and eighteenth centuries in the wake of Cossack uprisings in the east, invasions from the north and the south, and the military pressure on its borders from imperial Russia, Germany, and the Habsburg Empire. Paralyzed by internal squabbles and manipulated from without, the Commonwealth of Poland-Lithuania disappeared from the map of Europe in 1795 after a failed uprising led by Tadeusz Kosciuszko, a hero of the American revolutionary war.

The country's territory was divided up among Russia, Germany, and Austria, and for the following 123 years, until the creation of the Second Republic, the Polish-Lithuanian state ceased to exist. The modern Polish national identity was seared by the experience of outside domination and evolved in the context of multinational empires. Still, the memory of the glorious past lived on, nurtured by the Polish insurrectionary tradition. In the nineteenth century the Poles rose twice against Russian control, in 1830 and 1863, but both insurrections were suppressed.

Poland reemerged as an independent state in 1918 after World War I brought down the three empires that had controlled its territory for over a century. The collapse of the Romanov empire in the east, followed by the 1917 Russian Revolution and the defeat of Germany and Austria-Hungary by the Entente, created a historic opportunity for the Poles to reestablish their state in the power vacuum of Central Europe. As one of the successor states of World War I, Poland would face the intractable challenge of building a cohesive nation out of the remnants of the vanquished empires.

Led by Marshal Jozef Pilsudski, the restored Second Republic (*Druga Rzeczpospolita*) was a weak multiethnic state in which the Poles constituted only some 60 percent of its twenty-seven million citizens. Interwar Poland included large Ukrainian and Belorussian minorities, as well as Lithuanians, Germans, and about three million Jews. Pilsudski attempted to reclaim the territory of the historic Commonwealth through a 1919–1920 alignment with the nascent Ukrainian state. The Polish military campaign in the east ended in disaster, with the country barely escaping destruction at the hands of the invading Red Army.

Since Bolshevik Russia had temporarily withdrawn from European politics, the Second Republic was compelled to play great-power politics in Central Europe as the best ally France had to balance Germany's resurgent might in the east. The political fragmentation and the weakness of Poland's democratic institutions, combined with intractable economic problems and the rising international tension, ultimately undermined the very foundations of the country's parliamentary system. In 1926 a coup led by Pilsudski ushered in a period of authoritarian rule that continued in Poland until World War II. Throughout the interwar period Poland's economy remained predominantly agricultural, with the majority of the population living in rural areas. The government attempted several successful state-supported industrialization programs, in large part to shore up the country's fledgling defense industry, but the arrival of the Great Depression in the 1930s effectively stymied a more balanced industrialization.

The resurgence of the Russian empire under Stalin's communist leadership and the rise of Nazi Germany placed Poland in an untenable geopolitical position. Determined to resist Hitler's territorial demands, Poland was also rightly suspicious of Soviet offers of assistance. Faced with an impossible choice, Poland put its faith in the hollow British and French security guarantees. In 1939 Poland put up a desperate and ultimately futile resistance to the German military machine and the Soviet invader. Within a few weeks, the Second Republic was erased from the map of Europe, partitioned once more by its historical enemies Germany and Russia, as stipulated by the Ribbentrop-Molotov secret protocol.

The experience of defeat in 1939 and the trauma of six years of German occupation—Poland lost over six million of its citizens—left the economy devastated and the population exhausted by the ordeal. Although nominally one of the victorious Allied powers, Poland emerged from the war as a defeated and occupied country. Stalin's decision to rely on the empire for Russia's security meant that Poland would not be allowed to regain its prewar sovereignty. The Soviets set up a communist government, which after the stolen election of 1947 became firmly entrenched in power. Secret police terror against all potential opposition followed. The Poles were forced to restructure their economy after the Soviet pattern, with an emphasis on heavy industry, although the peasants successfully resisted the government's pressure for collectivization.

COMMUNIST LEGACY

Communism defined Poland's domestic politics, economic development, and foreign policy for half a century, from 1945 through 1989. During that time Poland developed heavy industry, especially coal mining, steel production, and shipbuilding as part of the "division of labor" within the Council for Mutual Economic Assistance (COMECON), set up by Moscow in 1949 to harness the resources of its East European clients. In the course of industrialization, the majority of Poland's employment shifted from agriculture to industry. However, most of the employees of the large state-run enterprises were first-generation workers. They retained their strong peasant roots, including their religious faith and loyalty to the Catholic Church. In effect, because the Catholic Church was not suppressed, the Polish United Workers' (Communist) Party (*Polska Zjednoczona Partia Robotnicza*; PZPR) never managed to win over the workers to the cause of building a "new society."

Poland proved the most difficult country for the Soviet Union to control. As the largest state in the Warsaw Pact after the U.S.S.R., with the largest non-Soviet Warsaw Pact army, Poland was essential to Soviet control over East Germany and continued influence in the West. During the half-century of communist domination, Poland remained overwhelmingly Catholic, steadfastly anticommunist, and staunchly anti-Russian. The Polish society's consistent rejection of communism, marked by recurrent crises in 1956, 1968, 1970, and 1976, was a powerful factor undermining the strength of the Soviet bloc. In the end, the 1980–1981 crisis in Poland and the rise of Solidarity proved instrumental in bringing down Stalin's East European empire.

Beginning with the 1956 Polish October, during which the hard-line Stalinist regime was replaced by the national communist group led by Wladyslaw Gomulka, the futility of the experiment to remake the Polish society in the image of the Soviet Union was ever more apparent. In 1956 Moscow conceded to the Polish communists a limited autonomy on domestic policy. The 1970 bloody riots at the Baltic Sea coast, which came two years after a series of student demonstrations in 1968, brought down Gomulka and forced the new regime of Edward Gierek to appease the workers' demands for a better living standard; by 1976 the workers had an effective veto power over governmental decisions when through a series of wildcat strikes they forced the communists to rescind food price increases. Throughout the communist era, the progressive political emancipation of the new working class became a uniquely Polish phenomenon.

The workers' determination in the 1970s to hold the regime accountable was a direct result of the deterioration of the economy. As a result of the failed economic modernization program pursued by the Gierek regime, which relied on Western credits to industrialize the country and increase consumption, Poland was quickly approaching bankruptcy. By the end of the decade Poland had accumulated a $30 billion foreign debt and exhausted all sources of Western credit. Again, the government's feeble attempt in August 1980 to balance the budget by increasing prices was met by a wave of sit-in strikes at the Baltic coast shipyards. This time the workers demanded not only economic restitution but also the creation of an independent trade union. After days of tortuous negotiations, the government capitulated to all the strikers' demands; the independent trade union "Solidarity" was born. A national coalition of workers, peasants, intellectuals, and the Catholic Church represented by Solidarity would chart the course of Polish politics for the next decade.

SOLIDARITY, THE NEW CIVIL SOCIETY, AND THE COLLAPSE OF COMMUNISM

During the sixteen months of Solidarity's independent existence, between its recognition by the regime in the early fall of 1980 until its December 1981 suppression under a martial law regime of General Wojciech Jaruzelski, Poland underwent a historic metamorphosis, with dramatic consequences for the entire Soviet bloc and for the politics of postcommunist Poland. For sixteen months the key Soviet client existed under the conditions of duality of political power.

Although Solidarity never formally claimed the powers of the government nor officially presented itself as an alternative political party, it became a great movement of national rebirth. Solidarity provided an umbrella that united all the forces of anticommunist opposition. The rise of Solidarity marked the implosion of the Polish United Workers' Party and the beginning of the anticommunist revolution. Although suppressed sixteen months later with the introduction of martial law by General Wojciech Jaruzelski, Solidarity endured as an idea that would ultimately accelerate the decomposition of the Soviet bloc.

The "self-limiting revolution"[2] of 1980 to 1981 remade the Polish society. It brought together the opposition forces, marginalized the communist regime, and laid foundations of the civil society. The ten-million-strong union became a party of national renewal, whose membership included not only workers but also members of the intelligentsia, the peasantry, and even communists. The final collapse of the Polish economy was accompanied by a complete paralysis of the state administration. Gradually, General Wojciech Jaruzelski emerged in the course of the crisis as the most powerful government figure in the country, moving from the position of defense minister to prime minister, to party first secretary, and eventually to president. Jaruzelski, an officer with a spectacular political career within the communist bureaucracy (at thirty-three years of age he became the youngest Polish general), used the army to suppress Solidarity and to restore the PZPR's monopoly of political power.

On December 13, 1981, Jaruzelski introduced martial law, cut off all communications in the country, outlawed Solidarity, and imposed military rule. Although the use of the army to suppress the union's organization was a complete success, Jaruzelski failed to destroy Solidarity as a moral force in Polish politics. Despite the arrest of the union's chairman, Lech Walesa, and the detention of key activists, Solidarity continued to operate underground. The Jaruzelski regime found itself isolated internationally and unable to address the country's economic problems. The introduction of martial law in Poland coincided with the deepening of the Brezhnev succession crisis in the Soviet Union, accompanied by effective paralysis in Soviet decision-making.

The introduction of martial law in Poland prolonged the existence of the communist-dominated political system but failed to save it from collapse. During the 1980s the Polish crisis festered, with the government and communist-party organizational structures becoming marginal to the ever-stronger Polish civil society. The continued deterioration of the Polish economy, to the tune of $40 billion owed to the West and an annual inflation rate in excess of 1,000 percent further undermined the credibility of Jaruzelski's regime. Jaruzelski's attempts to restore the Polish United Workers' Party and to reestablish governmental authority, as outlined in his so-called normalization program of 1981 to 1986, ended in failure.

The intra-Soviet bloc politics was also changing. Like the rest of Eastern Europe, after 1985 the Polish regime had to adapt to Mikhail Gorbachev's *perestroika* reforms. The turning point came in 1987 with Gorbachev's decision to renounce the Brezhnev doctrine that had been used in the past to justify Soviet military intervention in Eastern Europe. Gorbachev's 1987 proclamation that the Eastern European states would have to take the "responsibility for socialism" denied the communists in Poland the ultimate sanction of Soviet military power. In an unprecedented development, in 1988 the Polish government resigned from office.

The decomposition of communist power was accelerated by the collapse of the economy. By 1989 Poland was gripped by hyperinflation, with the government unable to provide for the most basic needs of the citizens. Deprived of Soviet military sanction, in 1989 Jaruzelski had no choice but to turn to the opposition for help. In April 1989 his minister of internal affairs, General Czeslaw Kiszczak, initiated talks with Solidarity chairman Lech Walesa and other representatives of the trade union. These "roundtable" discussions led to a historic breakthrough by allowing for free elections to a newly restored Senate and for partially free elections to the *Sejm* (the lower house of the parliament), with 60 percent of the seats reserved for the communists and their fellow-travelers.

THE SOLIDARITY GENERATION IN POWER: 1989 TO 1993

The June 1989 election gave the Solidarity candidates a clean sweep: 99 of the 100 seats in the Senate and all the freely contested seats in the *Sejm*. Furthermore, the so-called bloc parties that had traditionally collaborated with the communists (the United Peasant Party and the Democratic Party) broke ranks, making it impossible for Jaruzelski's appointee to form a government. With a constitutional crisis threatening to unravel the roundtable deal, Jaruzelski caved in, asking Solidarity to form the first noncommunist government in postwar Poland. In August 1989 Tadeusz Mazowiecki, a former editor of the weekly *Solidarnosc* and a politician closely associated with the Catholic Church, became the new prime minister. The Ministry of Defense and the Ministry of Internal Affairs remained in communist hands, and Jaruzelski was to retain the post of president for a full five-year term.

The negotiated arrangement between Solidarity and the communists proved untenable from the start, as the dramatic chain of events sweeping across all of Eastern Europe brought down the established communist regimes. Jaruzelski, who was elected to the presidency by only one vote in the Senate, was unable to maintain control without the ultimate sanction of Soviet military power. By the winter of 1989, as Romania's Nicolae Ceausescu fell to the wrath of his people, Jaruzelski accepted the inevitable. The Polish United Workers' Party announced its formal dissolution, with Jaruzelski becoming a caretaker president pending free and direct presidential elections scheduled for 1990.

In 1990 the relegalized trade union Solidarity began to shed its character as an anticommunist umbrella organization, breaking up into nascent political parties. The process polarized the movement, pitting the populist Solidarity chairman Lech Walesa against the group of liberal intelligentsia centered around Tadeusz Mazowiecki. Walesa, who had been instrumental in 1989 in selecting Mazowiecki as Poland's first noncommunist prime minister, felt increasingly pushed aside by his former associates centered around the prime minister. By 1990 Walesa became increasingly vocal in his criticism of Mazowiecki's cautious style of government, especially his reluctance to begin his tenure by settling accounts with the communists. Walesa spoke of the urgent need for economic reform that would accelerate the market reform program, introduced by Leszek Balcerowicz, Poland's minister of finance.

The confrontation between Mazowiecki and Walesa came to the fore early in 1990 during the presidential election campaign, which pitted the two men against each other in a race often marked by misstatements and unsubstantiated allegations of conspiracy. Walesa, who ran on the platform of a man of action who would "hack through" the ossified administrative structures, earned disdain from the intelligentsia, who branded him the "president with an ax." Mazowiecki ran a halfhearted and lackluster campaign amid the initial pain of economic reform. The presidential race was made even more bitter and unpredictable by the unexpected rise of a third candidate, Stanislaw Tyminski and his party "X." Tyminski, a "dark-horse" candidate and a former Polish emigre to Canada, appealed quite effectively to the populist discontent, charging both Walesa and Mazowiecki with selling out Polish national interests. Tyminski's appeal in the provinces, where the pain of the Balcerowicz economic program was more pronounced than in major cities, was especially damaging to Mazowiecki, whose government Tyminski blamed for the pauperization of the population.

Tyminski's attacks on Mazowiecki proved remarkably effective. On the election day in December 1990, Tyminski came in second after Walesa after the first round of balloting, with none of the candidates getting the required majority of votes. The result forced a runoff vote, which unexpectedly pitted Walesa against Tyminski, with Walesa coming out the winner. In the final days of the campaign in December 1990, Walesa alleged that Tyminski's candidacy represented a ploy by the ousted communist *nomenklatura* and pointed out that Tyminski's staff included a number of former members of the secret police.[3] Walesa's election as the first president of the Third Republic, in December 1990, was accompanied by the resignation of the Mazowiecki government, thus marking the end of the first phase of postcommunist transition in Poland.

Although with the election of Lech Walesa, Poland had its first democratically elected president, the legislature was still not fully representative, having been elected as part of the roundtable agreement between the communists and Solidarity. During the presidential campaign Walesa frequently attacked the *Sejm* as a "contract parliament" unrepresentative of the genuine will of the Polish nation. Immediately after the 1990 presidential election it became obvious that the parliament's lack of legitimacy had to be addressed if the country was to move forward with the postcommunist transformation.

In early 1991 Walesa chose Jan Olszewski, a lawyer close to Solidarity, to become prime minister. Two weeks later Olszewski withdrew his candidacy citing "significant differences of opinion between the president-elect and himself on the composition of the government."[4] Reportedly, Olszewski was opposed to the inclusion in the cabinet of Leszek Balcerowicz, the former finance minister and author of the IMF-endorsed economic reform program. After Olszewski's resignation, Walesa appointed Jan Krzysztof Bielecki, a young businessman committed to the Balcerowicz program of currency stabilization and market liberalization. Still, the protracted negotiation between Walesa and the parliamentary leaders that preceded Bielecki's appointment foreshadowed a difficult relationship between the two.

The parliamentary election took place in October 1991, almost two years after the January 1990 radical economic reform program and ten months after the December 1990 presidential elections. The parliamentary election campaign demonstrated how deeply fragmented the Solidarity movement had become during that period. On the eve of the *Sejm* election Poland had more than 160 registered political parties.[5] In addition to the more established groups, they included such bizarre organizations as the Party of the Owners of Video Cassette Recorders "V" (*Partia "V" Posiadaczy Magnetowidow*), the Polish Erotic Party (*Polska Partia Erotyczna*), and the Polish Friends of Beer (*Polska Partia Przyjaciol Piwa*). Among these organizations, the Polish Friends of Beer would win sixteen seats in the new parliament. The electoral law itself proved to be a bone of contention. The proposal had been vetoed twice by President Walesa before the final version was agreed upon after several protracted debates in the *Sejm* and the Senate.[6]

Indicative of the growing popular disenchantment with politics, the voter turnout on October 27 was low, estimated at only 40 percent of the 27.6 million in the Polish electorate. The voters chose from among some 7,000 candidates for the 460 seats in the *Sejm* and from among 612 candidates for the 100 seats in the Senate; no party received more than 13 percent of the vote for the *Sejm*. The fact that almost two-thirds of the Polish electorate did not vote raised a disturbing question about the strength of popular support for the future government.

The report on the final election results was published on October 31 by the State Electoral Committee. It set the voter turnout at 43.2 percent and announced that twenty-nine of the sixty-nine political groups contesting the elections won seats in parliament. The scope of the fragmentation was best symbolized by the fact that eleven of the twenty-nine political parties represented won only one seat each. The top ten parties in the *Sejm* were the Democratic Union (*Unia Demokratyczna*; UD), with sixty-two seats (13 percent); the Democratic Left Alliance (*Sojusz Lewicy Demokratycznej*; SLD) with sixty seats (13 percent); the Catholic Electoral Action (*Wyborcza Akcja Katolicka*; WAK) with forty-nine seats (11 percent); the Polish Peasant Party (*Polskie Stronnictwo Ludowe*; PSL) with forty-eight seats (10 percent); the Confederation for an Independent Poland (*Konfederacja Polski Niepodleglej*; KPN) with forty-six seats (10 percent); the Center Alliance (*Porozumienie Obywatelskie Centrum*; PC) with forty-four seats (10 percent); the Liberal-Democratic Congress (*Kongress Liberalno-Demokratyczny*; KLD) with thirty-seven seats (8 percent); the People's Alliance (*Ludowe Porozumienie Wyborcze*; LPW) with twenty-eight seats (6 percent); Solidarity Trade Union (*Solidarnosc*) with twenty-seven seats (6 percent); and the Polish Friends of Beer (*Polska Partia Przyjaciol Piwa*; PPPP) with sixteen seats (3 percent). Other parties garnered the remaining forty-three seats (10 percent) of the 460-member legislature.[7]

The most influential political parties remained the Democratic Left Alliance (former communists), which carried eleven of Poland's thirty-seven electoral districts; the center-right Democratic Union, which carried ten; and the peasant parties, which jointly won nine. The Catholic Electoral Action and the Center Alliance, both conservative, won two districts each, while the nationalist-conservative Confederacy for an Independent Poland, the conservative Liberal-Democratic Congress, and the German Minority Party had one district each. The two biggest winners, the Democratic Union and the Democratic Left Alliance, represented clearly different constituencies. Most of the electoral support for Mazowiecki's Democratic Union was concentrated in large cities throughout central and southern Poland; the Democratic Left Alliance remained the strongest in the northern and northwestern regions of Poland, in the formerly German areas settled after World War II by Poles from the eastern territories annexed by the U.S.S.R.[8] The largest winners in the Senate were as follows: Democratic Union (21), Solidarity (11), Center Alliance and Catholic Electoral Action (9 each), the Polish Peasant Party (8), Rural Solidarity (7), Liberal-Democratic Congress (6), and the Democratic Left Alliance or former communists (4).

The 1991 parliamentary election demonstrated that the Solidarity movement, which since 1980 had served as a grand national coalition opposed to communist rule, was nearing its end. The political fragmentation between the post-Solidarity left-wing parties and the center-right and conservative parties has become a dominant factor in Polish politics. The breakup of the Solidarity coalition, combined with the continued efforts by Lech Walesa to build a strong presidency, contributed in 1992–1993 to a perception of chaos at the highest level of the government. Between October 1991 and July 1992 Poland witnessed an intense confrontation among Walesa, the *Sejm*, and Jan Olszewski, the new conservative prime minister representing the Center Alliance, over the scope of executive power and legislative authority. The results were constitutional paralysis, uncertainty about the future of the economic reform program, and a growing perception abroad that Poland was becoming dangerously unstable politically. Poland's "war at the top" resulted in the collapse of two consecutive governments, led by Olszewski and Waldemar Pawlak, and was finally ended by the majority coalition government under Prime Minister Hanna Suchocka of Mazowiecki's Democratic Union. On August 1, 1992, the *Sejm* adopted the interim "Little Constitution," which, upon Walesa's approval in late November, superseded the 1952 basic law. The document outlined a compromise formula for Polish democracy, which combined elements of presidential and parliamentary systems.

The eight parties of the Suchocka majority coalition represented the entire spectrum of the post-Solidarity center-right movement, except for the Center Alliance, which refused at the last moment to participate. The new prime minister proved extraordinarily adept in forging consensus within the government and working with Walesa. As prime minister, Hanna Suchocka maintained the course of Poland's economic reform, resisted the inflationary budget policies of the *Sejm*, and took a hard line on the issue of work stoppages used by the trade unions to exact concessions from the government. Often described by the press as the "iron lady of Polish politics," Suchocka improved dramatically the relationship between the government and the president and restored the confidence of Western investors in Poland's economic future.

In light of her solid record, it became the supreme irony of Polish domestic politics that Suchocka's government collapsed in May 1993 after a no-confidence vote forced by Solidarity deputies. To make the defeat even more bitter, the no-confidence vote passed with a single-vote margin. The authoritative *Gazeta Wyborcza* called the vote in the parliament the most senseless development in Poland's postcommunist history.[9] Immediately after the no-confidence vote in the *Sejm*, President Lech Walesa dissolved the parliament and ordered the Suchocka cabinet to remain as a caretaker government until the new parliamentary election in September 1993.

The September 19, 1993, balloting was an earthquake in the politics of the Third Republic, with power shifting from the broad Solidarity elite to parties with their roots in the old communist system. The Democratic Left Alliance (SLD), a coalition dominated by the direct successor to the Communist Party won over 20 percent of the popular vote. The former official Polish Peasant Party (PSL) came in second with 15.3 percent. Because the current election law grants the biggest winners bonus seats in the parliament, the two postcommunist parties emerged with a full 65 percent of the seats in the lower house, with a similar result in the Senate. The only party from Suchocka's government coalition to pass the 5 percent threshold was the Democratic Union (UD), but its 11 percent of the vote was less than in 1991. The Union of Labor (*Unia Pracy*; UP), a social-democratic party with roots in Solidarity, won 7.3 percent, confirming the voters' general shift to the left. The Confederation for an Independent Poland and President Lech Walesa's Nonparty Reform Bloc (*Bezpartyjny Blok Wspierania Reform*; BBWR) squeaked in with 5.7 percent and 5.3 percent of the vote, respectively.[10] Among the parties that did not make it to the new parliament were the leading organizations of the Solidarity-era opposition, including the Solidarity trade union, the Liberal-Democratic Congress, the Catholic parties, and the anticommunist right wing. Three years after the collapse of communism the Poles voted for a left-wing government dominated by the former communists from the SLD and the PSL, with the Union of Labor as a coalition partner. The leader of the Polish Peasant Party, Waldemar Pawlak, became the new prime minister.

POLITICAL SYSTEM: THE "LITTLE CONSTITUTION"

The current Polish constitution, the so-called "Little Constitution" (*Mala Konstytucja*), is a compromise forged during the confrontation between Walesa and the *Sejm*. After the 1991 parliamentary election, the *Sejm* set up an extraordinary commission to recommend revisions to the 1952 constitution in the direction of greater parliamentary authority. For his part, President Walesa submitted to the *Sejm* his draft proposal for constitutional changes, the "Little Constitution," which would strengthen the presidency and the government. After protracted negotiations and concessions on both sides, the formula was finally adopted on August 1, 1992, by the required two-thirds majority of votes.[11] Three and a half months later the new constitution was ratified by the Senate and, on November 17, 1992, signed by Walesa into law.

The "Little Constitution"[12] has set up a hybrid presidential-parliamentary system. It seeks a middle ground between the *Sejm*'s insistence on overall supervision of the government and Walesa's demand for greater presidential powers, while it also strengthens the government. In a concession to Walesa, the "Little Constitution" does not include the previous formulation of the *Sejm* as supreme authority. Instead, chapter 1 on "General Principles" identifies the legislative (*Sejm* and Senate), the executive (President and Council of Ministers), and the independent judiciary as the three branches of government, without reference to their relative powers.

The parliament may be dissolved by the president if it fails over three months to pass the budget or approve the government (Articles 4 and 21). However,the president no longer has the authority to dissolve parliament even if the *Sejm* passes a law that (contrary to constitutional provisions) limits his powers. Legislation can be initiated by the *Sejm*, Senate, President, or the Council of Ministers (Article 15). In a departure from preexisting practice, a special "fast-track" legislative process has been established to accelerate parliamentary procedure, with the *Sejm* deciding which bills qualify for "fast-track" review (Article 16). In order to control government spending, all amendments to legislation introduced in the Senate have to be accompanied by a clear statement as to how they will be financed without adding to the budget (Article 17). The *Sejm* can empower the government to issue decrees with the force of law, except in the areas of constitutional change, presidential and parliamentary election laws, regional government, the budget, civil rights, and ratification of international treaties (Article 23). As in the case of parliamentary legislation, all such decrees must be signed by the president.

The president is elected through direct popular vote for a five-year term (Article 30). The president is the head of state and the commander-in-chief of the armed forces (Articles 29 and 36), who, upon consultation with the minister of defense, appoints the army's chief of the general staff, chiefs of the other services, and commanders of military districts. The president has the authority to introduce martial law for a period of up to three months, with one three-month extension permitted, provided it has been authorized by the *Sejm* (Article 38). However, the *Sejm* cannot be dissolved while martial law is in effect, nor can the constitution be amended during that time. The president also determines foreign policy and national security policy (Articles 33 and 35).

The "Little Constitution" imposes a constraint on presidential powers by requiring the prime minister's or a cabinet minister's countersignature on the president's decisions, on matters other than the dissolution of the parliament, calling a new parliamentary election, submitting new legislation, the presidential legislative veto, nominating a prime minister, calling a meeting of the Council of Ministers, initiating a referendum (provided the Senate approves), judicial appointments, nominating the president of the Polish National Bank, and calling for an investigation by the Constitutional Tribunal (Articles 47 and 48). The president can be impeached for violating the constitution or other crimes by a two-thirds majority in both houses of parliament, after which he will be tried by the Constitutional Tribunal (Article 51).

The president appoints the prime minister and, upon his recommendation, the cabinet (Article 58). The government appointed by the president must present its program to the *Sejm* within fourteen days, and it must win an absolute majority vote of confidence. If the government fails to win a vote of confidence, it is the *Sejm*'s turn within twenty-one days to appoint a new government, which then again must win an absolute majority of votes (Article 59). Should this government fail to win the requisite support, it is again the president's turn to appoint a government, which now has to win only a simple majority of votes in the *Sejm* (Article 60); again, should this fail, the *Sejm* has another twenty-one days to make its second attempt at forming the government, which also needs only to win a simple parliamentary majority for approval. If the two attempts by the president and the two attempts by the parliament to appoint a government fail, the president can either dissolve the parliament or within fourteen days make his final attempt to appoint a government, which then has six months to win a vote of confidence. Should that fail as well, the president must dissolve parliament and call a new election (Article 63).

The "Little Constitution" requires that the premier win the president's approval only for appointments of the ministries of internal affairs, national defense, and foreign affairs, regardless of the manner in which the government is being formed. The government can be dismissed by the *Sejm*, which then can form a new cabinet. If that cabinet fails to win a vote of confidence, the president appoints the replacement (Article 65). However, the president cannot ask for the government's dismissal and can change individual cabinet ministers only after the prime minister has requested it (Article 69).

ECONOMIC POLICY: THE BALCEROWICZ PROGRAM

In 1990 Poland became the first postcommunist country to launch a radical economic reconstruction and stabilization program developed with assistance from Western economists and the International Monetary Fund (IMF). Introduced on January 1, 1990, the "Balcerowicz Plan," named after the country's finance minister, Leszek Balcerowicz, concentrated on fighting hyperinflation, which by that time had approached in Poland 1,000 percent per year. The plan also aimed at making the Polish *zloty* convertible and began the process of privatizing the economy. On January 1, 1990, Warsaw freed the prices, froze wages, and virtually eliminated government subsidies in order to revive market forces.

The shock treatment administered to the economy by Balcerowicz exacted social costs in terms of unemployment and the initial dramatic price increases, but it proved essential to future economic growth. The inflation rate was brought down from 1,000 percent in 1989 to about 30 percent in 1993. The Polish *zloty* has become fully convertible internally, with an exchange rate set by the market. The transition to the convertible *zloty* was brought about without the government having to draw upon the $1 billion currency stabilization fund set aside by the IMF. In 1991 the Polish National Bank announced that in 1993 it would introduce the new "heavy zloty" worth a thousand times the nominal value of the present currency[13]; that date was subsequently put off until 1994.

The Balcerowicz plan has transformed the Polish economy, leading to a surge of private business activity in the country. Polish entrepreneurs imported food, clothing, durable goods, and even gasoline,[14] thereby increasing supply, lowering prices, and undercutting the monopoly of state-owned enterprises. Foreign investment in Poland accelerated, including acquisitions by Fiat, General Motors, and other multinational corporations. In addition to the growth of the industrial private sector, the market reform forced the traditionally private but inefficient Polish agriculture to undergo a difficult transformation toward greater consolidation and efficiency. By the end of 1990, the perennial food shortages of the communist period were a thing of the past.

The market reform program also revitalized Polish foreign trade. Already in 1990 Poland had achieved a $2.2 billion trade surplus from its convertible currencies exports.[15] In 1991 Warsaw resorted to barter to resuscitate its Eastern market. On December 24, 1991, Poland and Russia signed a trade agreement covering "strategic commodities," with Poland agreeing to provide Russia with coal and sulphur, as well as $500 million worth of food and $400 million worth of medicine in exchange for Russian natural gas and oil. The deal was valued at $1.4 billion for each side.[16]

On balance, despite initial problems with the implementation of the large-scale privatization plan, Poland has made remarkable progress on the road to market capitalism. Most important, the country's political elite, including the postcommunist coalition government led by Waldemar Pawlak, has remained committed to reform. The Suchocka government continued the Balcerowicz program, while reorganizing the country's tax system, including the introduction of a value-added tax (VAT), and outlining a program for improvements in infrastructure, including building a network of toll superhighways and installing fiber optic telephone systems. The Pawlak government has maintained the overall direction despite the earlier promises to increase spending.

In 1993 Poland was the most successful of the former communist states in Eastern and Central Europe in making the transition to market capitalism. Today Poland has the largest private economy among the former Soviet bloc countries, estimated at 40 to 55 percent of GDP, which reflects a rapid expansion of the new private business as well as several successful large-scale privatization efforts. In effect, with a projected growth rate of between 4.5 and 5.0 percent, in 1993 Poland was the only economy showing respectable growth in recession-ridden Europe. It was the supreme irony of Polish politics that as the austerity measures of the last four years were beginning to pay off, the electorate rejected the very people who have led the country through its revolutionary economic change.

FOREIGN AND SECURITY POLICY

Since 1989 Poland has been striving to build good relations with Germany and Russia, with the overall objective of full integration in the European Union (EU) and NATO. In 1990–1991 Polish policy toward Germany had two principal objectives: (1) to obtain German recognition of the Oder-Neisse line as the permanent border between the two countries and (2) to conclude a bilateral friendship and cooperation treaty with Germany. Since the collapse of communism the Polish government has developed good neighborly relations with Germany, based on the premise that Germany will pose no threat to Poland so long as it remains anchored within the Western security system.[17] Warsaw has hoped that Polish-German relations will continue to improve, eventually overcoming the historical legacy of mistrust, and that Germany will lead Poland into NATO.

The new policy resulted in significantly improved relations between Warsaw and Bonn. The Polish-German border treaty, which has confirmed the existing borders, was signed in November 1990. The Polish-German bilateral treaty on friendship, cooperation, and good neighborly relations was signed in June 1991. The latter has guaranteed legal protection to the approximately 200,000 ethnic

Germans living in Poland, including their religious, cultural, and educational rights. Germany extended the same guarantees to its Polish minority. In the course of the negotiations, Bonn also promised to support Poland's application for full membership in the EC. Polish Foreign Minister Krzysztof Skubiszewski, the architect of his country's German policy, described the two treaties as a "breakthrough in Polish-German relations."[18]

While Warsaw's German policy has been an unqualified success, the task of formulating a coherent policy toward the former Soviet Union has proved more difficult. The breakdown of Moscow's administrative authority and the surge of nationalism in the former republics created a level of uncertainty that all but precluded substantive negotiations. The December 1991 demise of the U.S.S.R. raised new challenges to Warsaw's foreign policy. Regional instability along Poland's eastern border has increased while the threat of direct Russian invasion has become hypothetical. Today, Poland shares a common border with four new neighbors: Lithuania, Belarus (Belorussia), Ukraine, and Russia (the Kaliningrad District).

Polish-Lithuanian relations have remained strained, even more so after Lithuania regained its independence. Only in late 1993 were there the first signs of normalization and renewed diplomatic activity between Warsaw and Vilnius. Still, leading Lithuanian politicians have continued to point to the history of past Polish interference in Lithuania's domestic affairs, especially during the interwar period, including the Polish seisure of Vilnius after World War I.

Relations between Warsaw and Vilnius are further complicated by the presence of a 260,000-strong Polish minority in Lithuania.[19] Polish Foreign Minister Skubiszewski maintained that the mistreatment of the ethnic Poles by Lithuania was the reason for the postponement until January 1992 of his visit to Vilnius, originally planned for November 1991.[20] Another potential problem is a territorial dispute between the two countries over the city of Vilnius/Wilno, which before World War II belonged to Poland but which historically has also been claimed by Lithuania. While Poland has declared repeatedly that the issue of Vilnius/Wilno is closed, Lithuania has remained suspicious of Polish irredentism.

Polish-Belorussian relations have largely been determined by the extent to which Minsk has been able to act independently of Moscow. Poland has maintained the position that the preservation of an independent Belorussian state is in its national interest as it reduces the likelihood of Russia resuming its imperial drive into Europe. In practice, however, Warsaw can do little to bolster Belarus's independence. Polish-Ukrainian relations are burdened with a history of mutual hatred and atrocities committed by both sides. A large segment of the Polish society has retained a strong sentimental attachment to the city of Lwow/Lvov in western Ukraine, which belonged to Poland before the war and has been traditionally considered the cradle of Polish culture in the East. Warsaw has viewed continued Ukrainian independence as critical to the independence of postcommunist Europe, for it makes the restoration of the former Russian empire impossible. Polish-Ukrainian relations improved in 1992–1993 at the state-to-state level, with Ukrainian President Leonid Kravchuk even suggesting the establishment of a Central European security system, with Poland and Ukraine as its principal members.

The Kaliningrad District, a remnant of former East Prussia that was incorporated into the Soviet Union after World War II, is today the only area where Poland and Russia share a common border. It remains a major Russian military base at the Baltic coast, and discussions of its future role have affected Polish-Russian as well as Polish-German relations. In 1990 Bonn and Moscow briefly considered resettling the two million Volga Germans in the district, an idea that was staunchly opposed by Poland on the grounds that it would recreate the prewar conditions.[21] In 1991 the Polish government informed Moscow and Bonn that it would view the implementation of the scheme to resettle the Volga Germans in the Kaliningrad District as a direct threat to Polish security, as it would in effect recreate the Polish "corridor" running between Germany proper and an area that would gravitate to Germany politically and economically. In 1993 the issue became moot as Russia shifted to a more assertive foreign policy in the region and the continued military presence in Kaliningrad once more became an asset.

Bilateral relations with Germany and the Soviet successor states have been viewed by Poland in a broader regional and pan-European context. In 1991, Poland took a step toward EC membership by signing, together with Hungary and Czechoslovakia, an associate membership agreement with the European Community. Poland has been slated for full integration into the EU (successor to the EC) as a "second tier" state, following the union of the European Free Trade Association Countries with the European Union. The Polish government expects a complete merger with the EU around the turn of the century. Since 1989, Warsaw has consistently viewed the continuation of NATO and the attendant U.S. presence in Europe as a necessary precondition of its security. The Polish government has regarded NATO as the only Western security structure capable of keeping Germany firmly anchored in the West, balancing the residual Russian military threat in central and eastern Europe and guarding against the resurgence of Russian imperialism. Polish overtures to NATO have been successful to the extent that in 1993 the question of expanding NATO eastward to include Poland, the Czech Republic, Slovakia, and Hungary was on NATO's policy agenda, even though the January 1994 NATO summit chose to delay the decision on new membership.

The Third Republic has reformed its armed forces to bring the military under civilian control. The military reform program has reorganized the Ministry of Defense into two branches, the civilian branch and the military branch. The civilian side includes the position of the undersecretary for education, the Information Bureau, the Institute for Social Research, the Field Church (*kuria*), the Defense Minister's Staff (*Urzad Ministra Spraw Wojskowych*), the *Sejm*

Liaison Office, the Personnel Office, the Finance Office, the Institute for Strategic and Defense Studies, the Legal Affairs Office, and the Military Police Directorate (*zandarmeria*).[22]

For the first time in over four decades questions about the utility of military force are at the center of Poland's national security concerns. This has been reflected in the new Polish military doctrine. The current doctrine describes Poland's national security policy and the role of its army as purely defensive, with the country's constitutional bodies retaining complete control over the military. The army has been redeployed to four new military districts to provide for an all-around defense of the national territory, as have the air force and the air defense units.

WHITHER THE THIRD REPUBLIC?

As 1993 drew to a close, the restored independent Polish state found itself at a crossroads. The scorecard of the first four postcommunist years is impressive: Poland managed to reverse its economic decline, to build a viable market structure, and to register impressive economic growth. It has developed the foundations of a democratic society, with a new constitution and a democratic electoral process in place. The fact that power was transferred in an orderly way to the postcommunist parties after the September 1993 elections speaks highly of the maturity of Poland's democratic institutions. Poland has made impressive progress in its efforts to integrate with the West, and its prospects for full membership in the European Union and NATO are among the best in postcommunist Europe. Finally, continued instability in the East notwithstanding, the Polish security situation is better today than at any time in this century, thereby giving the country the opportunity to overcome its historical dilemma of a medium-sized power caught between the great powers of Russia and Germany. Polish-German relations have improved dramatically following the 1990 and 1991 bilateral agreements between the two countries. The visa-free travel arrangement between Bonn and Warsaw has brought the nations closer, occasional friction notwithstanding, while Germany has become a driving force for including Poland in the existing European institutions. On the other hand, Poland's future relations with Russia remain uncertain as Moscow's resurgent imperialism could become a threat to Polish sovereignty.

Domestic problems remain, the most enduring among them being the unfulfilled public expectations of a rapid improvement in the living standards and the concomitant appeal of populist programs. The great coalition of the workers, peasants, intellectuals, and the Catholic Church that led Poland to independence has exhausted itself. The fragmentation of the center-right post-Solidarity parties, demonstrated in the 1993 election, facilitated the victory of the old communist parties.

The apparent return of the old communists into Polish politics may prove less damaging than Polish conservative and liberal-democratic politicians fear.

The SLD/PSL/UP coalition will not be able to deliver on the frequently contradictory promises made during the campaign. While both the SLD and the PSL advocate greater deficit spending, their room to maneuver will remain sharply limited by the policy constraints imposed by the International Monetary Fund. If implemented, the promised change in economic policy would reignite inflation and create additional social pressures that would most likely bring the government of Waldemar Pawlak down. Aleksander Kwasniewski, the chairman of the SLD, has gone to great lengths since the election to reassure the international lending institution and the Polish business community that there would be no reversal of market policies, although the government may slow down the pace of reform.

Real changes are more likely to take place in the Polish political arena, where the SLD pledged itself to work for a new constitution that would restore the primacy of the parliament and make the presidency a largely ceremonial institution. Since the communists and the peasant party have a 65 percent majority in the parliament, they would command the necessary votes to bring about constitutional change. It is impossible to anticipate how exactly President Lech Walesa might react to any attempt to undermine his position, but it is fair to assume judging from the past that he would not stand idly by. If the new Polish government chooses confrontation over cooperation with the president, Poland may be in for some very turbulent political times ahead.

NOTES

1. For an authoritative review of the history of the Polish-Lithuanian Commonwealth see Norman Davis, *God's Playground: A History of Poland* (New York: Columbia University Press, 1984).

2. The term was first used by Polish sociologist J. S. Staniszkis. See J. S. Staniszkis, *Poland's Self-Limiting Revolution* (Princeton, N.J.: Princeton University Press, 1984).

3. Radio Free Europe/Radio Liberty (RFE/RL), *Daily Report*, December 3, 1990.

4. *Daily Report*, December 19, 1990.

5. *Informator o partiach politycznych w Polsce* (Warsaw: Polska Agencja Informacyjna, October 1991), pp. 1–2.

6. "Wybory 91: Scena po pierwszym starciu," *Zycie Warszawy*, July 20–21, 1991.

7. *RFE/RL Daily Report*, November 4, 1991.

8. "Polska geografia polityczna," *Gazeta wyborcza*, November 7, 1991.

9. "Bez rzadu, bez sejmu, bez sensu," *Gazeta Wyborcza*, May 29–30, 1993.

10. "Poland Goes Left," *RFE/RL Daily Report*, September 21, 1993.

11. For the text of the "Little Constitution" see "Mala Konstytucja: ile komu wladzy," *Rzeczpospolita*, August 7, 1992.

12. The following discussion is based on *Mala Konstytucja z komentarzem* (Warsaw: Wydawnictwo AWA, 1992). See also Dariusz Dudek, *Konstytucja Rzeczypospolitej Polskiej: Wybor zrodel* (Lublin: Lubelskie Wydawnictwa Prawnicze, 1992); Piotr Zaremba, "Rownowaga wladz," *Zycie Warszawy*, August 3, 1992; and Louisa Vinton, "Poland's 'Little Constitution' Clarifies Walesa's Powers," *RFE/RL Research Report*, 35(1) (September 4, 1992).

13. This was subsequently confirmed by the president of the Polish National Bank, Hanna Gronkiewicz-Waltz. Conversation with the author, Stanford, California, November 24, 1992.

14. Polish Television, Channel 1 News, January 12, 1991.

15. *The Financial Times*, May 3, 1991.

16. *RFE/RL Daily Report*, December 30, 1991.

17. "Jeden Dzien z Januszem Onyszkiewiczem," *Zolnierz Rzeczypospolitej*, June 1–3, 1990.

18. "Wielkie zmiany," *Sztandar Mlodych*, April 19–21, 1991.

19. Ibid.

20. *RFE/RL Daily Report*, December 23, 1991.

21. "2 Million Volga Germans Pose Settlement Issue for Bonn, Moscow," *Washington Post*, February 4, 1991.

22. General Zdzislaw Stelmaszuk, "Nowy model armii (z obrad Sejmowej Komisji Obrony Narodowej)," *Polska Zbrojna*, November 22, 1990.

2 _____

THE CZECH REPUBLIC AND SLOVAKIA

CZECHS, SLOVAKS, AND THE INTERWAR FEDERATION

The Slav settlements in Bohemia and Moravia, the two principal regions of today's Czech Republic, date back to the fifth century A.D., with the first state formation of Western Slavs, the Great Moravian Empire, dating back to the ninth century. The proto-Czech Christian state was centered around the Nitra region and included Bohemia and Slovakia, as well as Moravia. The Moravian state was destroyed by the Magyars, with Slovakia becoming a part of Hungary until 1918. The medieval Czech kingdom was consolidated in the thirteenth century under the Premyslid dynasty, which ruled in Bohemia and Moravia. Exposed to Mongol raids as well as pressure from Hungary, the Czech kingdom peaked in the late fourteenth century under the rule of Charles IV, who expanded the state's territory by annexing Silesia, Lower Lusatia, and Brandenburg to the Czech crown. The cultural development of the kingdom was symbolized by the founding in 1348 of a university in Prague, one of the oldest and greatest centers of learning in medieval Europe.

The reformation of the fifteenth century sweeping across Europe resulted in the indigenous Jan Hus reform movement, with the city of Tabor in south Bohemia becoming a preeminent Hussite center. The subsequent wars and the eclipse of the Czech kingdom coincided with the rise of the Habsburgs in Germany and of the Jagiellonian dynasty in Poland-Lithuania. The Thirty Years' War brought about a dramatic transformation of the Czech society, with the nation's nobility virtually wiped out in 1620 in the Battle of the White Mountain, followed by the assertion of strong Habsburg domination over the region. The centuries of Germanization that the Habsburgs brought with them nearly wiped out any sense of national identity among the Czechs, while a similar process of Magyarization continued in Slovakia. Neither the Czechs nor the Slovaks sought full national independence prior to World War I.[1]

The early abolition of serfdom in the Czech Lands in 1781 and in Slovakia in 1785 accelerated urbanization and economic development. By the mid-nineteenth century, the Czech Lands and especially Bohemia ranked among the most industrialized parts of the Habsburg domain. The rising tide of nationalism in 1848 sweeping across Europe awakened Czech nationalism, bringing forth demands for greater political representation. The 1867 constitution granted basic civil rights to the Czechs within the overall imperial structure. The growing national aspirations of the Czechs and Slovaks resulted in an independence movement by the turn of the century. Efforts by Czech and Slovak political leaders prior to and during World War I to establish statehood coincided with the desire on the part of the Allies to replace the Austro-Hungarian Empire, leading to the federal formula for a joint Czech and Slovak state.

Czechoslovakia was declared independent in 1918 and recognized by the 1919 Treaty of St. Germain as a multinational state rather than simply a Czech and Slovak federation, the country's new name notwithstanding. At the time, about 35 percent of the fourteen million of its citizens were German, Magyar, Ukrainian, Polish, and Jewish minorities. Czechs constituted approximately 50 percent of the total and Slovaks 15 percent.[2] The new Czechoslovak state brought together people with the centuries of experience of being part of multinational empires but with very different experience of foreign rule. Under the Habsburgs, Bohemia and Moravia had been the industrial heartland of the empire, while Slovakia languished under Magyar rule. The task of forging a nation-state from the regions with such different levels of economic development would prove formidable. In addition, religious and cultural differences fueled the Czech-Slovak animosity during the interwar period.

Still, Czechoslovakia remained a model East Central European democracy throughout the two decades prior to World War II, at the time when other east and central European successor states experimented with authoritarianism and fascism. Interwar Czechoslovakia was a relatively highly developed economy, with levels of development in Bohemia and Moravia on par with those in Western Europe. It was also highly urbanized by the standards of the times, with 48 percent of the population living in cities of five thousand or more.[3] The country's large middle class, the high levels of literacy, and the absence of an aristocracy, combined with a strong tradition of local self-government and the experience of Habsburg administration, gave the Czechoslovak democracy its unique strength and stability. These factors were buttressed by the leadership of Tomas Masaryk, the first president of Czechoslovakia and its dominant political figure throughout the interwar period. Masaryk's unswerving commitment to Western democratic principles and to minority rights was a decisive factor in the political consolidation of the new republic.

Despite Prague's efforts to sustain the country's democracy, interwar Czechoslovakia remained an artificial creation with a strongly felt absence of an ethnic, cultural, or historical unity. In the final analysis, Czechoslovakia suffered not only from the centrifugal pressures exerted by its non-Czecho-slovak minorities but more fundamentally from the continued differences in national identity and the disparity in the national aspirations of Czechs and Slovaks themselves. Czechoslovakia's difficult ethnic situation at home was compounded by the hostility of its immediate neighbors and the concomitant threat of political isolation. Throughout the interwar period Poland, Hungary, and Germany maintained irredentist claims on Czechoslovakia's territory, which were compounded further by the rising national consciousness and territorial claims of western Ukrainians.

The most serious threat to Czechoslovakia's independent existence between the two world wars emanated from Germany and Hungary. Prague sought to build an alliance with France against Germany to be buttressed by the Little Entente (1920–1921) with Romania and Yugoslavia directed against Hungarian irreden-tism. With the rise of Adolf Hitler's Germany, in 1934 President Eduard Benes also shifted his efforts to build better relations with the U.S.S.R. Czechoslovakia extended diplomatic recognition to the Soviet Union in 1934 and two years later established a military alliance with the Soviets. In the end, however, both the French and Russian connections proved of little value when confronted with Hitler's determined effort to dismember the Czechoslovak state.

The pressures of Slovak separatism, German and Magyar grievances, pres-sure from Poland and Hungary, and the extension of German power into Austria in 1938 left Czechoslovakia completely isolated and vulnerable to attack. Western support, in particular French assurances, proved meaningless when Czechoslovakia was forced to accept German territorial demands, sanctioned by Britain, Italy, and France at the 1938 Munich conference. Next, in 1939 the Czech Lands were fully incorporated into the Reich as the Bohemian-Moravian protectorate, while the now nominally independent Slovakia became a puppet state of Nazi Germany.

The trauma of Munich and the war left deep scars and compelled the Czechoslovak political elite, led by President Benes, to reorient the country's foreign policy. Already during the war the Czechoslovak government-in-exile sought greater security by looking to the Soviet Union as the only regional check on German power. In 1943 Benes and Stalin signed a treaty of friendship, cooperation, and mutual assistance between the two countries. At the time Benes also agreed to cede Ruthenia, a part of Czechoslovakia's eastern territory, to the Soviet Union. After the American and Soviet troops liberated the country, Benes moved to expel the Sudeten Germans and to reestablish the federal Czechoslovak state.

Throughout the war the Czechoslovak government-in-exile believed that in the postwar Europe Czechoslovakia would play the role of a "bridge" between the East and the West. Benes accepted the notion of communist participation in the government and actively courted Soviet favor. At the same time, Czechoslovakia tried to secure ties to the West, with Foreign Minister Jan Masaryk approaching France in June of 1946 with a draft of an alliance treaty and in 1947 announcing Czechoslovakia's readiness to participate in the Marshall Plan.

The original support for the communists and the lack of a strong anti-Russian sentiment, combined with some loss of credibility among the Czechoslovaks for the Western-style republic after 1938, facilitated the communist takeover. In addition, many Czechs believed that the communists would be better at overcoming the secessionist pressure in Slovakia and hence better at keeping the federation together. Immediately after the war Soviet prestige was relatively high, as the U.S.S.R. was not blamed for Munich. In a free election held in 1946 the communists got 38 percent of the vote, leading Benes to ask Communist Party leader Klement Gottwald to form a government. From then on the nationalization of the economy proceeded apace. In 1947 the communists consolidated their position by taking control over the army and the police and on Moscow's orders staged the final coup in February of 1948 on the eve of national elections. Remarkably, the coup succeeded even though there were no Soviet troops stationed on Czechoslovak territory at the time.

COMMUNIST LEGACY

The Czechoslovak Communist Party controlled the Czechoslovak Federation from 1948 through 1989. It brought about a Soviet-style transformation of the economy and of the society. Despite the apparent willingness on the part of Czechoslovakia's leaders to accommodate Soviet wishes, the Russians ruled the country with an iron fist. Compared to the rest of Eastern Europe, Stalinism was particularly brutal in Czechoslovakia, with indiscriminate terror hitting the society at large, the military, the church, and the communist elite. The regime repressed all religious activity, and in 1952 it severed diplomatic relations with the Vatican. A large number of high-ranking Czechoslovak clergy were jailed, as were members of the prewar elite and all other potential "bourgeois enemies." The country's industry was nationalized starting already in 1945; by 1948 all industry was state owned.

The communists were not to be spared the terror they helped to unleash. The purge of the Czechoslovak Communist Party was long, building up momentum between 1950 and 1952. The most prominent communists executed at the time were Vladimir Clementis, the foreign minister and a ranking Slovak communist, and Rudolf Slansky, the former secretary general of the Czechoslovak Communist Party and the deputy prime minister; both were hanged in December 1952. The Czechoslovak brand of communism was made even more noxious by the fact that in 1956, in contrast to neighboring Poland and Hungary, Czechoslovakia was not de-Stalinized. Although Gottwald died in 1953, as did Stalin, Stalinist repression continued. Antonin Novotny, who succeeded Gottwald, remained the unquestioned leader; and the "thaw" of the early Khrushchev period all but bypassed Czechoslovakia. The 1960 Czechoslovak constitution proudly declared that the country had achieved socialism.

The 1960s in Czechoslovakia was a period of growing discontent with the Stalinist rigidity in all fields of life. Eventually, a rebellion within the Communist Party led to the removal of Novotny and his replacement by Alexander Dubcek, a Slovak reform communist. Dubcek's attempt to build "socialism with a human face" included freedom of the press and democratic competition for political power. At the same time, Czechoslovakia declared its loyalty to the COMECON and the Warsaw Pact and remained hostile toward West Germany. The goal of Dubcek's reform was not to terminate the communist system but to create a more democratic form of communism.

In 1968 Czechoslovakia's constitution was revised to accommodate the greater Slovak demands for autonomy within the federation. The 1968 constitutional law established the separate governments for the Czech Lands and for Slovakia, thereby creating three layers of state bureaucracy: the Czech, the Slovak, and the federal. The Czech and Slovak republics acquired some autonomy on matters of education and cultural policy, while the federal government continued to control defense, foreign policy, natural resources, mass media, industry, and agriculture.

The Soviet-led Warsaw Pact invasion of Czechoslovakia demolished all residual pro-Russian sentiment among Czechoslovak people. The disillusionment with Russia in 1968 was even more profound than the one with the West after the 1938 Munich sellout. Dubcek capitulated to Moscow under duress and reversed his reforms; he was subsequently removed from power altogether. From the 1968 invasion until the collapse of communist power the Soviet Union stationed troops in Czechoslovakia. In 1969 Dubcek was replaced by Gustav Husak, a hard-line communist whose policy of "consolidation" marked a return to the Stalinism of the Gottwald and Novotny eras. In 1975 Husak combined the offices of the president and the Communist Party first secretary, concentrating all political power in his hands. Czechoslovakia remained an obedient Soviet satellite to the end. Its relations with the West were frozen, save for a 1973 treaty with West Germany that declared the Munich agreement null and void and opened up the possibility of renewed trade.

After the 1975 Conference on Security and Cooperation in Europe in Helsinki, Czechoslovakia was repeatedly singled out as a principal human rights violator in Eastern Europe. Continued human rights abuses by the Husak regime gave rise to a Czechoslovak dissident movement. In January 1977 the Charter 77 was established with the goal of forcing the government to abide by the Helsinki commitments. Playwright Vaclav Havel, one of the founding members of the organization, became the country's premier dissident. The Charter included Catholics, Protestants, reform communists, democratic socialists, and even Trotskyites. It had no stated political agenda other than protecting the population from police terror, but it did speak out on other issues, such as the 1979 Soviet invasion of Afghanistan or U.S. policy in Central America in the 1980s. Although the organization attempted to reach out to both the Czechs and the Slovaks, when the Charter was signed in 1977 by some one thousand people, only four of the signatories were Slovaks.[4] In addition to the dissident movement, the Catholic Church began to reawaken, with its primate Cardinal Tomasek becoming an outspoken critic of the Husak regime.

The Czechoslovak economy under communism continued to stagnate. Bohemia and Moravia's industrial base of the interwar period, once the envy of all of Eastern Europe, became largely obsolete, while a substantial portion of new industrial development (especially in the defense sector) was now concentrated in Slovakia. Czechoslovakia remained a principal supplier of machine tools and building and construction equipment within the COMECON, but its wares were no longer competitive on world markets. It was also one of the key suppliers of military equipment, earning the country the sobriquet the "arsenal of Eastern Europe." Over a hundred defense and defense-related plants were built under communism, most of them sited in Slovakia. The communists also launched an ambitious nuclear power program, with 30 percent of the country's electricity in the 1980s generated by Soviet-designed nuclear power plants. Czechoslovakia's agriculture remained fully collectivized throughout the communist era.

Still, compared to other East European countries, communist Czechoslovakia did perform relatively well economically by drawing on its preexisting industrial base and its tradition of technological excellence. However, while in the 1960s and 1970s the economy grew at over 5 percent, by the mid-1970s it began to contract; by 1980 the growth rate was about 2 percent; and by 1985 the economy stagnated. As Gorbachev's reforms in the late 1980s rocked the systemic foundations in the Soviet Union, Czechoslovakia under the leadership of Milos Jakes remained an eerily calm bastion of old-style communism. The Czechoslovak Communist Party, thoroughly purged after 1968, could not play the role of its Hungarian or even Polish counterpart in the 1989 revolutionary upheaval.

THE VELVET REVOLUTION AND ITS AFTERMATH

Czechoslovakia awakened after the historic roundtable accords in Poland in August 1989 and the progressive transformation of Hungarian domestic politics toward party pluralism set the revolutionary forces in motion across Eastern Europe. On November 17, 1989, a wave of demonstrations swept the country, culminating ten days later in a national general strike. The demonstrators demanded free elections and the resignation of the hard-line communists. Deprived of Soviet military support, the rigid communist power structure imploded. Milos Jakes resigned on November 24; his successor Ladislav Adamec resigned on December 7; and the country's "president-for-life" Gustav Husak submitted his resignation on December 10.[5] On December 29, 1989, Vaclav Havel, the leader of Charter 77, was elected Czechoslovakia's president by a unanimous parliamentary vote. The speed of change and the nonviolent nature of the upheaval earned the national uprising in Czechoslovakia the name of "Velvet Revolution."

The first free and democratic elections in Czechoslovakia took place on June 8, 1990. In the six months leading to the election the Civic Forum (*Obcanske Forum*; OF) became the principal political organization in the country; its equivalent in Slovakia was Public Against Violence (*Verejnost proti nasiliu*; VPN). Even before the election, members of the Civic Forum took up key appointments in the government.[6] The primary function of the interim government was to prepare the country for the election. By the time of the June elections, 334 political associations and fifty-eight political parties were formally registered.[7] The communists also contested the election, offering the Czechoslovaks a new reformed image.

The elections to the Czech, Slovak, and federal legislatures were conducted according to a proportional representation formula, with a threshold set at 5 percent of the total vote to gain representation. It had a turnout of 96 percent of the registered voters and returned eight political parties to the parliament.[8] Alexander Dubcek, a former communist reformer who led the 1968 Prague Spring movement, became the speaker of the new federal legislature. The electorate returned a landslide victory for the Civic Forum/Public Against Violence coalition, which garnered more votes in the 300-member Federal Assembly than all the rest of the parties combined. The communists got 15 percent of the vote in the Czech republic and 13 percent in the Slovak republic, thereby winning forty-seven seats in the legislature and becoming the second largest political party in the parliament. Other groups elected to the Federal Assembly in June 1990 included the Christian and Democratic Union, the Association for Moravia and Silesia, which advocated greater autonomy for the country's regions, the Slovak National Party, and the minority Coexistence–Hungarian Christian Democratic Movement.[9]

The new federal parliament was elected to a two-year term with the principal tasks of drafting Czechoslovakia's new constitution and restructuring the state administration. The domestic political scene began to fragment shortly after the election, with the breakdown of the principal anticommunist umbrella organizations translated into the progressive fragmentation of the federal parliament. After its February 1991 congress, the Civic Forum gave rise to two new parties: the left-leaning Civic Movement (*Obcanske hnuti*; OH) led by Foreign Minister

Jiri Dienstbier and the conservative Civic Democratic Party (*Obcanska demok-raticka strana*; ODS) led by Vaclav Klaus, the country's finance minister. Subsequently, the Civic Forum gave rise to another party, the center-right Civic Democratic Alliance (*Obcanska demokraticka aliance*; ODA), thus effectively ending its existence as an anticommunist umbrella organization. Klaus's ODS became in 1991 the largest and strongest political party in the country.[10]

In Slovakia, the political devolution of the anticommunist opposition groups was quite different from the changes in the Czech Lands. By 1991, with the majority of the Slovak population opposed to market reforms, the Public Against Violence lost most of its support. Slovakia's first postcommunist prime minister, Vladimir Meciar, became a dominant figure in Slovak politics by appealing to the anti-Czech sentiment and to the seething national resentment over the alleged domination of Slovakia by the federal authorities in Prague. Although he was ousted from his job as prime minister in April 1991 by the Slovak parliament, Meciar capitalized on his overwhelming popular base of support to found his own political party, the Movement for a Democratic Slovakia (*Hnutie za demokraticke Slovensko*; HZDS), which soon became the most powerful pro-independence party in Slovakia.

The creation of the HZDS in March 1991 effectively destroyed the Public Against Violence umbrella organization. The other principal party in Slovakia, the Christian Democratic Movement (*Krestanskodemokraticke hnutie*; KDH) led by Jan Carnogursky, Meciar's successor as premier, appeared at times to endorse the secessionist program of the HZDS, while also speaking out in favor of preserving the federation. The militantly separatist Slovak National Party called for the immediate breakup of the federation and the creation of an independent Slovak state.

In the last months of Czechoslovakia's unified existence, the country's extreme political left and right were dominated by the remnants of the Czecho-slovak Communist Party and by the staunchly anticommunist Republican Party, respectively. The Communist Party of the two republics broke up in January 1991, with the Slovak communists adopting a reformist program and changing their name to the Party of the Democratic Left (*Strana demokratickej lavice*; SDL). Other political groups, such as the Czech communists' ally Democratic Left (*Demokraticka levice*; DL), remained minor players in Czechoslovakia's postcommunist politics.

FOREIGN AND SECURITY POLICY BEFORE THE BREAKUP OF CZECHOSLOVAKIA

Commitment to pan-European institutions and close cooperation with Ger-many characterized postcommunist Czechoslovakia's foreign policy after 1989. In May 1991 Czechoslovakia normalized fully its relations with Germany by signing a bilateral treaty on good neighborly relations that also addressed the bitter legacy of World War II. Also in 1991 Czechoslovakia was admitted into the Council of Europe and, together with Poland and Hungary, became an associate member of the European Community.[11] It moved to build better relations with Russia by negotiating and signing a bilateral treaty on good neighborly relations. On regional issues Prague supported close cooperation within the Visegrad Group (Poland, Czechoslovakia, and Hungary) and the Pentagonale initiative for the Danubian basin (Yugoslavia, Austria, Italy, Hungary, and Czechoslovakia).

The German-Czechoslovak treaty on friendship and cooperation was particularly important to Czechoslovakia, for it led to Germany's support for Prague's program to return the country to its rightful place among the Western European nations. The treaty was ratified by the Czechoslovak Federal Assembly on April 22, 1992. The document declared the 1938 Munich agreement that brought about the destruction of Czechoslovakia "null and void," reaffirmed the existing borders between the two states as "inviolable," referred to the expulsion rather than transfer of the Sudeten Germans, and pledged Germany's support for Czechoslovakia's membership in the European Community.[12]

Postcommunist Czechoslovakia moved quickly to emancipate itself from Soviet tutelage and to redefine its security policy. An agreement on complete Soviet troop withdrawal was negotiated in 1990, and the last Soviet army units left Czechoslovakia in June 1991. Prague placed great stress on collective security in Europe, as embodied by the Conference on Security and Cooperation in Europe (CSCE), and only gradually shifted to an unambiguous pro-NATO stance. In the second half of 1991, in light of the growing instability in the East, Czechoslovakia made renewed efforts to become an associate member of NATO. In April 1991 Havel made a highly symbolic visit to NATO headquarters in Brussels to explore the extent of Czechoslovakia's possible association with the North Atlantic alliance, in particular political and military cooperation between Czechoslovakia and NATO. The Czechoslovak security policy, outlined by Foreign Minister Jiri Dienstbier, emphasized collectivism and mutuality as the path to a regional and pan-European security system.[13] The stated security policy objective of the Czech and Slovak Federal Republic was to develop a cooperative pan-European security system within the broad context of the CSCE process and to "transfer security on the Continent from a bloc basis to an all-European one."[14] Dienstbier argued for the creation of a "confederated Europe" of shared economic and security interests.

The biggest problem facing postcommunist Czechoslovakia was the growing pressure of Slovak separatism, which by 1991 began to threaten the very integrity of the Czech and Slovak federation. The 1991 demand by the Slovak Prime Minister Jan Carnogursky that "in 1992 Slovakia join the new Europe under its own banner" generated enough concern in Prague to prompt the Czech parliament to consider a contingency plan for Bohemia and Moravia if the federation were to fragment.[15]

ECONOMIC REFORM

Prague began implementing market reforms a year after the Polish program had been put in place. Introduced in January 1991, the Czechoslovak plan was similar to the Balcerowicz program; it removed price controls and subsidies while holding down wage increases. The program also introduced the partial convertibility of the Czechoslovak *koruna* in order to open up the country's markets to international trade competition.[16] It called for a two-year transition period during which the country's price system would be readjusted to fall in line with the world market prices, the Czechoslovak *koruna* would become internally convertible, and the privatization program in industry and agriculture would begin in earnest. The federal government expected to have the key reforms in place by the end of 1993, with positive results apparent by the second half of the decade. The author of the program, then finance minister Vaclav Klaus, proved instrumental to its eventual success by holding fast to the principles of a free market economic system.

The plan for large-scale privatization became caught up in bureaucratic infighting inside the government, with Finance Minister Vaclav Klaus remaining a staunch proponent of a rapid transition to the market, while the social-democratic members of the federal administration, the Federal Assembly, and the government of Slovakia called for gradualism. The Slovaks were especially concerned about the unemployment that would inevitably accompany the radical privatization of industry. Since most of the Czechoslovak heavy defense industry is concentrated in Slovakia, the republic would bear the brunt of the social cost of unemployment if the course advocated by Finance Minister Klaus were adopted. Throughout, Prague feared that such a powerful shock to Slovakia's economy would fuel the separatist pressures and might contribute to the collapse of the Czechoslovak federation. In addition, various privatization schemes discussed in Prague in 1991 had to take into account the heavy indebtedness of Czechoslovakia's industry, especially of its heavy inefficient enterprises. Reportedly, as of spring 1991, Czechoslovak heavy industry plants owed in excess of fifteen billion *koruny*—close to 25 percent of all of their earnings in 1990.[17]

Privatization was announced in the government's 1991 reform program. It was implemented in Czechoslovakia in two phases: the "small-scale" privatization, which entailed auctioning off retail shops and service establishments to individuals, and the "large-scale privatization," including large state-owned factories. The large-scale privatization program was based on a voucher scheme (*kuponova metoda*), whereby the public obtained shares in state-owned enterprises. Both methods proved successful, with the state targeting 1,440 large state enterprises for voucher privatization. In 1991 the small-scale privatization scheme transferred 42 percent of all retail and service industry to private owners, with the figure reaching 75 percent in the grocery business.[18] The economic reform began to show results by early 1991, with a surge of business activity as shown by 200,000 Czechoslovaks registered to start private businesses.[19] The large-scale voucher privatization system was successfully introduced in Czechoslovakia on November 1, 1991.[20]

In 1991 several of the more profitable Czechoslovak enterprises were bought up by Western firms, including the acquisition of the Skoda car-manufacturing plant by the Volkswagen concern. Skolunion, the country's largest glass company, was acquired by the Japanese-controlled Glaverbell of Belgium. Although the actual German and Japanese equity investment in both Skoda and Skolunion, respectively, was relatively small, the deals included the long-term commitment by Volkswagen and Glaverbell to invest in new equipment and to market Czechoslovak-made goods worldwide. In 1991 Germany and Austria were the largest foreign investors in Czechoslovakia, followed by France and Holland. In January 1992 the French BSN and Swiss Nestle groups obtained approval from the Czechoslovak government to buy 21.5 percent of Cokoladovny Prague, Czechoslovakia's biggest confectionery, for $100 million.[21]

By mid-1991 the total direct foreign investment in Czechoslovakia amounted to $500 million, with the projection that it would go up to $1.5 billion by the end of the year and $3 billion by the end of 1992.[22] However, Prague's success in attracting foreign investment further aggravated the Czech-Slovak animosity. As in 1991 most of direct foreign investment in Czechoslovakia was concentrated in the Czech Lands, Slovakia charged that it was being intentionally left out of the process. The growing friction between the Czech and Slovak governments in 1991 over the distribution on direct foreign investment was yet another factor driving the two nations apart. The situation was compounded by the breakdown of the Czechoslovak-Soviet trade. The successful opening of the Czechoslovak economy to the West and the privatization program were offset by the collapse of its Eastern market. In the first half of 1991 Czechoslovak trade with the U.S.S.R. dropped by more than 50 percent.[23] This again contributed to the Czech-Slovak discord, with Slovakia suffering more as a result.

The greatest challenge facing the Czechoslovak economy during the early phase of postcommunist reconstruction was the prospect of a serious energy shortage. Considering that Czechoslovakia depended on supplies from Russia for 90 percent of its energy,[24] the need to diversify the country's oil supplies was brought home in November 1991, when Russia's President Boris Yeltsin announced the temporary suspension of all oil sales abroad in order to meet the domestic demand for energy faced by his republic in the winter of 1991. Since then Prague has sought to secure oil and natural gas supplies from other sources, including OPEC countries. Despite objections from the United States, the Czechoslovak government negotiated a series of barter agreements with oil-producing countries, trading Czechoslovak weapons for oil. In April 1991, Czechoslovakia agreed to supply Nigeria with L–39 trainer jets and spare parts in return for 100 million tons of Nigerian oil.[25] The deal envisioned additional deliveries of Nigerian oil in 1992 in return for a Czechoslovak ammunition-manufacturing plant to be built in Nigeria. Despite strong U.S. and Israeli opposition, in September 1991 Czechoslovakia agreed to supply Syria with 300 tanks in exchange for oil. Another Czechoslovak-Syrian barter deal called for the delivery of 150 Czechoslovak armored personnel carriers to Syria in 1992.[26] Over time, as Czechoslovak foreign exchange reserves increased, the barter deals became of secondary significance.

Prior to the breakup of the federation following the June 1992 parliamentary election, Czechoslovakia made considerable economic progress under the skillful leadership of Finance Minister Vaclav Klaus. In 1991 almost 40 percent of the country's exports went to the European Community, unemployment was kept low, the social welfare system remained in place, and the balance of payments and the trade balance remained in surplus.[27]

THE END OF THE CZECHOSLOVAK FEDERATION: 1992 ELECTIONS

The two-year period between the June 1990 and the June 1992 parliamentary elections witnessed a deepening internal political crisis in the Czechoslovak federation, which ultimately led to the separation of the Czech and Slovak nations into independent nation-states. The June 5 and 6 elections of 1992 reflected the division of political power between pro-reform right-wing Czechs and nationalist left Slovaks, becoming in effect a national referendum on the federation's future. The progressive fragmentation of Czechoslovakia's political parties gave the conservative parties the dominant voice in the domestic politics of the Czech Lands, while Slovakia became dominated by left and centrist nationalist parties. The biggest victors in the elections, Klaus's Civic Democratic Party (ODS) in Bohemia and Moravia and Meciar's HZDS in Slovakia, represented two radically different and, ultimately, mutually exclusive visions of the future of Czechoslovakia. In Bohemia and Moravia the ODS led by Vaclav Klaus committed itself to a liberal market reform, with tight monetary and fiscal policies, and rapid privatization. In Slovakia, Vladimir Meciar's Movement for a Democratic Slovakia and Jan Carnogursky's Christian Democratic Movement (KDH) opted for a much more gradual transition to the market and for continued state intervention in the economy.

Between 1990 and 1992 economic change in Bohemia and Moravia proceeded at a dazzling pace, while it increasingly lagged in Slovakia. Approximately 96 percent of $800 million invested in Czechoslovakia by Western firms was invested in the Czech Lands; unemployment in Bohemia and Moravia stood at 4 percent, while it reached 12 percent in Slovakia.[28] The rapid deterioration of the Slovak economy was triggered by the collapse of the former Soviet Union, whose markets had been principal customers for Slovakia's heavy and defense industries.

The postelection attempts at a negotiated settlement between Vaclav Klaus, the Czech premier-designate, and Vladimir Meciar, his Slovak counterpart, came to naught. Meciar's commitment to a three-point program calling for a declaration of sovereignty, drafting a new Slovak constitution, and the election of a Slovak president was an insurmountable obstacle, for it demonstrated to the Czechs that the Slovaks would accept at best a loose commonwealth of the two states. In the Meciar plan, Slovakia would have its own army and its own central bank, and it would pursue an independent economic policy that would include greater state intervention in the market, slower privatization, and the restoration of government subsidies to the industry.[29] The final breakdown in the negotiations came when Meciar ordered his deputies in the federal legislature to vote against the reelection of Vaclav Havel as president of Czechoslovakia. The slight to Havel, who was the most popular politician in Bohemia and Moravia, was received by the Czechs as a calculated insult.

The parliament of the newly established Czech Republic confirmed Vaclav Klaus as the country's prime minister, with Slovak premiership going to his rival Vladimir Meciar. In October 1992 the two states signed a series of agreements that would regulate the dissolution of the federation, maintain common currency during a transition period, provide for visa-free travel between the two countries, establish a customs union, and lay the groundwork for future negotiations on the division of Czechoslovak assets. After seventy-four years of existence, the federation was formally dissolved on January 1, 1993, and succeeded by the Czech Republic and Slovakia.

CZECH DOMESTIC POLITICS AND ECONOMIC POLICY SINCE INDEPENDENCE

Since the June 1992 election the Czech Republic has been governed by a conservative four-party coalition including the Civic Democratic Party, the Civic Democratic Alliance, the Christian Democratic Union-People's Party, and the Christian Democratic Party. The coalition holds 105 parliamentary seats, which gives it an absolute majority in the 200-seat parliament. The left-wing opposition in the parliament, which consists of the Communist Party of Bohemia and Moravia, the Social Democratic Party, the Liberal and Social Union, and the Movement for Self-Administrative Democracy–Association for Moravia and Silesia, has been largely ineffective in blocking the reform program of the Klaus government.[30] On January 26, 1993, the Czech parliament elected Vaclav Havel as the country's first president.[31] The domestic political agenda has been set by Klaus's Civic Democratic Party with its program of radical market reform, restoration of private property, tight monetary policy, and the rapid transition to democracy.

The Czech Republic has made a concerted effort to come to terms with its communist past. In July of 1993 the parliament passed a so-called lustration law, which bars the former secret policemen and communist officials from important political and economic positions in the country. The law condemns the entire period of the communist regime, beginning in 1948, which makes it possible to prosecute individuals for crimes committed in the name of communism. Although heatedly debated and controversial both at home and abroad, the new lustration law is a bold step to "de-bolshevize" the political life of the newly democratic Czech Republic. In contrast, Slovakia's Prime Minister Vladimir Meciar announced in 1992 that he intended to repeal the preexisting Czechoslovak lustration law.[32]

The constitution of the Czech Republic was adopted on December 16, 1992, by the Czech National Council.[33] It describes the new state as a parliamentary democracy, with the legislative powers concentrated in the hands of a two-chamber parliament. The lower house, the Chamber of Deputies, consists of 200 deputies elected to a four-year term; the Senate has eighty-one senators elected to a six-year term, with one-third of the senators elected every two years (Article 16). The Chamber of Deputies is elected in a direct election according to the principle of proportional representation, while the election to the Senate is direct but based on the majority principle (Article 18). The minimum age of twenty-one is required of a candidate to the Chamber, and the age of forty of a Senate candidate (Article 19). Both chambers of parliament are continually in session (Article 34).

The president has a largely ceremonial function as the head of state and commander-in-chief of the armed forces. He is elected by the parliament at a joint session of both chambers (Article 54). He appoints and dismisses the prime minister and his government, can dissolve the parliament, appoints judges to the Constitutional Court, appoints the president and vice president of the Supreme Inspection Office and members of the Bank Council of the Czech National Bank, and can veto legislation except for constitutional amendments (Article 62). The president also represents the republic abroad, negotiates and ratifies international treaties, receives heads of foreign diplomatic missions, accredits and recalls heads of Czech diplomatic missions, calls parliamentary elections, appoints and promotes army generals, confers state awards, appoints judges, and grants amnesty (Article 63).

In contrast to the largely ceremonial presidential functions, the Czech system makes the government the supreme executive authority of the state. The prime minister is appointed by the president. The government is also appointed by the president but on the recommendation of the prime minister; it must win a vote of confidence of the Chamber of Deputies within thirty days of the appointment (Article 68). The Chamber of Deputies can force the resignation of the government by passing a no-confidence vote by an absolute majority of the deputies (Article 72).

The constitutionality of legislation and government action is guarded by the fifteen-member Constitutional Court, appointed by the president to a ten-year term (Article 84). The constitution also provides for an independent judiciary consisting of the Supreme Court, the Supreme Administrative Court, and high, regional, and district courts (Article 91). The Supreme Court judges are appointed by the president to a life term (Article 93). The Supreme Inspection Office is an independent government watchdog organization; it is appointed by the president upon recommendations from the Chamber of Deputies. The nation's central bank, the Czech National Bank, is guaranteed an independent status and charged with maintaining the stability of the country's currency (Article 98).

The Czech constitution also includes key safeguards of individual rights and freedoms and refers specifically to the Charter of Fundamental Rights and Freedoms as an integral part of the republic's constitutional order (Article 3). The guarantees of civil rights and freedoms contained in the constitution are on par with the Western European standards. In addition to the universal constitutional safeguards, the rights of the Slovak minority have been addressed in separate legislation.

According to a 1991 census, there were over 300,000 Slovaks living in the Czech Lands and only some 40,000 Czechs living in Slovakia. The immigration law of the Czech Republic adopted in January 1993 gives preferential treatment until January 1, 1994, to Slovak nationals who wish to apply for citizenship, provided they can prove two years of residency in the Czech Lands prior to January 1, 1993, and do not have a criminal record. Anyone among the approximately 300,000 Slovaks living in the Czech Republic who are eligible for Czech citizenship can acquire it automatically by notifying the appropriate government agency of their decision. Other nationals can apply for citizenship after a five-year period of residency. In 1993, 63,000 Slovaks opted for Czech citizenship, in addition to some 46,000 who had applied in 1992; in contrast, only 200 Czechs opted for Slovak citizenship in 1993.[34]

The establishment of a conservative government led by Vaclav Klaus has brought about a further acceleration of economic reform in the Czech Republic. In contrast to Slovakia, where the continued government controls and subsidies have resulted in budget deficits and a dramatic drop in the foreign exchange reserves, in the first months of 1993 the Czech Republic registered a budget surplus, increased its foreign exchange reserves to $1.6 billion, and announced that it intended to make the *koruna* fully convertible in the near future.[35]

On January 1, 1993, the Czech Republic introduced a new tax system, including the value-added tax (VAT), and revamped the tax collection mechanism.[36] The consistent implementation of the Klaus program has generated renewed business activity, as evidenced by a substantial increase in savings deposits; the Czech Savings Bank reported an increase of close to 4 billion *koruny* in the first two weeks of 1993, compared to a 1.1 billion increase during the whole month of January 1992.[37]

While the country has done remarkably well in its trade with Western Europe, trade with the East continued to decline, including trade with Slovakia, where the estimated drop for 1993 was 30 percent.[38] According to the February projection of the Czech Statistics Bureau, the 1993 inflation rate in the Czech Republic would not exceed 16 percent, with its anticipated decline to 8 percent in 1994 and 6 percent in 1995; a corresponding inflation projection for the Slovak economy for 1993 is 27 percent.[39]

The Klaus government remains committed to a speedy transformation of the economy to a market system to facilitate the Czech Republic's full membership in the European Union at the earliest possible date.

CZECH FOREIGN AND SECURITY POLICY

The geopolitical location of the new Czech Republic is qualitatively different from that of the former Czechoslovakia. The new state has no direct contact with the East or the trans-Danubian region, while it is relatively more exposed to German influence. The Czech Republic is, therefore, a much more distinctly Western European state than was the former federation. In light of this change, membership in NATO and the EU is now the constitutive element of Czech foreign policy.

The key foreign policy objective of the Czech Republic is to achieve a speedy and complete integration with Western Europe. As outlined by Czech Foreign Minister Josef Zieleniec, the drive for return to Europe must be augmented by building good relations with the country's immediate neighbors, but most of all a strong relationship with Germany and Austria.[40] According to Zieleniec, the Western orientation will take precedence in Czech foreign policy over regional cooperation within the Visegrad Group, as it is the only option available to the country if it is to complete successfully the postcommunist transformation and ensure its future security. Prime Minister Vaclav Klaus went even further than Zieleniec in discounting the importance of the Visegrad Group by calling it "an artificial formation without natural roots."[41]

Klaus's views on regional cooperation make the Czech policy radically different from that outlined by Slovakia, which considers regional cooperation, including close ties to Ukraine, a viable alternative to Western integration.[42] For Klaus, integration with Western Europe is in the best interest of the Czech Republic for it would ensure its security and resolve the outstanding bilateral issues such as the Sudeten German demands for compensation for the loss of property after World War II, which has marred the otherwise strong relationship between Germany and the Czech Republic.

Full membership in NATO is the principal goal of Czech security policy. In preparation for this step, the country has undertaken to transform its military institutions in line with the West. Antonin Baudys of the conservative Christian Democratic Union was appointed Czech defense minister on the eve of the state's independence, on December 30, 1992. The appointment of Baudys, a civilian and a former vice premier in the Czech government, reaffirmed the principle of the civilian control over the military. Baudys called for substantial reform of the army that would entail its reduction in size and its professionalization.[43] He identified possible security threats to the Czech Republic emanating from the East, including Slovakia, should the postcommunist states in eastern Europe fail to create stable and economically prosperous systems.[44]

The appointment of Baudys as Czech defense minister was followed by substantial personnel changes within the army. Baudys announced at his first press conference in January 1993 that 674 former political officers would have to leave the new army; he referred to those officers who had approved the 1968 Warsaw Pact invasion of Czechoslovakia as "traitors" for whom there could be no place in the new democratic army. The new Czech army intends to build close cooperative relations with the German and Austrian armed forces.[45] The overall objective of the new policy is to create a "modern army of the Western European type."[46] In May 1993, Czech Defense Minister Antonin Baudys and German Defense Minister Volker Ruhe signed an agreement on military cooperation between the two countries.[47]

The Czech Ministry of Defense entered into specific negotiations with its German counterpart to assist the new army in developing an organizational structure and acquiring equipment compatible with NATO armies, as the necessary precondition for future integration in the North Atlantic alliance. Baudys's reforms include a 30 percent reduction in the numerical strength of the army by 1996 and an increase in rapid deployment capability. In addition, the basic military service will be reduced to twelve months, while the positions requiring the skill level that cannot be taught within one year's training will be staffed exclusively by career soldiers and NCOs. The units of the Czech army will be redeployed to reinforce the defense capability of South Moravia, while reducing the unit saturation of West Bohemia. The Ministry of Defense will be revamped and staffed with civilians who will set policy, while career military will refocus on policy implementation and day-to-day operation of the army. As outlined by Lieutenant Colonel Petr Luzny of the Czech Army General Staff, the transition to the new army will be completed by 1997. The force should number approximately 65,000 personnel, with about 40,000 career soldiers included in the total.[48]

DOMESTIC POLITICS AND ECONOMIC POLICY OF INDEPENDENT SLOVAKIA

Independent Slovakia is in for some difficult times ahead as it deals with its intractable economic problems and its difficult relations with other states in the region. The question of how to deal with Slovakia's ethnic minorities while the government relies on appeals to Slovak nationalism to consolidate its power base is bound to strain relations with the neighboring states and contribute to Slovakia's regional isolation. Should the economic situation in Slovakia deteriorate dramatically, the overall domestic political stability of the country could be put in question.

Slovakia's population of only over five million places the new country among the ranks of small European states. While the breakup of Czechoslovakia brought the Czech Republic closer geopolitically to the West, for Slovakia it has meant the end of its relative proximity to Western Europe. The country's weak and outdated economic base and the government's reluctance to implement market reforms have contributed to the further deterioration of economic conditions. Slovakia's large minority population, which accounts for over 12 percent of the total, has made for tense relations with the country's neighbors. In addition to the large Hungarian minority in the south, Slovakia has a sizeable Ukrainian and Ruthenian minority in the eastern regions.

In contrast to the Czech Republic where the political life has been dominated by conservative and center-right political parties, the left has dominated the Slovak political scene, with the population appearing to place considerable trust in the agencies of state power.[49] The dominant political party in Slovakia today is Vladimir Meciar's Movement for a Democratic Slovakia (*Hnutie za demokraticke Slovensko*; HZDS), which has seventy-four seats (49.33 percent) in the National Council. In addition to Meciar's holding the office of prime minister, another member of the HZDS, Michal Kovac, is Slovakia's president, although upon his election as president Kovac was compelled to resign his party membership. The HZDS has close to 50 percent of the seats in the parliament, which gives it an effective lock on the legislature. The next largest is the former Communist Party, now called the Party of the Democratic Left (*Strana demokratickej lavice*; SDL), led by Peter Weiss. The SDL has twenty-nine seats in the parliament (19.33 percent). The third largest party is Jan Carnogursky's center-right Christian Democratic Movement (*Krestanskodemokraticke hnutie*; KDH) with eighteen parliamentary seats (12 percent). The smaller parties represented in the parliament include the Hungarian Christian Democratic Movement (*Madarske krestanskodemokraticke hnutie*; MKDH), the Green Party (*Strana zelenych*; SZ), the Coexistence movement (*Egyutteles-Spoluzitie-Wspolnota-Souziti*; ESWS–Coexistentia), and the Conservative Democrats Party (*Strana konzervativnych demokratov*; SKD).[50]

Slovakia adopted a new constitution on September 3, 1992, three months ahead of the Czech Republic; the basic law became effective October 1, 1992.[51] The preamble of the new constitution speaks on behalf of the "Slovak nation" as the "bearer of political and cultural heritage," rather than the "citizens of Slovakia," as was the case in the first draft. The new wording implies the emphasis placed on the national character of the new republic. The preamble also suggests a distinction between ethnic Slovaks and Slovakia's minorities by stating that the constitution was adopted by the "Slovak nation together with members of national minorities and ethnic groups living on the territory of the Slovak Republic."

The constitution emphasizes the "national principle" over the "civic principle" by, among other things, declaring the Slovak language the official "state language" on Slovakia's territory (Article 6), although it allows for the use of other languages, subject to legal regulations. Minority rights are defined in terms that may lend themselves to a broad interpretation. In a throwback to the communist-era notion of rights, the Slovak constitution grants every citizen the right to work, the right to earn enough to maintain a decent standard of living, and the right to have "satisfactory working conditions" (Articles 35 and 36). Free medical care for Slovak citizens is also written into the constitution (Article 40).

All legislative power is vested in the unicameral National Council of the Slovak Republic, a parliament consisting of 150 deputies (Articles 72 and 73). Executive power is exercised by the president (Article 101) and the government, with the government being the "supreme body of executive power" (Article 108). The prime minister is appointed by the president; the cabinet is appointed by the president on the prime minister's recommendation (Article 111). The government is responsible to the National Council and must resign if it receives a no-confidence vote (Article 116). The president is elected by a three-fifths majority in the National Council to a five-year term; he is the head of state and the commander-in-chief of the army and has the authority to dissolve the parliament and to veto legislation (Article 102). The parliament can remove the president from office if he endangers the state's sovereignty, territorial integrity, or its democratic system (Article 106). The independent judiciary consists of the Constitutional Court composed of ten judges selected by the president to a seven-year term from among twenty candidates proposed by the National Council (Article 134). All court judges are elected by the National Council to a five-year term (Article 145).

Economic conditions in Slovakia have continued to deteriorate since the dissolution of the federation. The inevitable decline in military production has created pockets of high unemployment in the country, especially around the cities of Pavazska Bystrica, Martin, Dubnica nad Vahom, Detva, and Snina. According to government data, Slovakia's budget deficit as of April 1993 stood at Sk 13.5 billion (Slovak *koruna*),[52] but Czech sources have estimated the deficit to be closer to Sk 20 billion. According to the figures released in November 1992, Slovakia's trade deficit stood at Sk 1.3 billion,[53] and the country continued to run a substantial trade deficit into 1993.

Privatization has proceeded much slower in Slovakia than in the Czech Republic or Poland. In December 1992, the government announced that the private sector in Slovakia accounted for 20.5 percent of the GDP (compared to over 50 percent for Poland), while unemployment stood at 10.38 percent.[54] In order to improve economic conditions in the country without instituting radical market reforms, the Meciar government decided in 1993 to increase substantially Slovakia's weapons production for export. Slovakia's negotiations with the International Monetary Fund (IMF) in the spring of 1993 became deadlocked after Meciar refused to devalue the Slovak *koruna*, which led to an abrupt departure of the IMF delegation from Bratislava. In May 1993 Meciar disclosed that Slovakia would increase weapons production from the current 10 percent to 50 percent of the 1989 level in order to keep its defense factories working.[55] Meciar's decision on weapons production renewed concern in the West that Slovakia would be exporting arms to the potentially unstable regions of the Third World.

SLOVAK FOREIGN AND SECURITY POLICY

As outlined by Slovak Foreign Minister Milan Knazko, Slovakia's foreign policy emphasizes closer ties to the EC, but with equally strong ties with the country's Eastern neighbors.[56] In the regional context, Slovakia faces a complex and difficult relationship with Hungary on account of its five hundred thousand–strong Hungarian minority in the south. Slovak-Hungarian relations have also been complicated by a disagreement over the future of the controversial Gabcikovo hydroelectric plant. The Gabcikovo project initiated jointly by Hungary and Czechoslovakia in 1977 diverted a section of the Danube, causing concern about the ecological impact. After the collapse of communism, Hungary abandoned the project on account of environmental concerns, but Slovakia has proceeded with its part. Slovak-Hungarian relations have deteriorated considerably since the breakdown of Czechoslovakia, as Prague no longer exercises a moderating influence on the Slovak-Magyar ethnic tensions. Since Slovakia's independence, Budapest has accused Bratislava of discrimination against the ethnic Hungarians, pointing to a new Slovak language law that resulted in the removal of Hungarian street signs. For its part, the Slovak government charged Hungary with harboring irredentist designs against Slovakia, citing as evidence Hungarian Prime Minister Jozsef Antall's claim that he was the prime minister of all Hungarians.[57] Slovak Prime Minister Vladimir Meciar accused "some political forces in Hungary" of aspiring to revise the border with Slovakia.[58]

As outlined by Foreign Minister Knazko, Slovakia sees its place in Europe as an "East-West bridge."[59] However, Bratislava's relations with Western Europe have been complicated by Slovakia's reversal of the radical market reform policies. The increasingly complex relationship with the West, combined with the difficult relations with Hungary and the Czech Republic, has led in Slovakia to a growing sense of international isolation. Although in principle Slovakia considers joining the EU, NATO, and the Western European Union (WEU) to be important foreign policy objectives, its emphasis on pan-Europeanism is far less pronounced than that of the Czech Republic.

Slovakia's relations with the Czech Republic deteriorated rapidly in 1993. One month after the official dissolution of the Czechoslovak federation, on February 8, 1993, the two states canceled the treaty that would have maintained the *koruna* as the common currency. Trade between the two fell off sharply, followed by a series of confrontations between the two governments over the division of the assets of former Czechoslovakia. Prague demanded reimbursement for the stocks distributed to the Slovaks during the 1992 voucher privatization program.[60] Arguments over the division of the Czechoslovak army's equipment and the holdings of the Czechoslovak State Bank became especially heated. Prague and Bratislava also disagreed over the sharing of the cost of operating the Russian gas pipeline that supplies the two countries with energy. The bilateral agreement that was finally signed requires that the Czech Republic pay Slovakia $1.30 for every 1,000 cubic meters of gas flowing through every 100 kilometers of the pipeline on Slovak territory, a rate ten cents lower than the standard international rate.[61] In the spring of 1993 Slovak Prime Minister Vladimir Meciar caused an uproar in Prague when he intimated that Slovakia could cripple the Czech economy by shutting off its natural gas supplies.

In April 1993 Prague and Bratislava made some progress on the issue of dividing Czechoslovakia's assets. However, the question of how to divide the holdings of the Czechoslovak State Bank remained outstanding, as were the issues of how to divide up the Czechoslovak budget deficit, the Czechoslovak Airline (CSA) assets, and the Czechoslovak Travel Agency (CEDOK). The question of Slovakia's outstanding debt to the Czech Republic, estimated at about twenty-four billion *koruny*, remained unresolved.[62] Slovakia's claims on the Czech Republic escalated in the spring of 1993, when Slovak President Michal Kovac demanded compensation for the Czech Republic's continued use of the Czechoslovak flag and for a Slovak village transferred to Poland after World War II, for which Czechoslovakia had been given Polish territory now located in the Czech Republic. Czech Prime Minister Vaclav Klaus dismissed the demands and suggested instead a "super-zero option," whereby at an agreed date both sides would abandon all claims against one another.[63]

The considerable confusion over the priorities of Slovak foreign policy was underscored by an internal squabble within the government caused by Premier Meciar's call in February 1993 for Milan Knazko's resignation as foreign minister. Meciar accused Knazko, who is also the HZDS deputy chairman, of insufficient cooperation with other ministries, a poorly devised foreign policy concept, and the lack of adequate preparation of a series of foreign trips.[64] In the ensuing conflict, President Kovac sided initially with Knazko against Meciar, contributing to the perception that the Slovak government and the president were working at cross-purposes. On March 19, 1993, Kovac finally yielded to Meciar's pressure and dismissed Knazko as foreign minister but only after Meciar had threatened his own resignation if the demand for Knazko's removal was not fulfilled.[65] Jozef Moravcik, Meciar's associate from the HZDS and his legislative advisor, was appointed the new foreign minister.

In December 1992 Slovakia passed a National Defense Law, which provided for the creation of the Slovak Republic army. The law was described by Prime Minister Vladimir Meciar as an ad hoc measure, pending the development and approval of a national defense doctrine by the end of 1993. Also in December 1992, the Slovak parliament established the Slovak Defense Ministry.

The Slovak army is envisioned to number 35,000 soldiers and officers and is to serve strictly defensive purposes. It will rely on the domestic defense industry for its equipment and supplies. According to the legislation, the portfolio of the Slovak minister of defense is to be given to a military officer, who is to be assisted in his work by a civilian state secretary. General Imrich Andrejcak, former Czechoslovak minister of defense and the commander of the Eastern Military District, was selected by Meciar for the post of Slovak defense minister. Andrejcak was confirmed as Slovakia's defense minister in March 1993.[66] Major General Julius Humaj was appointed the commander of the Slovak army.[67]

GOING WEST, GOING EAST

The breakup of Czechoslovakia ended the seven decades of the Tomas Masaryk experiment of trying to satisfy the nationalist aspirations of the Czechs and the Slovaks in a common federal state. The two successors to Czechoslovakia are moving today in distinctly different political directions. The Czech Republic is no longer burdened with concerns over the integrity of the state and the ever-present Slovak separatism. As an inheritor of the interwar democratic tradition and a country deeply committed to rejoining Europe, the Czech Republic has very good prospects to complete its journey west. Bohemia and Moravia's traditional cultural ties to Austria and Germany have reasserted themselves once more, with Germany leading the way to bring the Czechs closer to NATO and the Western security system. The legacy of technological excellence and the historical industrial strength of the Czech Lands have contributed significantly to the rapidly growing foreign investment in the Czech Republic, while Klaus's privatization program and his consistency in implementing economic austerity measures have laid the foundations for a near-term economic recovery.

Conditions in Slovakia are less favorable, although the outcome of the postcommunist transition there is not foreordained. Still, the lasting influence of nationalism and the appeal of populism do not augur well for the country's future. The continued shift to the left in domestic politics of the Meciar government, including the slowing down of market reform and increased budget deficits, is bound to reignite inflation. Even though Meciar's government was ousted by the parliamentary vote of no-conficence on March 11, 1994, Slovakia's troubles are far from over. The country's relative isolation in the region, compounded by the significant ethnic minority problem and its proximity to the unstable East, will make stability at home more difficult to attain. Unless Slovakia faces up to the inevitable hardships of postcommunist economic transformation, it will continue to shift away from the center of the emerging new Europe, becoming eventually another trouble spot on its periphery.

NOTES

1. Vojtech Mastny, "The Historical East Central Europe after Communism," in Andrew A. Michta and Ilya Prizel, eds., *Postcommunist Eastern Europe: Crisis and Reform* (New York: St. Martin's Press, 1992), pp. 12–13.

2. Roy E. H. Mellor, *Eastern Europe: A Geography of the Comecon Countries* (New York: Columbia University Press, 1975), p. 5.

3. Sharon L. Wolchik, *Czechoslovakia in Transition: Politics, Economics, and Society* (London and New York: Pinter Publishers, 1991), p. 3.

4. Otto Ulc, "The Bumpy Road of Czechoslovakia's Velvet Revolution," *Problems of Communism*, May/June 1992, p. 28.

5. "Vaclav Havel's New Year's Address," *Orbis*, Spring 1990, p. 254.

6. "The Price of Freedom," *New Statesman and Society*, June 8, 1990. p. 25.

7. Ulc, "The Bumpy Road," p. 19.

8. Ibid., p. 21.

9. Jiri Pehe, "Czechoslovakia's Changing Political Spectrum," *RFE/RL Research Report*, January 31, 1992, p. 3.

10. Ulc, "The Bumpy Road," p. 27.

11. Ibid., p. 22.

12. Jan Obrman, "Czechoslovak Assembly Affirms German Friendship Treaty," *RFE/RL Research Report*, May 22, 1992, p. 20.

13. Jiri Dienstbier, "Central Europe's Security," *Foreign Policy*, Summer 1991.

14. Statement by the Deputy Prime Minister and Minister of Foreign Affairs of the Czech and Slovak Federal Republic Jiri Dienstbier in the Federal Assembly on April 9, 1991 (Prague: Ministry of Foreign Affairs, 1991), p. 3.

15. *RFE/RL Daily Report*, May 23, 1991.

16. Vaclav Klaus, "Transition—An Insider's View," *Problems of Communism*, January-April 1992, p. 75.

17. Interview with Dr. Cestmir Konecny, Institute of International Relations, Prague, May 2, 1991.

18. Ulc, "The Bumpy Road," p. 25.

19. Karel Dyba and Jan Svejnar, "Czechoslovakia: Recent Economic Developments and Prospects," *American Economic Review* 81 (2) (May 1991): 190.

20. Klaus, "Transition," p. 74.

21. *RFE/RL Daily Report*, January 9, 1992.

22. "Czechs Hang 'For Sale' Sign on 50 of Republic's Key Companies," *The Financial Times*, June 14, 1991.

23. "Czech Bank Chief Appeals for More Aid," *The Financial Times*, April 16, 1991.

24. *Atlas of Eastern Europe* (Washington, D.C.: Central Intelligence Agency, August 1990), p. 11.

25. *RFE/RL Daily Report*, April 29, 1991.

26. *RFE/RL Daily Report*, January 2, 1992.

27. Otto Pick, "Eastern Europe II: Czechoslovakia's Divisions," *The World Today*, May 1992, p. 84.

28. "Czechoslovakia: One Country, Two Elections," *The Economist*, May 30, 1992, p. 50.

29. "Czechoslovakia: Velvet Divorce?" *The Economist*, June 13, 1992, p. 53.

30. Jan Obrman, "Czech Opposition Parties in Disarray," *RFE/RL Research Report*, April 16, 1993, p. 1.

31. "Parliament Elects Havel First President," *FBIS-EEU-93-016*, January 27, 1993, p. 13.

32. Paulin Bren, "Lustration in the Czech and Slovak Republic," *RFE/RL Research Report*, July 16, 1993, p. 22.

33. The discussion of the constitution is based on *Constitution of the Czech Republic of December 6, 1992*, published by the Czech government.

34. Jiri Pehe, "Slovaks in the Czech Republic: A New Minority," *RFE/RL Research Report*, June 4, 1993, p. 60.

35. Jiri Pehe, "Czech-Slovak Relations Deteriorate," *RFE/RL Research Report*, April 30, 1993, p. 4.

36. "Economy Minister Comments on New Tax System," *FBIS-EEU-93-005*, January 8, 1993, p. 10.

37. "Extraordinary Increase in Deposits Reported," *FBIS-EEU-93-014*, January 25, 1993, p. 19.

38. "Dlouhy Estimates Decline in Trade with Slovakia," *FBIS-EEU-93-031*, February 18, 1993, p. 21.

39. "Inflation Prognosis for 1993–1995 Released," *FBIS-EEU-93-033*, February 22, 1993, p. 11.

40. "Foreign Minister Views Policy Objectives," *FBIS-EEU-93-010*, January 15, 1993, p. 9.

41. "Klaus Says Visegrad Group Is 'Artificial,' " *FBIS-EEU-93-053*, March 22, 1993, p. 20.

42. "Foreign Minister Stresses Western Orientation," *FBIS-EEU-93-011*, January 19, 1993, p. 14.

43. "Defense Minister Announces Army's 'Radical Steps,' " *FBIS-EEU-93-003*, January 6, 1992, p. 18.

44. "Minister Sees Possible Military Threat from East," *FBIS-EEU-93-007*, January 12, 1993, p. 19.

45. "Minister Outlines His Ideas about Czech Army," *FBIS-EEU-93-016*, January 27, 1993, p. 14.

46. "Baudys Analyzes State of Army, Ministry," *FBIS-EEU-93-017*, January 28, 1993, p. 10.

47. "Defense Minister Views NATO Integration," *FBIS-EEU-93-103*, June 1, 1993, p. 10.

48. "General Staff Officer Outlines New Army Concept," *FBIS-EEU-93-028*, February 12, 1993, p. 12.

49. *Aktualne Problemy Cesko-Slovenska* (Bratislava: Centrum pre socialnu analyzu, January 1992), p. vi.

50. Based on *Political Parties* information sheet released by the Slovak Embassy, Washington, D.C., July 1993.

51. The discussion of the Slovak constitution is based on *Constitution of the Slovak Republic* (Bratislava: CSTK, 1992).

52. *Trend*, April 28, 1993, an information sheet released by the Slovak Embassy, Washington, D.C., July 1993.

53. *Basic Figures on Slovak Economy* (Bratislava: Slovak National Agency for Foreign Investment and Development), January 1993.

54. Ibid.

55. "Meciar on Ties with Czech Republic," *FBIS-EEU-93-097*, May 21, 1993, p. 7.

56. "Foreign Minister on Country's Future Ties," *FBIS-EEU-93-005*, January 8, 1993, p. 8.

57. Jan Obrman, "Slovakia Forges a Foreign Policy: Relations with the Czech Republic and Hungary," *RFE/RL Research Report*, December 11, 1992, pp. 40–41.

58. "Meciar Accuses Hungary of Seeking Border Changes," *FBIS-EEU-93-001*, January 3, 1993.

59. "Knazko Discusses Foreign Policy Concept," *FBIS-EEU-93-013*, January 22, 1993, p. 24.

60. Pehe, "Czech-Slovak Relations Deteriorate," p. 1.

61. Ibid., p. 2.

62. Ibid.

63. Ibid., p. 3.

64. "Knazko Refuses to Resign," *FBIS-EEU-93-024*, February 8, 1993, p. 21.

65. "President Dismisses Knazko as Foreign Minister," *FBIS-EEU-93-053*, March 22, 1993, p. 21.

66. "New Minister of Defense Appointed," *FBIS-EEU-93-050*, March 17, 1993, p. 18.

67. "Law on Establishing Slovak Army Passed," *FBIS-EEU-92-245*, December 21, 1992, p. 12.

3

HUNGARY

THE MAGYAR HERITAGE

Hungary claims one thousand years of statehood. The Hungarian ancestors moved into the Danubian River basin from the Russian steppe between the Volga and the Ural Mountains in the fifth century A.D., fighting and displacing the Huns in the process. The Magyars accepted Christianity and became recognized as a kingdom by the papal authority in the tenth century under St. Stephen I of the Arpad dynasty. During his rule, the Magyars conquered Slovakia and consolidated the state. At his coronation in 1001 Stephen was given the title "Apostolic Majesty," which Hungarian kings would hold until the abolition of the monarchy in 1918.

Throughout their history the Hungarians have considered themselves culturally apart from the other peoples in the region, an island against the onslaught of the Slavs and the Turks. In addition to the geographic sense of vulnerability (Hungary is completely landlocked), the sense of separateness has been underscored by the cultural and linguistic differences. The Hungarian language is unique in Central Europe, being a part of the Ugro-Finnish group separate from Slavic, Germanic, or Romance languages.

The Magyar nobility, like the gentry of the Commonwealth of Poland-Lithuania, considered itself the bearer of national culture and national identity.* Even after Hungary found itself under Habsburg control, the Hungarians retained the key symbols of state institutions, including the

---

*Poland and Hungary have maintained historically close ties, including the election of Hungarian King Istvan Bathory (Stefan Batory) as the king of Poland-Lithuania in the sixteenth century.

parliament and, beginning in the mid-nineteenth century, a separate constitution. During the 1848–1849 "spring of the peoples" in Europe, the Hungarians under the leadership of Lajos Kossuth briefly freed themselves from Austrian control, only to see their independence from Vienna crushed at the hands of the Russians, intervening at Austria's request. However, the defeat only further strengthened Hungarian nationalism; twenty years later in the wake of the Prussian-Austrian war the Magyars won a coequal status with the Austrians within the Dual Monarchy (Austria-Hungary) after the Austro-Hungarian compromise (*Ausgleich*). Throughout their association with Austria, the Magyars prided themselves on their national culture, their political heritage, and their distinct national identity.

Hungary emerged from World War I as a defeated nation, one that had to come to terms with the retribution imposed upon the Dual Monarchy by the Paris accords. The 1919 Treaty of Trianon created an independent Hungarian state with a territory substantially smaller than the area historically claimed by the Magyars. The treaty left large concentrations of Magyars living outside the state boundaries of the Hungarian state in Czechoslovakia (southern Slovakia), Romania (Transylvania), and Yugoslavia (Vojvodina). The territorial settlement imposed upon it by Trianon made interwar Hungary a revisionist power par excellence. Hungarian policies in the interwar period were driven by a "victim complex," while initial domestic instability, including reaction to the failed 1919 communist seizure of power under the leadership of Bela Kun, pushed its domestic politics to the right. Following the suppression of the Kun revolt, interwar Hungary was a monarchy ruled by Regent Admiral Miklos Horthy and dominated by two policy imperatives: right-wing nationalism at home and staunch irredentism toward its neighbors in foreign policy.

The demands for territorial revisions deemed necessary to restore Greater Hungary led Horthy into an alliance with Nazi Germany during World War II, which again put Hungary on the side of the defeated powers at the end of the conflict. In the event, the country lost more territory and found itself firmly within the Soviet sphere of influence. Hungary's underdeveloped agricultural economy of the interwar period was further undermined by wartime devastation, as the defense of Budapest against the advancing Soviet armies ravaged the city. The anti-Russian sentiment of the Magyars was strengthened by the experience of Soviet occupation and by the imposition of the Stalinist experiment. The anticommunism of the largely Catholic Hungarian population was exacerbated by the renewed territorial losses sanctioned by the U.S.S.R. The Hungarian nation, which prided itself on its independence, was confronted once again with the material and human costs of the war and once more felt itself the victim of historical circumstance.

LEGACY OF COMMUNISM

As a former satellite of Nazi Germany Hungary could not count even on Western moral support after the war. The country was subjected to the full force of Stalin's policies, but the process of communist consolidation in Hungary was slower and more gradual than in neighboring Romania. In addition, the Hungarian communists exhibited a degree of self-restraint, possibly on account of the experience of the failed 1919 Bela Kun revolution. The Hungarian Communist Party, led by Matyas Rakosi, returned to Hungary with the Red Army and took part in the November 1945 free elections, in which the communists got only 17 percent of the vote, with a 57 percent majority going to the Smallholders' Party. The first postwar Hungarian government denied the communists their trump card by instituting a land reform and thus addressing a major popular grievance.

The communists reacted to the electoral loss with a campaign of terror against alleged "war criminals." They attacked the Smallholders' Party as reactionaries and, capitalizing on the temporary absence from Hungary of the Smallholders' Prime Minister Ferenc Nagy, forced his resignation. A revised electoral law was then introduced that favored the communist-led Leftist Bloc; it won 60 percent of the vote in the subsequent 1947 election, even though the communists still got only about 22 percent of the total. The nationalization of the economy, which had proceeded at a slow pace at first, was accelerated in 1948 on express orders from Moscow. Hungary quickly became another East European satellite of the Soviet Union, with secret police terror unleashed against the nation.

The death of Stalin and the beginning of the 1956 "thaw" in Eastern Europe precipitated a crisis in Hungary. The liberalization in Poland in the aftermath of the "Polish October," which installed the national communist regime of Gomulka, further encouraged the Hungarians to pursue reform. The economic conditions in the country were desperate, because the communist policies that had been applied to the relatively primitive economic structure of Hungary exacted an especially high price for both collectivization and nationalization. The Rakosi regime, which had been exceptionally brutal (in the late 1940s and early 1950s Hungary went through a series of violent purge trials) became the target of popular wrath.

In 1955 Khrushchev induced Rakosi to resign the premiership and to appoint Imre Nagy, the leader of a reformist faction within the Hungarian Socialist Workers' (Communist) Party. Nagy's call for wage increases, reduction in taxes on the peasantry, greater religious and political tolerance, and amnesty for political prisoners set in motion in Hungary a drive for emancipation from Soviet tutelage. In the end, the popular outcry against communist oppression led to the 1956 Hungarian Revolution and its bloody suppression by the Soviet army. The invasion was followed by the reinstatement of communist power and the execution of Imre Nagy and other leaders.

Janos Kadar was put in power by the Soviets as the new Hungarian Communist Party boss. The subsequent three decades of Hungarian communism bore the indelible stamp of Kadar's policies. Kadarism would eventually come to stand for economic reform and greater political liberty in the country, earning Hungary the reputation for being the most liberal of the East European communist regimes. In the process, Kadar shed his image of a proverbial Soviet stooge to became recognized by his people as the man who brought about the liberalization of "goulash communism."

The most dramatic reforms in communist Hungary began in the early 1960s, when the elements of a market economy and greater political liberalization were first introduced. The "New Economic Mechanism" (NEM) as Kadar's economic reform was called, was formally introduced in January 1968. It came after a period of substantial political liberalization, starting with the 1963 amnesty for political prisoners, the gradual lifting of restrictions on travel to the West, the relaxation of censorship, and the tolerance of greater diversity on political issues in the media. Although Hungarian agriculture remained fully collectivized, Kadar encouraged the peasants to maintain private plots. His economic reforms benefited from the fact that in the mid-1960s the Soviet Union itself engaged in some economic experimentation. The Hungarian New Economic Mechanism abolished some of the central planning indicators, shifted a portion of the production decision-making responsibilities from the ministries to plant managers, and simplified the central planning process by treating the plan as an outline of national economic objectives rather than a minutely detailed prescription for each branch of the economy. A partial price reform was introduced, with some 50 percent of all prices set by the market. A modicum of competition was thereby generated in the industrial sector, allowing individual enterprises to select their own suppliers on the wholesale level. The overall objective of the NEM was to create a mixed economy that would in turn generate a higher standard of living and, combined with political relaxation, serve as a source of legitimacy for Hungarian communists. This was the essence of Kadar's "social contract" for the Hungarian people.

The NEM program never worked as expected, in part because of the contradiction inherent in the very notion of a "mixed economy" and in part because of Soviet pressure to restore uniformity within the bloc after the 1968 invasion of Czechoslovakia. Another reason for the NEM's collapse was the aftershocks of the 1973 oil crisis, especially the 120 percent increase in the price of Soviet-supplied oil in 1975. The economic contraction in Western Europe caused by the oil crisis in the late 1970s dealt the final blow to Kadarism because it reduced the demand for Hungarian exports. After the oil shock the Hungarians had to borrow from the West at a growing rate, while their ability to earn foreign exchange declined. By 1980 Hungary owed over $9 billion to the West, which constituted the highest per capita debt of any East European country, exceeding even the indebtedness of Gierek's Poland. The NEM experiment was finished, with the Hungarian regime becoming painfully aware that mixed-market experiments had no long-term viability. In 1982 Hungary became the first East European state to be admitted to the International Monetary Fund and received credits to help it meet its international obligations.

Overall, although the NEM program ultimately failed, Hungary's experience with market reform, especially its de facto legalization of the "second economy," would prove a crucial asset in the postcommunist transition. The experience was a good lesson, in that it compelled the Hungarian communists to look for real market solutions to the country's economic problems.

DOMESTIC POLITICS AFTER 1989

The Hungarian Communist Party accepted the changes of 1989 while trying to capitalize on them. It formally abandoned the Leninist program, renamed itself the Hungarian Socialist Party, and campaigned for votes in the free elections in the spring of 1990. The first free parliamentary elections since the collapse of communism, in which 386 seats in the National Assembly were contested, were held in Hungary in March and April of 1990. The law provided for the direct election of 176 representatives from their constituencies, with the remainder of the representatives gaining entrance from their party lists. The clear winner in the election was the Hungarian Democratic Forum (MDF), which won 165 of the seats (42.7%); the Alliance of Free Democrats (SZDSZ), with ninety-four seats (24.4%); the Independent Smallholders' Party (FKgP), with forty-four seats (11.4%); the Hungarian Socialist Party (MSZP—former communists) with thirty-three seats (8.5%); the Alliance of Young Democrats (FIDESZ), with twenty-two seats (5.7%); and the Christian Democratic People's Party (KDNP), with twenty-one seats (5.5%); seven seats in the parliament (1.8%) went to independent deputies.[1]

The MDF, the dominant party in postcommunist Hungary, formed the government in coalition with the Independent Smallholders' Party (FKgP) and the Christian Democratic People's Party (KDNP), thereby gaining a clear majority in the parliament with 230 votes. Jozsef Antall, the chairman of the MDF, became the new prime minister.

The MDF and its coalition partners represent the center-right movement in Hungarian politics. The MDF was created in 1987, while the FKgP and the KDNP represent the continuity of the pre–World War II Hungarian politics, both having existed prior to the communist takeover. The opposition in the Hungarian parliament is represented by the left-leaning Alliance of Free Democrats, the Alliance of Young Democrats, and the Hungarian Socialist Party.

The governing coalition consists of three conservative parties. The Hungarian Democratic Forum (MDF) is currently the majority party in the Hungarian government. The MDF was founded in 1987 and by 1991 had a registered membership of thirty-eight thousand. The party's program emphasizes conservative Christian democratic values and a market reform program modeled after Western Europe. In foreign policy the MDF is committed to Hungary's return to Europe, including membership in the European Union, the Western European Union, and NATO.[2] The Independent Smallholders' Party (FKgP) is the second largest in the current coalition. It is one of the so-called historic parties, dating back to the pre–World War II era; it was originally founded in 1930. Quintessentially a party of the middle class, the Smallholders' Party emphasizes market reform with the stress on private ownership, national culture, and the "embourgeoisment" of society. It shares with the MDP a strong commitment to Christian values. The FKgP's membership in 1991 was about sixty-one thousand. The Christian Democratic People's Party (KDNP) is the smallest of the three governing coalition parties. It sees its intellectual origins in the French Catholicism of the 1930s and considers itself the political successor to the Hungarian Democratic People's Party, which existed prior to 1949. The KDNP's program is built around fundamental Christian values and individual human rights. The KDNP membership in 1991 was estimated at 15,300.

The opposition in the parliament after 1990 has been led by the Alliance of Free Democrats (SZDSZ). The party was established in 1988 based on a network of Hungarian anticommunist dissident groups. The SZDSZ sees itself in the mainstream of Hungarian and European liberalism. Its program is committed to human rights, a "social market economy," and Europe's social democratic tradition. Its membership in 1991 was over thirty-three thousand. The second largest opposition part in the parliament is the Hungarian Socialist Party (MSZP), the successor to the former ruling Communist Party. The MSZP was formed in 1989. The party's program professes commitment to "democratic socialism" based on the 1989 Stockholm declaration of principles of the Socialist International. It had about thirty-five thousand members in 1991. The smallest opposition party in the parliament is the Alliance of Young Democrats (FIDESZ). FIDESZ was formed in 1988 by academic radical liberal dissident groups. It subscribes to a radical liberal political program and professes allegiance to radical activism and ecological concerns. The membership of FIDESZ in 1991 stood at less than ten thousand.

In anticipation of the upcoming 1994 parliamentary election, on October 3, 1993 three social democratic parties united and adopted the name Social Democratic Party of Hungary. Putting aside personal rivalry, which had crippled the left in the parliament, the party elected Zoltan Kiraly as its chairman. The program of the Social Democratic Party of Hungary calls for continuing the process of democratization, joining Europe, and market economic reforms.[3] The rise of the Hungarian left in the wake of continued social dislocations caused by the transition to the market may foreshadow a shift in Hungarian politics similar to the change engendered in Poland in the fall of 1993.

The new Hungarian constitution,[4] introduced on October 23, 1989, describes the country as a democracy based on the rule of law (Article 2), with a European-type parliamentary system. The constitution vests all supreme state and legislative power in the National Assembly, a unicameral parliament in keeping with the post-1945 elimination of the two-chamber legislature. The National Assembly elects the president and the prime minister, as well as members of the Constitutional Court, the National Assembly commissioner of civil rights, the National Assembly commissioner of national and ethnic minority rights, the president and vice presidents of the State Audit Office, the president of the Supreme Court, and the chief public prosecutor. It enacts the constitution, approves the state budget, ratifies international treaties, and declares war (Article 19). The National Assembly is elected to a four-year term (Article 20).

The Hungarian political system provides for a largely ceremonial presidency, similar to the German system. The president is the nominal head of state and the commander-in-chief of the armed forces. He is elected by the parliament to a four-year term, and can be reelected to office only once (Article 29). In addition to the usual representative function, the president has the right to initiate legislation and national plebiscites (Article 30) and may return legislation sent to him by the National Assembly for signing for reconsideration if he disagrees with its provisions; if the parliament sends the law to him again, he can request an opinion of the Constitutional Court on the subject, but otherwise must sign the bill into law (Article 26). The president can be impeached by a two-thirds majority of the votes in the National Assembly, in which case jurisdiction is transferred to the Constitutional Court (Articles 31 and 32).

The prime minister is elected by a majority vote in the National Assembly upon the nomination of the president (Article 33). The prime minister then selects his cabinet, which is formally appointed by the president. The government is accountable to the National Assembly and reports periodically to the parliament on its work. The government may be removed by the parliamentary vote of no-confidence (Article 39). The constitution also outlines the structure of the independent judiciary, including the Supreme Court of the Republic of Hungary, the Metropolitan Court, and county and local courts (Article 45).

The constitution contains a bill of rights and duties, which outlines the fundamental civil rights and responsibilities of each Hungarian citizen (Articles 54 through 70). A special feature of the Hungarian constitution is the constitutionally outlined offices of the National Assembly commissioner of civil rights and the National Assembly commissioner of national and ethnic minority rights (Article 32). The two are ombudsmen for civil and minority rights empowered to investigate any apparent violation of individual and minority rights in Hungary. The minority rights ombudsman in particular is a unique institution that sets the Hungarian political system apart from other parliamentary systems.

It also reflects the continued concern Budapest has exhibited over the fate of Hungarian minority groups in neighboring countries.

ECONOMIC REFORM

Rather than introducing a comprehensive "shock therapy" program along the lines of Poland or Czechoslovakia, Hungary relied on general liberalization of the economy to develop a market system. The most important of the changes in the area of economic policy was the 1989–1990 liberalization of government rules on foreign investment. As a result, in 1990 half of all foreign investment in Eastern Europe, including eastern Germany, went to Hungary; direct foreign investment in Hungary for the year is estimated at between $750 million and $1 billion.[5] Although relative to investment in southeast Asia or southern Europe this was a modest figure, nevertheless, compared to the figure for 1989, foreign investment in Hungary rose dramatically in 1990. A better indicator of the trend in foreign investment in Hungary is the increase in the number of joint ventures registered in Budapest in 1990. According to the Hungarian Central Statistical Office, as of the end of March 1990, 7,500 joint ventures had been registered, compared to only 900 in 1989. In addition to joint ventures, there were some 1,200 Hungarian companies with substantial foreign capital.[6] More important, Hungary has managed to attract a diverse pool of investors from Europe, the United States, and even Japan; Budapest is the only capital in Eastern Europe where the two largest Japanese banks have opened their offices.

Despite the impressive number of foreign firms operating in Hungary, the country endured the usual problems associated with market reform. The inflation rate in 1991 stood at 30 percent. Another major problem for Budapest is the loss of its Eastern market, due to the collapse of Hungary's trade with the Soviet Union. In 1991, the Soviet Union owed approximately 1.7 billion transferable rubles to Hungary; and, according to Lajos Berenyi, deputy state secretary for the Ministry of International Economic Relations, Moscow had refused to negotiate with Hungary an installment repayment plan.[7] As a result, entire Hungarian companies, which had been geared within the COMECON to produce for the Soviet market, including the huge Ikarus bus complex and several audio and electronics firms, faced major layoffs.

In 1992 and 1993 Hungary continued to liberalize the market, while striving to enhance its export opportunities in the West. Nevertheless, the Hungarian economy continued to contract. As reported by the National Bank of Hungary, the country's real GDP contracted by 11.9 percent in 1991 and 4.5 percent in 1992.[8] The halving of the rate of decline, however, combined with signs of renewed economic activity in the industrial sector in early 1993 and the decline of unemployment from 13.6 percent in February 1993 to 12.6 percent by the end of June,[9] suggested that, like Poland, Hungary was finally poised for economic recovery.

Hungary has nearly completed the reform of the regulatory, legal, and institutional framework of a market economy. In 1993 the price liberalization program has, on the whole, been completed, with subsidies in 1992 amounting to roughly 5.3 percent of the GDP. The currency, the *forint*, is internally fully convertible, and privatization has progressed substantially. High inflation remained a problem in 1993. Since the privatization program began in Hungary in March 1990, nearly 1,000 state-owned enterprises have been privatized; in 1993 the State Property Agency sold 100 percent of its holdings in 165 companies. As of mid-1993 45 percent of the Hungarian GDP was produced by the private sector.[10] In 1992 new laws were introduced to compensate individuals deprived of property between 1939 and 1989. In August 1992, the government began the process of auctioning off the farmland held by collective farms.[11]

In December 1991 Hungary signed the Central European Free Trade Agreement with Poland, the Czech Republic, and Slovakia (effective March 1, 1992) to phase out tariffs and import quotas within the Visegrad Group. In addition to the associate membership agreement with the EC, also signed in December 1991 (effective March 1, 1992), Hungary concluded in March 1993 a free trade agreement with the European Free Trade Association (EFTA), effective October 1, 1993. Hungarian exports to EFTA countries account for 15 percent of all its exports, and Hungarian imports from EFTA countries comprise 21 percent of the total.[12]

FOREIGN AND SECURITY POLICY

Since 1989 Hungary has focused its foreign and security policies on the goal of becoming a full member of the European Union at the earliest possible date. During his visit to Brussels in July 1990, Prime Minister Antall told the EC officials that Hungary would seek an associate membership in the Common Market by January 1, 1992, and full membership by 1995. In 1991 Hungary was indeed granted associate membership status. Antall stated that Hungary wanted to be the first East European country to join the EC; EC Commission President Jacques Delors agreed that the associate membership deadline for Hungary was "reasonable."[13] Most important, the Hungarians hope that their cooperation with Italy and, in particular, with Austria, which has expressed an interest in filing a joint application with Hungary for EU membership, will help Budapest achieve its ultimate goal of full integration in Europe. Hungary was admitted as a member of the Council of Europe in November 1990, which Budapest views as an important landmark on the road to reintegration with Europe.

Hungarian foreign policy is aimed at gaining entrance into Western European political, economic, and security institutions. Hungary has also attached considerable importance to regional cooperation, being one of the founding members of the Pentagonale regional group including Hungary, Austria, Yugoslavia, and Italy in 1989. The organization was expanded in 1990 to include Czechoslovakia; in 1991 Poland was added as a member. The Pentagonale has been viewed by Budapest as a formula for entry into the EU and closer ties to EFTA. The initiative is also aimed at improving the infrastructure in the region. The regional cooperation agreement, which is often referred to as Adria-Danube or the Central European Initiative, has undergone substantial transformation following the implosion of Yugoslavia and the disintegration of Czechoslovakia. In 1993 the Central European Initiative included nine states: in addition to Hungary, Poland, Austria, and Italy, the membership consisted of Croatia, Slovenia, Bosnia-Herzegovina, the Czech Republic, and Slovakia. The future of the infrastructure projects remained very much in doubt on account of the continued instability in the Balkans, the collapse of Bosnia-Herzegovina, and the larger question of the group's viability as a conduit to the EU.

Hungary looks at Germany as its premier political and economic partner and the leading power in Central Europe. Therefore, relations with Germany are among the highest foreign policy priorities of the Antall government. Hungary also considers ties to France, Great Britain, and the United States to be essential factors for the country's continued independence and sovereignty. Hungary's tense relations with neighboring Romania, Slovakia, and Serbia-Montenegro over the question of the rights of Hungarian minority populations in those countries have contributed a sense of urgency to Hungarian attempts to integrate with the existing Western political and security institutions.

Hungarian relations with Russia have been dominated by the determination to shed all vestiges of the fifty years of dependency on the U.S.S.R. Budapest has been a strong supporter of Russian President Boris Yeltsin's efforts to remake Russia into a democratic state. Hungary also welcomed the creation of an independent Ukrainian state as both a potential economic partner and a buffer against resurgent Russian imperialism.

Since 1989 Hungary has viewed membership in established Western security organizations, especially NATO, as the best solution to its security needs. Faced with instability in the East and the Balkan war on its southern border, Hungary has regarded NATO as the only institution capable of guaranteeing its security. Hungary's determination to join NATO goes back to early 1990, when Foreign Minister Gyula Horn argued in a lecture at the Hungarian Political Science Association that Hungary's membership in NATO's political structures should be feasible within a few years.[14] Although NATO rejected the idea, cautioning Hungary not to force the membership issue as it was unacceptable to the Soviet Union, Horn's statements set the course of Hungarian security policy for years to come.

In 1990 and 1991, Hungary worked for a speedy dissolution of the Warsaw Pact, while continuing to explore the possibility of joining NATO. On June 28, 1990, during a visit to NATO headquarters, Hungarian Foreign Minister Geza Jeszenszky raised the issue of Hungary becoming an associate member of NATO.[15] Although rebuffed by NATO's Secretary General Manfred Woerner,

Jeszenszky has remained committed to the notion of Hungary building a bridge to the North Atlantic alliance as a step to future membership.

Through persistent diplomacy, Budapest succeeded in placing the issue of security in eastern and central Europe on the West European agenda. NATO responded to pressure from Budapest by issuing official statements expressing continued interest in the region. Secretary General Manfred Woerner during a November 1990 visit to Hungary told his hosts that the Atlantic alliance would help Hungary "to overcome both economic and stabilization problems."[16] In November 1990 Hungary was offered associate membership in the NATO Assembly, which was formally accepted by the Hungarian parliament on January 29, 1991.[17] In May 1991 NATO reaffirmed its interest in the region's security and independence. Hungarian diplomacy, especially its persistence in pushing for membership in NATO, has contributed significantly to the initiation of a special relationship between the Visegrad Group (Poland, Czechoslovakia, Hungary) and NATO. In 1992 and 1993, after the demise of the Soviet Union and considering the escalation of violence in former Yugoslavia, Hungary shifted from inquiries about the feasibility of NATO membership to direct calls for its inclusion in the alliance. Feeling vulnerable on account of the Hungarian minority in Vojvodina and Transylvania and uncertain about the outcome of the confrontation between Russia and neighboring Ukraine, in 1993 Hungary asked directly for a timetable to bring it into NATO.

Reform of the Hungarian armed forces began in 1988, and it was accelerated after the collapse of communism. A new military oath was introduced on August 20, 1989, speaking of the soldier's obligation to his nation.[18] The Hungarian defense ministry also moved to depoliticize the armed forces. On October 12, 1989, Defense Minister Colonel General Ferenc Karpati signed an order dissolving Communist Party youth organizations in the army.[19] In late November 1989, the Hungarian government announced the plan to cut army personnel by up to 25 percent by the end of 1991. The reductions amounted to between 30,000 and 36,500 men and, according to new Hungarian Defense Minister Lajos Fur, would reduce the size of the Hungarian army to under 90,000 by the year 1992, with the target size of 75,000 troops.[20] The Hungarian border guard units were also restructured. The size of the Hungarian army went down from 91,000 in 1989 to about 80,000 by the end of 1990, thus reaching the approximate size of the army outlined in the new legislation.[21] The defense ministry also proposed that a territorial defense force be created as a home-guard reserve for the regular army. This home-guard force would be equipped with small arms stored in regional depots, and it would undergo periodic retraining.[22]

The government has also reaffirmed civilian control over the military. The reform program stipulates that although the day-to-day professional management of the Hungarian army is the prerogative of the commander-in-chief, the defense ministry sets policy and develops the nation's military doctrine. The commander-in-chief of the Hungarian army has the rank of a state secretary;

the position was created on December 1, 1989, with the office going to Lieutenant General Kalman Loerincz. Under the current reform program, the commander-in-chief is responsible for the implementation of military policy, as well as all personnel decisions and training programs. He is directly subordinated to the president of Hungary, who under the new constitution is the supreme commander of the Hungarian armed forces.

In 1990 the Hungarian government broke with the long-standing tradition of appointing a military man to the post of defense minister. Since May 16, 1990, the Hungarian Ministry of Defense has been headed by Lajos Fur, a civilian and a founding member of the Hungarian Democratic Forum.[23] Fur's appointment as defense minister was followed by changes in the deployment pattern of the armed forces on the Hungarian territory. During Hungary membership in the Warsaw Pact, the bulk of its army had been deployed in the western part of the country. This had reflected the role assigned to Hungary's by Soviet military planners to serve as a springboard for Warsaw Pact offensive operations through Austria and Yugoslavia against NATO. At the time, the majority of the Hungarian army had been concentrated in the 1st Army with headquarters in Budapest, the 5th Army at Szekesfehervar about thirty miles southwest of Budapest, and the 3rd Mechanized Corps with headquarters at Cegled about thirty-two miles southeast of Budapest.[24] In 1990 Fur reviewed the old deployment pattern in light of the country's new defensive doctrine and ordered an increase in the number of Hungarian military units stationed along the Romanian, Soviet, and Yugoslav borders. In early 1991 the Hungarian defense ministry asked the parliament for the authorization to create several new military districts.

The new deployment calls for the creation of four new military districts: (1) the Western District, (2) the Central District, (3) the Eastern District, and (4) the Budapest District. The new district system replaces the old "Western Zone" and "Eastern Zone," resulting in a balanced deployment of forces throughout Hungary in line with the new defense doctrine. According to the new plan, in wartime the Western, Central, and Eastern Districts would become three army corps, while the Budapest District would constitute an autonomous defense force assigned to the defense of the nation's capital.

The new Hungarian military doctrine allows the army to train only for defensive purposes and to operate only on the country's territory, except for peacekeeping missions authorized by a two-thirds vote in the parliament. This restriction on the use of the armed forces has been written into law.

LOOKING WEST

Freed from Russian tutelage, Hungary is committed to return to its traditional place as one of the historic nations of Central Europe. The country is grappling with a multitude of political and economic problems, some generated by the five decades of communism, some inherent in the geopolitics of the region. The Hungarians are trying to come to terms with their communist past. In February 1993, the parliament adopted two laws intended to bring those responsible for abuses under communism to justice.[25] However, there appears to be no firm consensus yet as to whether the guilty ones ought to be prosecuted or simply named publicly.

Hungary is also dealing with the consequences of the ongoing war in former Yugoslavia, which has the potential of spilling across its borders. Budapest has also been confronted with a serious refugee problem, as the Croats and Bosnian Muslims flee the fighting. Hungary is not able to deal on its own with a continued influx of refugees. Hungary's strained relations with Romania, Slovakia, and Serbia-Montenegro over the treatment of their Hungarian minority populations are likely to deteriorate further as regional instability increases. Furthermore, the social costs of economic reform and apparent disarray within the governing coalition after the sudden death of Prime Minister Antall may bring about a political realignment after the 1994 parliamentary election.

Overall, however, despite the increased visibility of extreme nationalist politicians within the ruling Hungarian Democratic Forum, Hungary has continued to project a positive image of internal progress and considerable political stability. Although not yet a member, Hungary has established regular consultations with NATO and concluded a number of bilateral military cooperation agreements with Western European countries. Already an associate member of the European Union, Hungary awaits a decision on the timetable for bringing it into the EU structures. Considering the continued improvement in its trade with Western Europe, despite the continued decline in the Hungarian GDP, the country has good prospects to rejoin the West as a less developed but nevertheless modern European state.

NOTES

1. Alfred A. Reisch, "Roundtable: Hungary's Parliament in Transition," *RFE/RL Research Report*, December 4, 1992, p. 29.

2. The discussion of the political programs of the six key parties is based on "Political Parties in Parliament," *Fact Sheets on Hungary* (Budapest: Ministry of Foreign Affairs, 1991).

3. "Hungarian Social Democratic Parties Unite," *RFE/RL Daily Report*, October 5, 1993.

4. The discussion of the Hungarian basic law contained in this section is based on *The Constitution of the Republic of Hungary*, an English translation of the document published by the Hungarian government in 1990; the English translation of the text was validated on December 31, 1990.

5. "Hungary Takes the Lead on Foreign Investment," *The Financial Times*, May 14, 1991.

6. Ibid.

7. "Official on Trade Problems with USSR," *FBIS-EEU-91-099*, May 22, 1991, p. 18.

8. *Recent Economic Developments in Hungary: Main Report* (Budapest: National Bank of Hungary, 1993), p. 7.

9. Ibid., p. 8.

10. Ibid., p. 11.

11. Karoly Okolicsanyi, "Hungarian Compensation Programs Off to a Slow Start," *RFE/RL Research Report*, March 12, 1993, p. 49.

12. *Recent Economic Developments in Hungary: Main Report*, p. 56.

13. *RFE/RL Daily Report*, July 18, 1990.

14. Alfred Reisch, "The Hungarian Dilemma: After the Warsaw Pact, Neutrality or NATO," *Report on Eastern Europe* 1 (15) (Munich: RFE/RL, April 13, 1990): 17.

15. *RFE/RL Daily Report*, June 29, 1990.

16. "NATO's Woerner Continues Official Visit," *FBIS-EEU-90-227*, November 26, 1990, p. 33.

17. "National Assembly Meets in Extraordinary Session, Approves Vote on NATO Membership," *FBIS-EEU-91-020*, January 30, 1991, p. 21.

18. "Oath Omits Reference to Party Loyalty," *FBIS-EEU-89-160*, August 21, 1989, p. 11.

19. "Youth Organizations to Disband," *FBIS-EEU-89-198*, October 16, 1989, p. 42.

20. "Fur Comments on Country's Future Defense Policy," *FBIS-EEU-90-119*, June 20, 1990, p. 28.

21. *The Military Balance, 1989–1990* (London: International Institute of Strategic Studies, 1989), pp. 44–48.

22. "Defense Ministry Airs Future Army Issues," *FBIS-EEU-90-152*, August 7, 1990, p. 15.

23. Fur, who holds a doctorate in history, was active in the 1956 Hungarian Revolution and was arrested after the Soviet invasion of the country. Shortly after his release in December 1956, Fur escaped to the West and briefly settled in France. Upon his return to Hungary he was prohibited from following his academic career until 1964; in the meantime Fur worked as a manual laborer.

24. "Warsaw Pact Forces in Europe," *Jane's Defence Weekly*, April 4, 1987, p. 598.

25. Edith Oltay, "Hungary Attempts to Deal with Its Past," *RFL/RL Research Report*, April 30, 1993, p. 6.

II

THE BALKANS

4

ROMANIA

THE LATINS OF EASTERN EUROPE

The Romanian nation harkens back to ancient Dacians, the original inhabitants of the Carpathian-Danubian region. The Roman conquest of Dacia brought with it the Latin language and Christianity, laying the foundations for the distinct Romanian culture. The Romanians claim kinship with the Spaniards, the French, and the Italians and regard their Latin identity as separate from the Slavic, Magyar, or Turkish traditions of their neighbors.

As Roman power waned, the Dacians were confronted by the Magyars and the Slavs. By the eleventh century northwestern Dacia (Transylvania) came under Magyar rule. Southern and eastern Dacia (Wallachia and Moldova) became briefly united in the late sixteenth century by King Michael the Brave, and (until Michael's assassination) constituted the proto-Romanian medieval state. As Turkey expanded into the Balkans, Wallachia and Moldova became protectorates of the Ottoman Empire administered by Greek officials in Turkish service.

The eighteenth century marked the beginning of modern Romanian nationalism, with Transylvania regarded by Romanian nationalists as the cradle of their culture. The 1848 revolutions reawakened Romanian nationalism at the time when the power of the Porte was declining. Romanian territory was now contested by Russia and Austria, with the former occupying briefly eastern Moldova (Bessarabia) and the latter northern Moldova (Bukovina). The modern independent Romanian state emerged in 1859 in the wake of the collapse of the Ottoman Empire. The first monarch, Prince Alexandru Ioan Cuza, was elected by both Wallachia and Moldova; he was succeeded in 1866 by King Carol, who finally expelled the Turks in 1877 and established the monarchy. Romania formally declared independence in 1881.[1]

Prior to World War I Romania ranked among the most developed Balkan states, as its agricultural base rapidly expanded and its productivity rose. In World War I Romania fought on the side of the Allies and was rewarded in 1920 with the return of Transylvania, Bessarabia, and Bukovina. After the war the country undertook a largely successful industrialization program. With the rise of Nazi Germany, Romania attempted to play a balancing game between Hitler and the Western powers. For a time King Carol II managed to resist the radical fascist Iron Guard, while maintaining Romania's traditional pro-French orientation. The policy began to shift after the Anschluss, when the king saw no alternative but to move closer to Germany with the hope that Hitler's favor would prevent the amputation of Romanian territory gained in 1920. Ultimately Romania sided with the Axis and took part in German offensive operations against the Soviet Union.[2]

In the course of World War II Romania suffered losses of territory to Hungary, Bulgaria, and the Soviet Union. Following Carol's abdication and the assumption of power by his son Michael, until 1941 Romania was briefly ruled by an uneasy condominium of the Iron Guard and the army. In January 1941 General Ion Antonescu staged a coup that after several days of bitter street fighting in Bucharest destroyed the Iron Guard and made the military the sole guardian of the country's politics. Under Antonescu's stewardship, Romania was a loyal German ally until August 1944, when it switched sides to the Allies after an anti-Antonescu coup engineered by Prince Michael. The coup opened the doors to the Balkans to the approaching Soviet armies.[3]

In 1944 Romania was quickly overrun by the Soviets and was placed under communist control in February of 1945. The country's strategic location across the Soviet border made it a prime target for a Soviet satellite as a buffer state on the U.S.S.R.'s periphery. The Soviet takeover occurred with little opposition from the Allies, who regarded it in part as a form of retribution for the Romanian atrocities committed on Soviet territory during the war. By 1945 Winston Churchill effectively wrote Romania off.

In March 1945 the king created on Soviet orders a communist-dominated government, headed by Petru Groza. The sham monarchy lasted through 1947, while the Soviet-style communist transformation of Romanian politics and economy was instituted. The communists, led by Gheorghe Gheorghiu-Dej, gained a modicum of popular support by stressing the Soviet Union's willingness to give Romania the Transylvanian lands, at the expense of Hungary. The Groza regime argued that only the communists could secure Soviet support necessary to guarantee the regained territories. The land reform of 1945 also proved quite popular with the peasantry and contributed to the communist power base, while the opposition was paralyzed by "war crimes" trials against former Romanian leaders. By 1946 the communists were firmly in control in Romania. In the 1950s the country under the leadership of Gheorghiu-Dej followed the Soviet pattern of the complete nationalization of industry, collectivization of agriculture, and terror by the secret police. Romania continued the course through the 1950s largely unaffected by the 1956 de-Stalinization campaign of Nikita Khrushchev. In 1965, after Gheorghiu-Dej's death, Nicolae Ceausescu was appointed the Communist Party first secretary.

THE CEAUSESCU YEARS

The story of the Ceausescu regime is one of the most hideous instances of repression and human rights abuses in the history of communist Europe. Nicolae Ceausescu was only forty-seven when he assumed office. He had risen through the ranks of the communist youth movement and was clearly groomed for succession; at the age of thirty-seven he had become one of the youngest members of the Romanian Politburo. His selection in 1965 was one of the smoothest communist successions in history.

The twenty-five years of the Ceausescu regime were marked by a Romanian brand of Stalinism at home, coupled with a modicum of national autonomy on matters of foreign policy. The Romanian dictator developed a cult of personality by playing up to the nationalist sentiment of the population. The key party and government positions went to Ceausescu's relatives in what has been referred to as the "party familialization" process.[4] Repression at home was in sharp contrast to Ceausescu's assertiveness in the foreign policy arena. For example, in 1968 Romania denounced the Soviet-led Warsaw Pact invasion of Czechoslovakia, insisting that Czechoslovak domestic politics was the business of the Czechoslovaks. Ceausescu's denunciation of the invasion brought Romania worldwide attention, and it served to improve dramatically Romania's relations with the West. At the same time, Ceausescu launched a campaign that glorified the "greater Romania" of the past, emphasizing the Dacian origins of the Romanian people as being equally as important to the country as their Roman roots.

The rising tide of state-sanctioned nationalism was instrumental in Romania's resistance to complete Soviet domination. At the core of Ceausescu's communist nationalist policy was his dispute with Moscow over the direction of Romania's economic development. Bucharest rejected the Soviet recommendation that Romania halt its industrialization drive and become an agricultural economy par excellence within the COMECON system. Ceausescu argued that such a policy would cripple the country's economy, as he pointedly noted that the Soviet Union did not place any such structural specialization constraints upon itself.

Romanian opposition to direct Soviet pressure became more vocal in the 1960s because of the 1958 Soviet military withdrawal from Romania.[5] The departure of Soviet troops removed an important psychological barrier in Romania and contributed to the new boldness of its foreign policy. Finally, the rising Sino-Soviet dispute presented Romania with a historic opportunity to reassert its independence vis-à-vis Moscow. Ceausescu personally derived considerable benefit at home from his opposition to direct Soviet control, while also scoring points with the West. However, Ceausescu's policy of resisting the Russians never threatened a direct break with Moscow, as the Romanians knew that such a move would have in all likelihood led to a Soviet invasion. Instead, Ceausescu worked for an increased autonomy in relations with the U.S.S.R.

By the 1970s Ceausescu had developed his own cult of personality and become a full-fledged communist despot. Aided by his wife, Elena, he brought his family directly into the government, transforming the communist regime into a family business of sorts. In foreign policy Ceausescu courted the West, especially the United States, Germany, and France, as well as the People's Republic of China. He also developed a special relationship with Tito, which in effect became a Yugoslav-Romanian defensive axis against a putative attack by the Soviet Union. Like Yugoslavia, Romania was the only other communist state and the only member of the Warsaw Pact to have a true national defense doctrine whose objective was to deny the country's territory to any outside aggressor. It was also the only Warsaw Pact country that maintained full diplomatic relations with Israel despite the Soviet decision to break off relations with the Israelis after the Six-Day War. Ceausescu's Romania became an active proponent of the rights of small and medium powers, established close ties with the nonalignment movement to increase its margin of safety from the Soviets, and offered to help mediate international disputes, including the quarrel between the U.S.S.R. and China. Romania's "maverick" reputation was strengthened in 1974 when Ceausescu suggested that the position of the commander-in-chief of the Warsaw Pact should be rotated and not given exclusively to the Soviets, when he successfully resisted Soviet pressure in 1978 to increase Romania's military spending, and when he condemned the 1979 Soviet invasion of Afghanistan.[6]

In sharp contrast to its independence in foreign policy, Romania's domestic politics under Ceausescu degenerated into a neo-Stalinist cult of personality. Increasingly megalomaniac, Ceausescu experimented with his own variety of "cultural revolution" after his 1969 visit to China. His wife, Elena, was included in the Permanent Bureau of the Party, while his three brothers were placed in key government positions and his son Nicu made a member of the Central Committee. Romania's communist regime became notorious for relegating its Hungarian, Jewish, Turkish, Serbian, and German minorities (about 20% of the country's population) to the status of second-class citizens. The result of repression at home and assertiveness in the international arena was a caricature of nationalism fueled by Ceausescu's Stalinist megalomania.[7]

The last years of Ceausescu's rule were particularly notorious for human rights abuses and Romania's continued economic decline. In large part the dire economic conditions of the country were a direct consequence of Ceausescu's determination to repay his country's foreign debt. During the 1980s Romania repaid the $11 billion it had owed to the West, and by 1989 it had earned a $2.5 billion surplus.[8] Another of Ceausescu's experiments in social engineering was his program of "systematization" (*sistematizare*), introduced in 1988, whereby the dictator announced his intention to raze about half of Romania's 13,000 villages and reconstruct them into "agro-industrial centers."[9] The program had its roots in the 1972 and 1974 Romanian Communist Party decisions, but in 1988 Ceausescu renewed his pressure for its full implementation when he announced that the program would be completed by the turn of the century. Ceausescu's grand experiment was interrupted by the wave of the 1989 anti-communist revolutions, which brought down his regime amid a violent confrontation between his loyal *Securitate* secret police and the army siding with the rebels.

The brutal fighting in Bucharest lasted for eleven days and produced carnage unseen in Europe since 1945. The uprising culminated with the capture and execution of Ceausescu and his wife; tapes of their interrogation were played on national television, which also showed the bodies after the execution. Devastated by four decades of communist dictatorship whose harshness became notorious throughout Europe, twenty-three million Romanians were now faced with the intractable task of rebuilding their economy and state administration virtually from scratch. In a country with no democratic tradition, with a problem of national minorities on its territory, and with no allies in the region, prospects for developing a working democratic system were slim at best.

AFTER THE REVOLUTION: BETWEEN TWO ELECTIONS

The 1989 revolution was largely a rebellion against Ceausescu. The rebels came both from within the ruling elite, as exemplified by Ion Iliescu and other "recycled communists" who led the movement, and from the masses of embittered and desperate Romanians. The determination of the army to side with Iliescu decided the outcome. Still, the new regime that emerged in the aftermath of the rebellion remained firmly in communist hands, only this time the communists were of the anti-Ceausescu faction.

The majority of the Romanians were desperate to improve their economic lot, to remove the constant fear of police terror, and to restore freedom of speech and religion. The society at large had very little notion of what democracy would entail and hence welcomed the advent of the National Salvation Front (NSF) led by Iliescu, as an alternative to the Ceausescu regime.[10] The Iliescu regime was accepted by the majority of the population as legitimate, but it continued to be challenged by the opposition at home and abroad. Iliescu's personal popularity among the blue-collar workers in Romania's cities and among the peasants in the countryside, as well as his skillful use of nationalist themes in the May 1990 election campaign, secured the NSF an electoral victory. The balloting gave the NSF two-thirds of the seats in the parliament, with 66 percent of the votes; Iliescu was elected president with 85 percent of the vote. The Hungarian Democratic Union, representing two million ethnic Hungarians, came in second with 7 percent of the popular vote, while the opposition National Liberal Party won 6 percent of the vote.[11] The remaining opposition parties, including the right-wing National Peasant Party and the Green Party, were pushed into the fourth and fifth places, respectively. The new parliament became Romania's constituent assembly, with its term limited to two years and with the primary goal of drafting the new basic law. The new constitution was passed in 1991.

The NSF's power base was further enhanced by the postelection progressive fragmentation and splintering within the National Liberal Party, the only genuinely democratic alternative to Iliescu's reformed communists. The Civic Alliance, an organization created after the May election and committed to resisting the NSF also failed to unify the opposition, and became yet another weak political party in Romania's postcommunist political mosaic. In November 1991 the Civic Alliance's popular support stood at 12 percent.[12] On the right of the political spectrum, nationalist fears that the collapse of communism might lead to territorial claims against Romania by Hungary led in February 1990 to the creation of *Vatra Romaneasca*, an ultranationalist party that a month later instigated a pogrom on Hungarian political activists, killing eight people and leaving scores wounded. Since then, *Vatra Romaneasca*'s membership has increased to about four million, making the organization an important ally of the NSF.[13]

The NSF monopoly power position did not remain unchallenged for long. The political situation in Romania between May 1990 and the subsequent parliamentary election in September 1992 was marked by splintering within the government, with President Iliescu firing Prime Minister Petru Roman in October 1991. Roman was being blamed for embarking on an ambitious market reform program, which Iliescu's old communist guard disavowed. Theodor Stolojan, who succeeded Roman as prime minister, proved unable to arrest the country's economic decline. The rapidly deteriorating economic conditions led to miners' riots in Bucharest in the fall of 1991 and to a growing popular dissatisfaction with the Iliescu regime. Moreover, the breakup between Iliescu and Roman resulted in March 1992 in the fragmentation of the NSF itself into Iliescu's hard-line neocommunist Democratic National Salvation Front (DNSF) and the more market-oriented remnants of the NSF, led by Roman.

As popular support for the NSF eroded, the opposition united into an umbrella organization, the Democratic Convention of Romania (DCR), to challenge the government in the upcoming elections. The Democratic Convention consisted of eighteen groups, the four principal groups among them being the Liberal Party, the Peasants' Party, the Hungarian Union of Democratic Magyars, and the Civic Alliance.[14] Despite the obvious diversity of political programs among the four, they were united by the principal common objective of completing the revolution, that is, getting rid of the communists. By February 1992, the Democratic Convention was showing remarkable strength in local elections in the country's largest cities, especially in Bucharest and Timisoara.

Still, despite expectations that the September 27, 1992, balloting would finally unseat the communists, the Democratic Convention failed to win the parliamentary majority and failed to replace Iliescu as president. Iliescu's DNSF won 27.71 percent of the parliamentary votes, winning 114 of the 341 seats in the Chamber of Deputies, and 28.29 percent of the Senate votes, winning forty-nine of the 143 seats in the Senate. DCR candidates came in second, with 20.09 percent of the lower house vote and eighty-two seats, and 20.16 percent of the senate vote and thirty-four seats.[15] In the runoff presidential election, Iliescu won 61.43 percent of the vote, beating DCR's Emil Constantinescu, who received 38.57 percent of the vote.[16] Roman's NSF became the third-strongest party in the parliament, with the Party of Romanian National Unity (PRNU) and the Hungarian Democratic Federation of Romania (HDFR) coming in fourth and fifth, respectively.

The most disturbing aspect of DNSF's 1992 electoral victory was that it constituted a mandate for Iliescu's economic program of continued central controls and for reversing the market reforms previously initiated by the Roman and continued by the Stolojan governments. In effect, the election constituted a national vote against economic change. It also marked gains for the "national communists" represented by the Greater Romania Party (GRP) and the Socialist Labor Party (SLP), who in October 1992 formed in the senate the National Bloc.[17] The greater fragmentation of the legislature after the 1992 election, where no single party holds a majority, has raised questions about the parliament's ability to put together a stable coalition, while increasing the influence of neocommunists (represented by the SLP) and radical nationalists (represented by the GRP and the Party of Romanian National Unity; PRNU) in Romania's politics. As a case in point, the new government of Nicolae Vacaroiu managed to win a narrow majority only thanks to the support of the GRP, the SLP, and PRNU. The Vacaroiu minority cabinet, which consists largely of technocrats with no party affiliations, including the DNSF, can easily be removed by a parliamentary vote of no-confidence.[18]

Iliescu's power base has remained strong among the old-time *nomenklatura*, the blue-collar workers, and the peasants. The effectiveness of government's central control has been assisted by the preservation of the remnants of the secret police, now called the Romanian Intelligence Service, and the continued support of the army.[19]

POSTCOMMUNIST POLITICAL SYSTEM

In postcommunist Romania the office of the president clearly dominates the country's political scene. The 1991 constitution[20] has vested in the office of the president of Romania the overall responsibility for the national sovereignty and territorial integrity and, more important, has assigned to him the special task as a "mediator between the Powers of the State, as well as the State and society" (Article 80). The president designates the prime minister and appoints the government once the cabinet has been approved by the parliament; once the government is constituted, the president has the authority to appoint ministers recommended by the prime minister, without having to consult with the parliament (Article 85). The president has the right to participate in the meetings of the government on key matters of foreign policy, defense, public order, or any other matter if the prime minister requests his presence; all meetings where the president is present are chaired by him (Article 87). In effect, the president can exercise strong influence over day-to-day operation of the government.

The president is the commander-in-chief of the armed forces, and he chairs the Supreme Council of National Defense (Article 92). He concludes international treaties negotiated by the government (Article 91) and has the right to declare the state of emergency, provided he submits his decision to the parliament within five days (Article 93). The president can dissolve the parliament if his candidates to form the government fail to obtain the parliamentary votes of confidence within sixty days after the first request has been made (Article 89). The president can exercise his power by issuing decrees; decrees on matters of foreign policy and defense require the countersignature of the prime minister (Article 99). A motion to suspend the president from office can be brought to the floor if supported by at least one-third of the deputies and senators. The motion must pass by a majority vote in a joint session of both chambers, in which case a referendum must be held within a month to decide if the president is to be removed from office (Article 95). In effect, even if the parliament votes to remove Iliescu, he can overcome the challenge by appealing directly to the public.

The parliament, divided into the Chamber of Deputies and the Senate, is elected to a four-year term (Article 60). It is Romania's supreme legislative body. In some consideration of Romania's minority population, the constitution guarantees symbolic parliamentary representation to the minorities even if their parties fail to clear the electoral vote threshold to gain a seat in the parliament. Should the party representing a minority group fail to win a representation in the parliament, it is automatically entitled to one seat in the Chamber of Deputies; however, ethnic minorities are allowed to be represented only by one party (Article 59).

In keeping with the overall concentration of power in the hands of the president, the prime minister is designated by the president and then has to win parliamentary approval (Article 102). The government is responsible for its actions only before the parliament, but the president also has the right to demand criminal prosecution against government members for acts committed in exercising their office (Article 108). Once criminal prosecution against members of the government has been requested, the president may suspend the ministers from their office. In practice, therefore, the government is accountable to both the parliament and the president.

The 1991 constitution outlines the structure of the Supreme Court of Justice appointed by the president to six-year terms (Article 125) and the Constitutional Court, with three Constitutional Court judges appointed by the lower house, three by the Senate, and three by the president (Article 140). It also contains articles that guarantee the protection of property rights (Articles 134 and 135).

ECONOMIC POLICY

Romania's economic reform has been in disarray since the September 1992 election, which strengthened the hand of the old *nomenklatura* opposed to a Western-style market system. The continued communist domination of the country's political scene, combined with reports of human rights abuses, has substantially retarded the flow of foreign investment and resulted in the October 1, 1992, decision by the U.S. Congress to withhold most-favored-nation (MFN) status from Romania.[21]

Romania's industry built in the Ceausescu era is obsolete and uncompetitive, while its raw-material base, especially oil, which in the past served as the primary source of foreign exchange, has been depleted. The country's agriculture, still the principal sector of the economy, is inefficient and unproductive, while access for Romania's foodstuffs to Western markets is severely restricted.

The economy continues to shrink, with the 1992 economic decline in GDP reaching 16.5 percent and the overall decline in industrial production for the year at 23.5 percent. The downward trend in the economy has continued uninterrupted since 1990, with unemployment reaching one million or 9 percent of the labor force by the end of 1992, with official forecasts projecting an additional 400,000 to 600,000 unemployed by the end of 1993. The shrinking economic base and soaring inflation made 43 percent of all Romanian families destitute, with 16 percent of all families living below the official poverty line.[22]

Privatization has been largely ineffective, with partial restoration of collectivized land to previous owners and with the voucher industrial privatization program still to be fully implemented. The July 1990 Privatization Law calls for the reorganization of state-owned enterprises into so-called *regies autonomes* (self-sufficient state entities) or joint stock companies. While joint stock companies are to be privatized, *regies autonomes* will remain state property.[23] Although Romania's private sector increased substantially in the areas of trade and tourism, as of 1993 it remained small relative to the continuously dominant large-scale state sector. In April 1991 a liberal foreign investment law was passed by the parliament, resulting in some increase in activity by foreign investors, notwithstanding the continued political uncertainty. Direct foreign investment picked up in late 1991 through mid-1992, with multinationals such as Coca-Cola, Colgate Palmolive, Amoco, and Siemens investing in Romania. According to the Romanian Development Agency, as of December 1992 the main source of foreign investment in Romania was Italy, with the total investment estimated at about $70 million, followed by the Netherlands with $65 million, the United Kingdom with $64 million, the United States with $63 million, Germany with $58 million, and France with $57 million invested.[24] The perception abroad of continued political instability and the lack of credibility with potential foreign investors have continued to plague Romania's effort to attract Western capital.

Bucharest has tried to change this perception by lobbying the U.S. Congress for the restoration of MFN status, as was done by Iliescu during his visit to the United States to attend the opening of the Holocaust Memorial Museum in April 1993. The government also hired the APCO public relations firm to induce the American business community to consider Romania a good place for business.[25] In addition, in November 1992 Romania initialed an association accord with the EC, subject to ratification by the European Parliament, thus becoming the fourth former Soviet bloc country, after Poland, Czechoslovakia, and Hungary, to sign an association agreement with the EC.

FOREIGN AND SECURITY POLICY

Postcommunist Romania's foreign policy is predominantly regional. It is driven on the one hand by the nationalist fear of Hungarian irredentism in Transylvania, and on the other hand by the national claim on Moldavian territories annexed by the U.S.S.R. in 1939 after the Ribbentrop-Molotov Pact. The fact that Romanian nationalists captured about 15 percent of the vote in the September 1992 election, with most of their support coming from Transylvania, has raised questions about the future of Romania's relations with Hungary and given new credence to the "two Romanias" argument advanced by the nationalists, by which Bessarabia of the former Soviet Republic of Moldova ought to reunify eventually with Romania proper.

Beyond the regional concerns, Romania has worked to improve relations with the European Community and to establish ties to NATO in order to break the country's continued isolation. The rejection by the U.S. House of Representatives of the bilateral trade agreement that would have restored MFN status to Romania can be traced directly to the outcome of the election. On the positive side, among the visible achievements of Romanian diplomacy since 1990 have been closer ties with France and an expressed commitment by Italy, articulated by Italian Foreign Minister Gianni de Michelis in July 1991, to support Romania's efforts to become fully integrated in the EU.[26] Romania has also sought to normalize relations with Russia by negotiating and signing a bilateral treaty that included a security clause pledging each side not to participate in an alliance hostile to the other and not to allow its territory to be used for hostile actions against the other. Iliescu called the treaty a "positive event that reflects the changes in European interstate relations."[27]

Romania's security policy, with its orientation toward a future membership in NATO, is rooted in a pervasive sense of insecurity, as the country borders on two highly unstable states, Moldova and former Yugoslavia. Officially Romania has recognized Moldova's independence; still, pressure for the return of Bessarabia to Romania has remained considerable. In light of the dwindling support in the Moldovan parliament for the idea of reunification, which in 1993 was favored only by 8 percent of Moldovians,[28] Iliescu's hands-off approach may mark a return to political realism. Romania's concern over the war in the Balkans remains high, as the country's support for the U.N. sanctions against Serbia-Montenegro has strained relations between Bucharest and Belgrade.

In an effort to compensate for the growing instability in southeastern Europe and the region's progressive marginalization in the emerging post-Cold War security system, Romania has sought to build regional alliances. In 1992 Romania concluded a cooperation treaty with Bulgaria, several technical agreements with Turkey, and economic agreements with Greece. Bucharest has sought to improve relations with Ukraine by opening up an embassy in Kiev, and in June 1992 it signed the so-called Istanbul Declaration, which created the Black Sea Economic Cooperation Zone.

Romania's relations with Hungary have continued to deteriorate since 1990, when tension over Transylvania prompted Hungarian Defense Minister Lajos Fur to order an increase in the number of Hungarian units stationed along the border with Romania. At the core of the quarrel lies the Hungarian concern over the treatment of its minority in Transylvania. In light of a rapidly deteriorating security situation along the Romanian-Hungarian border, in May 1991 the two countries concluded an "open skies" agreement intended as a confidence-building measure. The convention provides for overflights of Romania and Hungary's respective air spaces four times a year by specially designated aircraft from each country to ensure that no troop concentration across the border can take place undetected. France provided the monitoring equipment for the Romanian and Hungarian aircraft engaged in the operation.[29]

The Romanian General Staff has been reassessing the country's security situation with the goal of developing a new military doctrine. In an April 1991 interview for the newspaper *Romania Libera*, Defense Minister Colonel General Victor Atanasie Stanculescu asserted that the military reform under consideration would require between three and five years to implement.[30] As according to Stanculescu the Romanian army has relied on domestic suppliers for 80 percent of its weapons and equipment needs, the breakdown of the system and the impact of market reforms had a negative effect on the army's readiness level. The Defense Ministry proposed to redress the deteriorating supply situation by instituting long-term supply programs, for a period of five to ten years, to modernize military equipment by drawing upon foreign sources.

The Romanian army concluded in the fall of 1990 a technical cooperation agreement with Hungary and began in 1991 negotiations with France, as well as Bulgaria, Serbia-Montenegro, and the former Soviet Union. According to Major General Constantin Nicolae Spiriou, who succeeded Stanculescu as Romania's defense minister, the country's military doctrine proper, which had been based on the principle of the "war of the whole people," would remain the foundation of Romania's military planning.[31] The new military doctrine emphasizes the need to develop a pan-European security system and places an emphasis on diplomatic efforts to provide for Romanian security.[32]

NATO membership remains Romania's ultimate security policy objective, but realistic prospects for its attainment are slim. This position was outlined by Romanian Foreign Minister Theodor Melescanu, as he began a visit to Brussels on September 20, 1993. During Melescanu's meeting with NATO Secretary General Manfred Woerner, Melescanu stressed that in the long term Romania is striving for full integration into NATO's structures.[33]

BACK TO THE FUTURE

The political program espoused by the Romanian government appears to be more along the lines of Gorbachev's "democratization," with an emphasis on gradual change, than a radical democratic and market reform. In part this can be explained by Iliescu and his associates' communist background, as well as the weakness and political naivete of the indigenous dissident movement in Romania. The staunchest opponents of Iliescu were to be found among emigre politicians, led by Iliescu's chief contender for the office of the president, Ion Ratiu, who however lacked sufficient support at home.

As during the anti-Ceausescu rebellion, the army remained the key to domestic politics in Romania. In 1989 the army and the neutral elements in *Securitate* were willing to back up Iliescu because he was a known quantity. After 1989, the combination of the Iliescu career background, the position of the military in Romania, and the residual security apparatus retarded democratic reform. The situation has been further complicated by the weakness of the democratic anticommunist opposition in Romania. The strongest popular support for opposition parties has gone to the "historic parties": the National Liberal Party led by Radu Campeanu and the National Peasant Party led by Ion Ratiu.[34] Most of the support for the two formerly emigre parties came from the intellectuals and students, while support among the peasants and workers remained very limited.

Opposition to the NSF has also come from protofascist groups which tapped into the anti-Hungarian, anti-Russian, and anti-Semitic sentiments of the population. These groups have proclaimed Marshal Ion Antonescu, the wartime dictator in Romania who had fought alongside the Germans against the Soviet Union, as their national hero.[35] Their political demands include the return of Bessarabia and northern Bukovina as well as northern Transylvania.

The attacks on Hungarians in the town of Tirgu Mures in March 1990 further undermined the NSF's credibility with the West, which accused the Romanian government of failing to protect the rights of the Hungarian minority. Iliescu's treatment of the opposition confirmed the Western concerns about the future of Romania's democracy. In June 1990, in what one observer described as the "most alarming and aggressive anti-intellectual outburst in East-Central Europe,"[36] the government brought in miners to Bucharest to break antigovernment student demonstrations by force. The action led to the condemnation of the NSF by the European Community and the United States for gross violations of human rights, as well as the suspension of Western aid and a growing international isolation of the Iliescu regime.

The majority of the post-Ceausescu *nomenklatura* has remained in positions of power and authority, adjusting quickly to the new regime. The current situation in Romania is largely determined by nationalist attitudes of the population, which have changed little since World War II and which are skillfully exploited by the government. The Romanian leaders have shown little interest in and genuine appreciation of Western democratic principles. In that sense Iliescu's political views seem to reflect the general political desiderata of the Romanians.[37] As the historical political parties have no real power base in Romania, the question of whether the NSF will remain in power depends almost exclusively on its ability to solve the country's economic problems. The real alternative to the DNSF and the NSF at the moment appears to be the democratic parties, but these have support only among the intellectuals and students. To complicate matters, the radical nationalist and protofascist parties have attracted considerable support by playing up to Romanian xenophobia.

The plight of postcommunist Romania is in part due to the fact that the collapse of communist power occurred in a truly revolutionary fashion, without the gradual politicization of society and the rise of effective dissident movements that were the hallmarks of the Polish or Hungarian transition to democracy. The majority of Romanians still have a long way to travel to acquire the requisite skill of democratic politics. For now, the old communist guard appears in control.

NOTES

1. Barbara Jelavich, *History of the Balkans: Eighteenth and Nineteenth Centuries* (Cambridge: Cambridge University Press, 1990), pp. 287–299.

2. Barbara Jelavich, *History of the Balkans: Twentieth Century* (Cambridge: Cambridge University Press, 1990), pp. 23 and 250.

3. Michael Shafir, *Romania: Politics, Economics and Society* (London: Frances Pinter, 1985), p. 31.

4. Ibid., p. 79.

5. J. F. Brown, "Conservatism and Nationalism in the Balkans: Albania, Bulgaria, and Romania," in William E. Griffith, ed., *Central and Eastern Europe: The Opening Curtain* (Boulder, Colo.: Westview Press, 1989), p. 289.

6. A. Ross Johnson, "Soviet Military Policy in Eastern Europe," in Sarah Meiklejohn Terry, ed., *Soviet Policy in Eastern Europe* (New Haven, Conn.: Yale University Press, 1984), p. 263.

7. Juliana Geran Pilon, *The Bloody Flag: Post-Communist Nationalism in Eastern Europe, Spotlight on Romania* (New Brunswick, N.J.: Transactions Publishers, 1992), p. 61.

8. "What Follows the Deluge," *U.S. News & World Report*, January 8, 1990, p. 39.

9. *Revolt Against Silence: The State of Human Rights in Romania* (Washington, D.C.: U.S. Commission on Security and Cooperation in Europe, 1989), p. 1.

10. Stephen Fischer-Galati, *Rumania in Transition* (Ruston, La.: American Foreign Policy Center, 1991), p. 2.

11. "Romania: Back to Front," *Economist*, May 26, 1990, p. 33.

12. Florin Bican and Noel Malcolm, "Through the Looking Glass," *National Review*, November 4, 1991, p. 44.

13. Paul Hockenos, "Romania: Bigots' Brew," *New Statesman and Society*, July 26, 1991, p. 20.

14. "Romania: Grabbing Back the Revolution," *Economist*, February 29, 1992, p. 58.

15. "Parliamentary and Presidential Elections," Embassy of Romania News Release, October 1992, p. 1.

16. Michael Shafir, "Romania's Elections: Why the Democratic Convention Lost," *RFE/RL Research Report*, October 30, 1992, pp. 2–3.

17. Michael Shafir, "Romania's Election: More Change Than Meets the Eye," *RFE/RL Research Report*, November 6, 1992, p. 5.

18. Michael Shafir and Dan Ionescu, "Romania: Political Change and Economic Malaise," *RFE/RL Research Report*, January 1, 1993, p. 110.

19. "Iliescu Accused of Complicity with Securitate," *FBIS-EEU-91-160*, August 19, 1991, p. 23.

20. The discussion of Romanian basic law contained in this section is based on *Constitutia Romaniei 1991* (Bucharest: Monitorul Oficial, 1991). The constitution was adopted in a national referendum on December 8, 1991.

21. Tom Gallagher, "Electoral Breakthrough for Romanian Nationalists," *RFE/RL Research Report*, November 13, 1992, p. 20.

22. Shafir and Ionescu, "Romania: Political Change and Economic Malaise," p. 110.

23. *Investment in Romania* (Toronto: KPMG Peat Marwick Thorne, 1992), p. 41.

24. *Romania's Competitive Strength* (Bucharest: Romanian Development Agency), December 1992, p. 4.

25. "Romania Launches Image Building Campaign in the United States," *Business Tech Romania* (Washington, D.C.: ASE World Enterprises), May/June 1993, p. 1.

26. "Treaty Hailed," *FBIS-EEU-91-142*, July 24, 1991, p. 22.

27. "Iliescu Views USSR Treaty as 'Positive Event,' " *FBIS-EEU-91-080*, April 25, 1991, p. 31.

28. Vladimir Socor, "Moldova: Another Major Setback for Pro-Romanian Forces," *RFE/RL Research Report*, February 26, 1993, p. 16.

29. " 'Open Skies' Agreement Detailed," *FBIS-EEU-91-094*, May 15, 1991, p. 32.

30. "Stanculescu on Domestic, Foreign Issues," *FBIS-EEU-91-084*, May 1, 1991, p. 36.
31. "Spiriou: Army Serves the 'Country's Defense,' " *FBIS-EEU-91-092*, May 13, 1991, p. 41.
32. "Defense Minister Spiriou Interviewed," *FBIS-EEU-91-143*, July 25, 1991, p. 33.
33. "Romanian Foreign Minister in Brussels," *RFE/RL Daily Report*, September 21, 1993.
34. Fischer-Galati, *Rumania in Transition*, p. 4.
35. Ibid., p. 5.
36. Pilon, *The Bloody Flag*, p. 66.
37. Fischer-Galati, *Rumania in Transition*, p. 11.

5

BULGARIA

EASTERN SLAVIC HERITAGE

The Bulgarian state traces its roots to a seventh-century pagan kingdom of the Bulgars, a Turanian people from the Sea of Azov and Kuban areas, who had migrated to the Balkans and had gradually been assimilated by the indigenous majority Slav population. When Bulgaria adopted Christianity in the ninth century under the rule of King Boris, all the Bulgarians were Slavic speaking.[1]

With its early emphasis on Christian Orthodox scholarship, Bulgaria was the first major center of Slavic culture. Old Bulgarian or Church Slavic became the language of the Orthodox Church, while the Cyrillic alphabet that developed from the original script of Cyril and Methodius in Preslav in Bulgaria was eventually adopted by the majority of Eastern Slavs, including the Serbs and the Russians. The development of Slav literacy accelerated the process of state building and effectively forestalled the cultural absorption of the Slavic people by the neighboring Greeks.

The early Bulgarian empire peaked in the tenth century and subsequently declined when confronted by the power of Byzantium. As the Byzantine influence began to wane, the second Bulgarian empire was established, which lasted from the late twelfth to the late fourteenth century. The conquest of the Balkans by the Ottoman Empire then ushered in the almost five centuries of Turkish domination over Bulgaria. During that time the Bulgarian national identity and culture were preserved in the rural areas, but they did not drive the national self-determination movement until the late eighteenth century, when the Ottoman Empire was clearly in decline.[2] The eighteenth century brought the development of the modern Bulgarian vernacular and a rise of cultural nationalism in the region. By the mid-nineteenth century Bulgaria experienced a powerful cultural revival, which translated into a movement for the establishment of a national church and the growing national aspirations for self-determination. In the 1860s armed struggle against the Porte became a part of the Bulgarian drive for statehood.

The April 1876 uprising against the Turks failed, but the resulting massacres of some thirty thousand Bulgarian men, women, and children fueled a powerful groundswell of nationalism in the country. It also placed the issue of Bulgarian independence on the all-European agenda. In 1877 Russian troops crossed the Danube and, with the assistance from Bulgarian volunteers, defeated the Turkish army. In 1878 Moscow dictated to the Porte the Treaty of San Stefano, which created a vast Bulgarian state, encompassing most of Macedonia and having access to the Aegean. Subsequently, under pressure from Britain and Austria, who feared that a large Bulgarian state would vastly contribute to Russian power in the Balkans, the size of Bulgaria was reduced by two-thirds in the 1878 Treaty of Berlin.

The Treaties of San Stefano and Berlin provided for the convocation of a national assembly to elect a prince and to institutionalize a future government. In the meantime, the provisional tsarist governor in Bulgaria prepared the country's first constitution, which ushered in the constitutional monarchy. In 1879 the assembly convening in Tirnovo (an ancient Bulgarian capital) established a unicameral parliament and adopted the new constitution, which included guarantees of absolute political and civil liberties. The Tirnovo Constitution, although subsequently amended and often violated, would remain the foundation of the Bulgarian state for sixty-five years.

In 1885 and 1912 Bulgaria made additional territorial gains at the expense of Turkey, but the territorial expansion strained severely Bulgaria's relations with Russia and Greece and led in 1885 to a war with Serbia. In the process, the domestic situation was further destabilized, resulting in a series of failed as well as successful military coups, the deposition of Prince Alexander Battenberg, and continued turmoil. In the course of two Balkan wars at the beginning of the twentieth century, Bulgaria broke out of the confines imposed on it by the Treaty of Berlin, as symbolized by the adoption of the title of king by Prince Ferdinand. However, the second Balkan war contributed to Bulgaria's territorial losses to neighboring Balkan states.

It was largely in the hope of regaining the lost territory and acquiring additional land that King Ferdinand chose in late 1915 to side with the Central Powers against the Entente in World War I by attacking the neighboring Serbia. After initial successes Bulgaria suffered the devastation of the war, economic collapse, and the defeat and disintegration of its army. The peace treaty signed in 1919 with the victorious Entente compelled Bulgaria to give up territory, including western Thrace to Greece and a part of the western frontier to

Yugoslavia, which left close to a million Bulgarians separated from the ethnic core. The Bulgarian army was limited to twenty thousand men, and the country was to pay reparations. Interwar Bulgaria emerged as a revisionist state with a deep sense of humiliation and national resentment toward the Entente powers.

In World War II Bulgaria repeated the mistake of two decades earlier by becoming in 1941 a German ally with the goal of obtaining the territories originally promised Bulgaria by the Treaty of San Stefano. As a German satellite during the war, Bulgaria occupied parts of Greece and Yugoslavia, to which it believed it had legitimate claims. By 1944, when the defeat of the Third Reich appeared inevitable, Bulgaria sought to break away from Germany by opening a dialogue with the Allies and pleading for armistice. The Soviet Union disregarded Sofia's overtures to the West, declared war on Bulgaria, and swiftly occupied the country. Once again, under the terms of the armistice, Bulgaria was forced to evacuate the territories it had occupied in Greece and Yugoslavia.

ZHIVKOV'S BULGARIA

The Soviets moved swiftly to consolidate their position in Bulgaria by supporting the seizure of power by the communist Fatherland Front already in 1944. In 1946 a phoney plebiscite eliminated the monarchy and declared Bulgaria a republic. In 1947 rigged elections to a new general assembly were held, and a new constitution was enacted. This so-called Dimitrov Constitution, patterned after the Stalin constitution, laid the foundation for the rapid sovietization of Bulgaria, including the nationalization of industry and banking and the collectivization of agriculture. For the next fifty years Bulgaria would rank among the most obedient Soviet clients. Todor Zhivkov, the leader of communist Bulgaria, came to power in 1954, replacing Vulko Chervenkov,[3] and ruled the country until the collapse of communism in 1990. During his tenure as Bulgaria's leader Zhivkov was regarded by Moscow as one of the most loyal servants, while the Bulgarian People's Republic remained an important strategic Soviet asset on NATO's southern flank.

Bulgaria does have a history of an indigenous communist movement going back to the interwar period, when in 1923 the communists, led by Georgi Dimitrov, attempted a failed coup. Still, the postwar communist variety had little in common with that tradition, notwithstanding the fact that Dimitrov became the country's first leader. Communist Bulgaria served as a classic example of the Soviet client state. Under Zhivkov's leadership Bulgaria remained fully dependent on the U.S.S.R. for economic assistance, while the Soviets guaranteed Zhivkov's continued domination of the country's politics. Although occasionally Zhivkov displayed some fascination with "shortcuts to communism," as evidenced in communist China, he never pushed for genuine autonomy from Moscow. The most pliant and obedient Soviet satellite, in 1968 Bulgaria participated in the invasion of Czechoslovakia.

In contrast to Poland or Hungary, Bulgaria had precious little contact with the West during the communist era. Travel abroad for Bulgarian citizens was severely restricted, limited predominantly to Soviet-bloc countries. In keeping with its status of the most loyal Soviet ally, Bulgaria's communist constitution, revised in 1971 again after the Soviet model, presented the country as an advanced socialist society. For over three decades, communist Bulgaria bore an indelible mark of Todor Zhivkov's personal leadership.

A man of peasant stock, Zhivkov joined the Communist Party during World War II and rose to the position of power during Nikita Khrushchev's de-Stalinization campaign. Zhivkov's unequivocal pro-Soviet orientation and his unswerving loyalty were rewarded by substantial economic assistance from Moscow, including Soviet purchases of Bulgarian agricultural products and the sales of heavily subsidized Soviet oil and natural gas within the COMECON. Zhivkov's pro-Moscow orientation was buttressed by Bulgaria's historical affinity for Russia as the defender of Slavic interests in the Balkans and the power instrumental in Bulgaria's liberation in the nineteenth century from Turkish domination.

Zhivkov's Bulgaria earned international notoriety in the late 1970s and early 1980s for the alleged involvement of its secret police in Soviet proxy operations around the globe, including charges that the Bulgarian KGB was behind the assassination attempt against the pope in 1981. Zhivkov's determination to repress all opposition, including discrimination against the country's minority populations, especially against the Turks, singled communist Bulgaria out as a country with one of the worst records on human rights.

In foreign affairs, Zhivkov's Bulgaria had strained relations with Yugoslavia. At the center of Bulgaria's hostility toward Yugoslavia was a territorial grievance over Macedonia which was claimed by both countries. Relations with Greece and Turkey were strained throughout the postwar period. The Bulgarian-Turkish relations were defined by Zhivkov's policy of state-sanctioned discrimination against its Turkish minority, including forcing the Turks to "Bulgarize" their names and changing the Turkish names of villages. The discriminatory policies against the Turks were particularly pronounced in 1984–1985, leading to charges from Turkey that Bulgaria was engaged in cultural genocide. In contrast to the strained relations with its immediate neighbors, communist Bulgaria maintained very good relations with West Germany, albeit within the limits prescribed by the Soviet Union. In addition to the pro-Russian sentiment, the German connection was a historical strand in Bulgarian foreign policy harking back to the origins of Bulgaria's modern statehood.

In the area of economic policy, Zhivkov pursued the Soviet model of central planning and collectivization. At the close of World War II, Bulgaria's economy ranked among the least developed in Eastern Europe, with only Albania ranking behind it. After 1945 the economy continued to rely on agricultural production, with selected industrial sectors targeted for investment. Forced industrialization and an almost complete collectivization of the land proceeded faster in Bulgaria than in any other Soviet satellite in Eastern Europe after World War II, with collectivization of agriculture completed by the 1950s.

During the communist period, Bulgaria's economy relied mostly on agricultural exports, which constituted about a quarter of all its exports. Coal mining was the major heavy industry, in addition to food processing and some electronic equipment production, as in the 1980s Bulgaria specialized within the COMECON in building hard disk drives for Soviet-designed computers. Bulgaria also produced basic industrial robots and forklifts for the COMECON markets. In addition to its traditional agricultural exports, the country's foreign exchange was derived from the resale of refined oil and oil products based on Soviet oil supplies. Consequently, Bulgaria's economy was severely affected by the Soviet increase in oil prices within the COMECON after the oil shocks in the 1970s.

The Bulgarian economy began to suffer in the late 1980s due to energy shortages and the overall downturn in agriculture, the latter due in part to the decline in Soviet subsidies because of the revision of the intra-COMECON pricing mechanism for energy and the reduction in the deliveries of Soviet oil. The overall deterioration of the Bulgarian economy was accompanied by rampant corruption among the Communist Party apparatchiks and the security police. Since the 1970s Bulgaria had become a transit route for drug shipments from the Middle East to Western Europe, with drug money used for payoffs to high-level party and police officials. By the 1980s Sofia gained a dubious reputation as an international crime capital of Eastern Europe.

Reform came to Bulgaria in 1987. Under pressure from his Soviet patrons, Zhivkov began experimenting with *perestroika* by inaugurating the "July Concept of Reform," to include a degree of democratization and administrative reform. The proposed changes called for multicandidate elections, but in reality the old methods continued unhindered. The February 1988 election was manipulated by the government to ensure the victory of the candidates selected by the regime. The reform also promised greater freedom of the press, only to bring about a swift reimposition of the censorship after a few stories exposing official corruption. In effect, as long as Zhivkov remained firmly in the saddle, Bulgaria continued to operate along the tried and true communist methods.

Zhivkov's rule ended abruptly on November 10, 1989, when an intraparty coup removed him from power the day after the fall of the Berlin Wall. The collapse of communism in Bulgaria began not so much as a revolution but rather as an attempt by the communists to restructure the domestic politics to ensure their continued position of power, even if it meant sacrificing their leader. The man who was the country's unquestioned dictator for thirty-five years would subsequently be tried, convicted, and sentenced to seven years in prison on charges of high treason.

FROM COMMUNISM TO POSTCOMMUNISM:
JUNE 1990 ELECTIONS

Dissident movement in Bulgaria during the Zhivkov years had been small and ineffective, especially in comparison with the powerful opposition in Poland or even the dissident intellectual movement in Czechoslovakia. In 1989 several opposition groups were organized to challenge, albeit ineffectively at first, the communist monopoly of political power. The most important among them were the trade union *Podkrepa* (Support) and the environmental movement *Ecoglasnost,* operating initially in the city of Russe, a major petrochemical center. The most powerful challenge to the communist monopoly of power would emanate from the Union of Democratic Forces (UDF) umbrella organization of some nineteen political movements, led by Zhelyu Zhelev, a philosopher by training and a lifelong anticommunist. The UDF called for a rapid transition to democracy and a market economy. Still, in 1990 and early 1991 the communists, led by former foreign minister Petar Mladenov, were quite successful in neutralizing the opposition.

Mladenov committed himself to reform, ended press censorship, and abandoned the persecution of the ethnic Turks in Bulgaria, while inviting those who had fled the country to return. Mladenov allowed the opposition groups to register as legal entities and promised to eliminate the domestic role of the secret police. A series of peaceful demonstrations in early 1990 compelled the government to remove from the constitution the clause affirming the Communist Party leadership role. The manner in which Mladenov handled these demonstrations would ultimately cost him his job when it became public that he had initially advocated that tanks be used to disperse the crowds. Mladenov was forced to resign amid scandal in July 1990.[4]

In 1990 the communists were gearing up to continue playing the dominant role in Bulgaria's politics. In January 1990 a special extraordinary congress of the Bulgarian Communist Party was held in Sofia, during which Mladenov resigned the party leadership and became the titular head of state. Andrei Lukanov was chosen for prime minister, and Alexander Lilov became Bulgarian Communist Party secretary. In the aftermath of the congress Mladenov ordered a party referendum, which approved the change in name from the Bulgarian Communist Party to the Bulgarian Socialist Party (BSP). The BSP subsequently split into three parties, whereby in addition to the core BSP the so-called Alternative Socialist Party (ASP) and the Road to Europe faction were created. The ASP's program called for a more radical democratization in the country, while the Road to Europe demanded an outright reconciliation with the West. However, despite the fragmentation, the communists remained firmly in control for the time being.

The initial strength of the former communists both in the government and in the legislature was a direct consequence of the lack of an organized alternative to the BSP within the budding Bulgarian anticommunist opposition. While some fifty political parties were registered in 1990, they were small and organizationally ineffective. Before the election the UDF engaged the communists in a televised roundtable debate during which the BSP and the UDF agreed to elect the Grand National Assembly (400 deputies). According to the deal, for eighteen months the assembly would function as Bulgaria's parliament and general assembly all in one, with the primary task of designing a new political system in the country. The agreement provided for the legalization of all political parties, except for those formed on an ethnic or religious basis. Apparently, at least as far as controlling the national minorities was concerned, the BSP and the UDF seemed to have shared a common position.

The June 10 and 17, 1990, free elections to the constituent assembly gave the communists over 52 percent of the popular vote, with 36 percent going to the UDF. The UDF won only 144 seats, compared with 211 going to the BSP.[5] The new legislature, though it elected Zhelev as its president because some reform communist delegates refused to support BSP candidates, remained largely under the influence of the former communists. On the other hand, the election of Zhelev as Bulgaria's president was a landmark in the country's postcommunist transformation, because the president had the constitutional authority to call fresh elections to the parliament. Furthermore, recriminations over Zhelev's election eventually polarized and weakened the BSP internally, thereby reducing its effectiveness in government.

The opposition's poor performance in the June 1990 free elections to the Grand National Assembly was made worse by the fragmentation within the opposition movement, with the trade union *Podkrepa* rejecting the roundtable deal outright. The election, with a turnout of close to 84 percent of the electorate, gave the Bulgarian Socialist Party a two-to-one margin of victory and hence effectively a popular mandate that would keep the communists in control of Bulgaria until November 1991. Still, the June balloting unleashed forces of change in the Bulgarian body politic that would eventually sweep the communists from power. In a gesture symbolizing the collapse of the old order, in July 1990 the embalmed body of Georgi Dimitrov, a hero of the Communist International and Bulgaria's leader from 1946 until his death in 1949, was removed from its mausoleum in the heart of Sofia and cremated.

BUILDING THE FOUNDATIONS OF DEMOCRACY: BSP VS. UDF

The growing popular discontent with the regime and the rapid politicization among the Bulgarians forced the communists into a compromise with the opposition. Street demonstrations in December of 1990, which culminated in a four-day national strike, compelled the communists into a coalition government with the UDF. The UDF selected a deputy prime minister and controlled the Ministry of Finance and the Ministry of Industry and Commerce. On July 12, 1991, a new constitution was passed that eliminated the key legal foundation of communist power. Articles 17 and 19 restored private property rights in Bulgaria and reaffirmed the country's commitment to a market economy. The Bulgarian constitution was the first postcommunist basic law adopted after the collapse of the Soviet bloc.

The stranglehold by ex-communists on Bulgaria's political life finally ended on October 13, 1991, with another round of free elections. The election law provided that a 4 percent margin of the popular vote was required to win a seat in the parliament. The election was contested by forty-two political parties.[6] The new parliament reduced the number of seats from 400 to 240. During the campaign, other contenders emerged in addition to the UDF and the BSP: the Bulgarian Agrarian National Union led by Tsanko Barev, and the Bulgarian Agrarian National Union "Nikola Petkov," both of which organized the country's peasantry. The UDF itself fragmented into four groups, thereby laying foundations for Bulgaria's nascent party system. Another strong contender in the election was the Movement for Rights and Freedoms (MRF), representing Bulgaria's 1.3 million Turks.

In October 1991 the UDF won a majority of the seats, the BSP came in second, and the Movement for Rights and Freedoms won twenty-four seats in the new legislature. Following a negotiated arrangement with the MRF, in November a one-party UDF government was approved by the parliament. The October balloting marked Bulgaria's first decisive break with the past and a step toward genuine democracy. The UDF majority victory in the parliament was accompanied by the election of Zhelyu Zhelev as Bulgaria's first democratically elected president. The new noncommunist government, led by Filip Dimitrov, was installed on November 8, 1991.[7] Until its resignation a year later, the Dimitrov cabinet presided over progressively pluralist change in the country's political life, which was accompanied by considerable and probably inevitable turmoil.

At the core of the conflict was a growing polarization within the Union of Democratic Forces parliamentary caucus, as well as a growing antagonism between Dimitrov and the Turkish-dominated Movement for Rights and Freedoms over the continued policy of economic austerity, which hurt the MRF's impoverished rural constituency. The UDF government was also challenged by organized labor. The *Podkrepa* Confederation of Labor and the Confederation of Independent Trade Unions in Bulgaria accused Dimitrov of abandoning dialogue on economic policy with the trade unions. The confrontation between the UDF government and the trade unions worsened in the second half of 1992, resulting in a wave of wildcat strikes throughout the country.

The process of political polarization and the growth of political parties continued. In 1990 some of the key political parties in Bulgaria began to emerge.[8] The principal among them were the Bulgarian Socialist Party

(*Bylgarska Sotsialisticheskaya Partiya;* BSP), the successor to the Bulgarian Communist Party, which during its 39th Congress adopted the *perestroika* program. The stated goal of the BSP is to become a new party of "democratic socialism," although in practice it serves to preserve the power and influence of the old communist guard. The main noncommunist organization is the Union of Democratic Forces (*Syyuz na Demokratichnite Sili;* SDS), established on December 7, 1989, as an anticommunist umbrella organization by several independent organizations, including the Glasnost and Democracy Club (*Klub na glasnost i demokratsiya*); the *Ecoglasnost*; the Independent Association for the Defense of Human Rights (*Nezavisimo druzhestvo za zashchita pravata na choveka*); the Independent Trade Union *Podkrepa*; the Committee for the Defense of Religious Rights, Freedom of Conscience, and Spiritual Values (*Komitet za zashchita na religioznite prava, svobodata na syvestta i dukhovnite tsennosti*); the Bulgarian Social Democratic Party (BPSDP); the Bulgarian Agrarian National Union; the Bulgarian Agrarian National Union "Nikola Petkov" (*Bylgarskiya zemedelski naroden syyuz "Nikola Petkov"*); the Radical Democratic Party (*Radikaldemokraticheskaya partiya*); the Green Party (*Zelena partiya*); and the Democratic Party (*Demokraticheskaya partiya*). Later in 1990 *Podkrepa* separated itself from the UDF. The UDF remains a loose organization, whose general policy position is coordinated by the so-called Coordinating Council (*Koordinatsionen syvet*). The UDF publishes the daily *Demokratsiya*.

In 1992 a new government, supported this time by both the MRF and the BSP and led by President Zhelev's former economic advisor Lyuben Berov, vowed to concentrate on the economy and to deal with Bulgaria's deteriorating national security position. In addition, addressing public concern over the dramatic increase in the crime rate figured prominently on Berov's agenda. In contrast to the Dimitrov government, Berov has pledged to concentrate on privatization rather than the restoration of previous property rights.[9] It remains to be seen whether Berov can sustain sufficient support from the uneasy MRF and BSP coalition to implement the necessary reform. In terms of domestic politics, Berov's selection marked a reassertion of the former communists' influence in Bulgaria's postcommunist politics, as the BSP support has proved essential to the coalition's survival.

DOMESTIC POLITICS

The new noncommunist constitution of Bulgaria[10] was adopted by the Grand National Assembly on July 12, 1991. It describes the Bulgarian state as a republic with a parliamentary system of government (Article 1). The legislative powers are vested in the National Assembly (*Narodno Subranie*) of 240 representatives (*narodni predstaviteli*) elected to a four-year term (Articles 62, 63, and 64). The chairman of the National Assembly (*Predsedatelyat na*

Narodnoto Subranie) presides over the parliamentary sessions and certifies with his signature all approved legislation (Article 77).

The office of the president is weak relative to the extensive powers of the legislature. The president (*Prezident na Republikata*) is elected in a direct election to a five-year term (Article 93). He "schedules" the parliamentary election, but the decision to hold the election is made by the parliament (Article 98). The president concludes international treaties and performs other usual representative functions. The president's role in forming the government is also limited. He merely presents to the parliament the candidate for prime minister who had been nominated by the majority group in the parliament (Article 99). The executive powers on domestic and foreign policies are vested in the Council of Ministers (Article 105), which governs as long as it is supported by the National Assembly. In case of a vote of no-confidence, the prime minister submits the resignation of his entire cabinet (Article 111).

Bulgaria's independent judiciary consists of the Supreme Court of Appeals (*Vurkhovniyat Kasatsionen Sud*), the Supreme Administrative Court (*Vurkhovniyat Administrativen Sud*), and the appeal (*apelativni*), district (*okruzhni*), military (*voenni*), and regional (*rayonni*) courts (Article 119). The Constitutional Court consists of twelve judges; four of these are elected by the National Assembly, four are appointed by the president, and four are elected jointly by the Supreme Court of Appeals and the Supreme Administrative Court. The Constitutional Court justices serve one nine-year term (Article 147).

The question of Bulgaria's ethnic minorities remains a continued political problem. The constitution reaffirms the unitary nature of the state and the primacy of the Bulgarian language as the official state language (Articles 2 and 3), while making the study and knowledge of Bulgaria a constitutional obligation (Article 36). On the other hand, the basic law guarantees equal protection under the law to all its citizens (Articles 4 and 6). While the constitution establishes a separation between the church and the state and guarantees religious freedom to its citizens, it does reaffirm Eastern Orthodoxy as the "traditional religion of the Republic of Bulgaria" (Article 13). The constitution reaffirms the inviolability of private property and guarantees the right of inheritance (Article 17), but it denies the right to own land to non-Bulgarian citizens (Article 22).

The first free and direct presidential and vice presidential elections in Bulgaria's postwar history were held in January 1992. Zhelyu Zhelev was elected president on the UDF platform, with another UDF activist, the poet Blaga Dimitrova, elected vice president. The election was a testimony to the continued strength of the BSP, as the Zhelev-Dimitrova ticket won only by a slim margin in a second round of balloting.[11] The election also demonstrated that the ethnic problem, especially the anti-Turkish sentiment among the Bulgarians, can be used effectively to win votes. Among the candidates contesting the presidential election, only UDF's Zhelev and Dimitrova refrained from engaging in outright attacks against Turkish ethnics, and that restraint may have cost them votes.

Ethnic animosities remain high on the domestic political agenda. Among the approximately nine million Bulgarian citizens, Bulgarian Turks constitute close to one million, Gypsies (Roma) close to 600,000, and Pomaks (Bulgarian Muslims) about 300,000.[12] Pomaks, while they are considered ethnic Bulgarians, are Muslim and are regarded by Bulgarians as their separate third ethnic group and often discriminated against by the Orthodox Bulgarians.[13] In addition to the residual undercurrent of ethnic animosity, the political affiliation of various ethnic groups plays a role in Bulgaria's politics today. The UDF seems to have some support among the ethnic Turks, while the BSP has greater support among the Pomaks. The MRF has the strongest base of support among Bulgaria's Turks and the country's Islamic population in general, while Christians and Roma tend to support the BSP. The substantial minorities who are only now finding a voice in Bulgarian politics are bound to play an increased role in the future if the trend of the country's politics becoming progressively more open and democratic continues.

ECONOMIC POLICY

Bulgaria's economy has suffered a crippling blow as a result of the collapse of the COMECON system. Even though in 1991 Bulgaria managed to reach a debt rescheduling agreement with the Paris Club, in 1992 the country's indebtedness to the West still stood at about $12 billion, with no realistic near-term prospect for increasing its exports to the West to raise foreign exchange. Hence, the neighboring Balkan states as well as Turkey are potentially the most promising markets for Bulgarian exports. Bulgaria has attached considerable importance to the proposed establishment of the Black Sea Economic Cooperation Zone (BSECZ), to include Turkey as well as Bulgaria, Romania, Russia, Ukraine, and possibly Greece and Albania. The idea for the BSECZ was first raised in 1990, and its framework was formally established during the Black Sea summit on June 26, 1992; Bulgarian President Zhelyu Zhelev attended the signing ceremony.[14] The BSECZ's goals are to stimulate infrastructure projects, to eliminate barriers to trade, and to promote technological cooperation and tourism. If implemented, the BSECZ initiative may provide the needed incentive to stimulate regional trade as an alternative to exports to the West as long as the region's economies remain uncompetitive in the Western markets.

Since November 1991, on advice of the International Monetary Fund (IMF) and the World Bank (Bulgaria joined the IMF and the World Bank in September 1990), the UDF government has pursued a policy of economic austerity. The austerity program was a condition of the March 1991 structural adjustment loan and the technical assistance loan agreements with the World Bank.

Since then Bulgaria has been undergoing a painful adjustment to the new market conditions. By mid-1992 the decline of industrial output reached 23 percent relative to the analogous period in 1991, making Bulgaria's economic crisis one of the worst in postcommunist Eastern Europe. By the end of 1992, Bulgarian unemployment reached 14 percent.[15] High inflation has remained a problem. In 1991 alone, prices rose tenfold and interest rates reached 50 percent.

By 1993, however, there were some encouraging signs that the worst crisis might have passed. On the positive side, the Bulgarian currency, the *lev*, has stabilized as a result of the government's tight monetary policy. The restoration of precommunist property rights has generated a resurgence in small business activity. In addition, as part of the economic reform program, in 1991 Bulgaria received, on top of the $250 million loan from the World Bank, another $800 million from the Group of 24 wealthy countries.[16]

Once the BSP stranglehold on the government was broken, Bulgaria made considerable headway in laying the foundations for a market economy. Among the key economic legislation passed by the parliament are the Land Law, the Law on the Protection of Competition, the Law on Commerce, and the Foreign Investment Law. The law on foreign investment ranks among the most liberal such legislation in postcommunist Europe, as it lifts all limits on foreign ownership of Bulgarian companies, streamlines the registration process, and imposes no limits on the repatriation of profits.

The Privatization Law, passed by the parliament in May 1992, constitutes a significant landmark in Bulgaria's transition to the market economy. The law is complemented by a piece of legislation providing for a restitution for the property seized by the communists in the 1940s. Another law regulates the expropriation of communist property. Because of domestic political constraints, especially the powerful pressure from labor unions, Bulgaria had waited until 1992 to tackle the privatization issue head on. However, during the October 1991 election campaign the UDF ran on the platform of making privatization its number-one priority, only to concentrate on political rather than economic issues once the election was over.[17] The renewed commitment to privatization in 1993, which will require the government's determination to confront the labor unions, is essential to bring about the badly needed turnaround in the condition of Bulgaria's economy.

On March 8, 1993, Bulgaria took an important step in the direction of gaining greater access to Western markets when it signed an association agreement with the EC. The EC (EU) associate status, in addition to a 1992 agreement with the European Free Trade Association (EFTA) and the Black Sea Economic Cooperation Zone agreement, is Bulgaria's best hope to date to reverse its economic decline through increased exports.

Bulgaria sustained considerable losses to its economy during the Gulf War, when it supported the trade embargo against Iraq. In addition, the country's traditionally export-oriented defense industry has suffered as a result of the collapse of Bulgaria's traditional weapons export markets.[18] More important,

Bulgaria's adherence to the U.N. sanctions against Serbia-Montenegro severely hampered the country's economy. The Bulgarian government estimates the losses for the first half of 1993 at between $40 and $60 million per month; Western sources have estimated that the cost of enforcing sanctions and the use of alternative routes for Western European trade have generated a net loss for Bulgaria in excess of $1.2 billion.[19]

FOREIGN AND SECURITY POLICY

Since 1990 Bulgaria has been making an effort to build support in the West for its political and economic reform program. President Zhelev visited the United States twice, in September 1990 and September 1991. He also visited Germany, Great Britain, and France in an effort to secure Western aid. As a small Balkan state exposed to the rising tide of regional instability, Bulgaria has looked to the United States for support in its effort to build stronger ties to NATO. Following the 1991 visit to Bulgaria by NATO's Secretary General Manfred Woerner and the reciprocal visit by President Zhelev to Brussels, Bulgaria was granted observer status in the North Atlantic Assembly and was brought in as an observer to the Western European Union Parliamentary Assembly. Since 1992 Bulgaria has also been a member of the Council of Europe. Sofia has attempted to reorient its foreign policy to emphasize greater bilateral ties with Germany and France.

Bulgaria has worked to improve relations with its neighbors, especially Greece and Turkey, and to maintain traditionally good relations with Russia. Bulgaria's relations with Russia in particular expanded significantly in 1992, following the signing of a bilateral treaty on good neighborly relations, which covers among other things the matters of national security. The agreement reaffirmed Russia's role as an important partner for Bulgaria, as well as Moscow's interest in strengthening the relationship as a means for regaining influence in the Balkans.[20] The historical Russian-Bulgarian ties have been strengthened by a warm personal relationship between Presidents Yeltsin and Zhelev, after the latter expressed his complete support for Boris Yeltsin during the failed communist coup attempt of 1991.

The greatest threat to Bulgaria's security today is the danger of the Balkan war spreading into the neighboring republic of Macedonia. A Serbian invasion of Macedonia would reawaken the historic competition between Bulgaria and Serbia over the possession of Macedonia. In the event, the likely rise of Bulgarian nationalism might force Sofia to react. As the Balkan war increased in intensity in 1993, Bulgaria has attempted to maintain a low profile, not to antagonize Belgrade, while complying with the United Nations sanctions against Serbia-Montenegro. The U.N. decision to tighten the sanctions increased Western pressure on Bulgaria to contribute to their enforcement. Bulgaria's compliance with the U.N. demand generated an angry reaction from

Belgrade and has brought Bulgaria closer to a possible conflict with Serbia. In 1993 Bulgaria expressed concern about the possible expansion of the Balkan war into Macedonia and the possibility of Bulgarian-Serbian confrontation. The deterioration of relations with Belgrade has raised questions in Sofia about the fate of some 25,000 Bulgarian ethnics living in eastern Serbia.

In light of the perceived vulnerability to Serbian aggression, Bulgaria has sought to improve its relations with Turkey, whose strategic position, NATO membership, and an 800,000-strong army have made it an emerging great regional power. Already in December 1990, while the communists still remained in power, Bulgaria and Turkey signed a confidence-building agreement, with an exchange of military visits following later in 1991.[21] The new spirit of Bulgarian-Turkish cooperation resulted in the reduction of troop deployment on both sides of the common border. The Bulgarian-Turkish rapprochement was their joint response to the marginalization of both in European politics after the Cold War.

In an effort to compensate for the loss of the Soviet security umbrella, Bulgaria has tried to improve relations with the key regional powers as well as with the leading European democracies. Since 1991 Bulgaria has signed military technical cooperation agreements with Greece and Turkey as well as Germany and France. It has also concluded officer-exchange agreements with the United States, United Kingdom, France, Greece, Turkey, Germany, and NATO. Bulgaria has regarded continued U.S. presence in Europe as important to the Continent's security.

AGAINST THE ODDS

Bulgaria's democratic accomplishments, however imperfect, are remarkable considering the Zhivkov legacy and the relative weakness of its democratic institutions. As a country that now finds itself on the periphery of the new European order, Bulgaria has limited prospects for extensive Western aid. At the same time, the proximity of the Balkan conflict, combined with the historical quarrel with the Serbs over the future of Macedonia, has given Bulgaria a precarious security position in the region.

The country still has some way to travel before its economy begins to grow again, and it is not certain that the continued pressure for concessions by organized labor will not derail the entire process of reform. As is any postcommunist country, Bulgaria is susceptible to the appeal of populist political slogans; the return of the communists to support the governing coalition is a sign that the UDF may be exhausting its popular power base.

As an almost archetypal client state, Bulgaria needs a strong ally to improve its security situation and to provide assurances against the threat of regional instability. While Russia has been historically such an ally, today it is in no position to intervene directly on Bulgaria's behalf. Germany, a natural alternative to Russia as a desirable Bulgarian ally, is preoccupied with its own domestic problems attendant to the problem of incorporating the five eastern *Länder* into the Federal Republic.

For the foreseeable future, Bulgaria's closest partner is likely to be its historical enemy Turkey, with whom it shares common regional security and economic concerns. However, in light of the historical burden of relations between the two nations, as well as the religious divide that separates them, it is unlikely that the Bulgarian-Turkish cooperation will be much more than a temporary expedient.

NOTES

1. Barbara Jelavich, *History of the Balkans*, vol. 1 (Cambridge: Cambridge University Press, 1990), p. 15.

2. R. J. Crampton, *A Short History of Modern Bulgaria* (Cambridge: Cambridge University Press, 1989), pp. 8–9.

3. J. F. Brown, *Eastern Europe and Communist Rule* (Durham, N.C.: Duke University Press, 1988), p. 316.

4. "Bulgaria: Into the Dustbin," *Economist*, July 28, 1990, p. 41.

5. "Bulgaria: A Surprise at the Top," *Time*, August 13, 1990, p. 28.

6. "Bulgaria: Spoilt for Choice," *Economist*, October 5, 1991, p. 57.

7. Kjell Engelbrekt, "The Fall of Bulgaria's First Noncommunist Government," *RFE/RL Research Report*, November 13, 1992, p. 1.

8. All data are based on *Politicheski Partii i Dvizheniya v Republika Bylgariya* (Sofia: Konfederatsiya na Nezavisimite Sindikati v Bylgariya, 1990). East European Collection, "Bulgaria" Collection, Hoover Institution Archives, Stanford, California, pp. 6–9.

9. Kjell Engelbrekt, "Technocrats Dominate New Bulgarian Government," *RFE/RL Research Report*, January 22, 1993, p. 2.

10. The discussion of Bulgaria's constitution is based on the text published in *JPRS-EER-91-126-S*, August 22, 1991, pp. 1–15.

11. Rada Nikolaev, "The Bulgarian Presidential Elections," *RFE/RL Research Report*, February 7, 1992, p. 11.

12. Ivan Ilchev and Duncan M. Perry, "Bulgarian Ethnic Groups: Politics and Perceptions," *RFE/RL Research Report*, March 19, 1993, p. 35.

13. Hugh Poulton, *The Balkans: Minorities and States in Conflict* (London: Minority Rights Group Publications, 1991), p. 111.

14. Duncan M. Perry, "New Directions for Bulgarian-Turkish Relations," *RFE/RL Research Report*, October 16, 1992, p. 38.

15. Engelbrekt, "The Fall of Bulgaria's First Noncommunist Government," p. 2.

16. "Bulgaria: Spoilt for Choice," p. 58.

17. Kjell Engelbrekt, "New Bulgarian Government Hopes to End Delays," *RFE/RL Research Report*, April 24, 1992, p. 80.

18. Antoaneta Dimitrova, "The Plight of the Bulgarian Arms Industry," *RFE/RL Research Report*, February 12, 1993, p. 48.

19. Kjell Engelbrekt, "A Vulnerable Bulgaria Fears a Wider War," *RFE/RL Research Report*, March 19, 1993, p. 7.

20. Kyril Haramiev-Drezov, "Bulgarian-Russian Relations on a New Footing," *RFE/RL Research Report*, April 9, 1993, p. 33.

21. Perry, "New Directions," p. 37.

6

YUGOSLAV SUCCESSOR STATES AND ALBANIA

THE SOUTHERN SLAVS

The former Yugoslavia was the most heterogeneous country in Europe, once described as a state with two alphabets, three religions, four languages, five nationalities, and six republics.[1] Indeed, considering the diversity of its population and cultures, it is remarkable that the federation endured for most of the twentieth century as a unified state. Literally the "land of South Slavs," Yugoslavia's territory has been historically a passageway between Western Europe and Asia.

The Serbian state, established in the mountainous region of the Balkans in the tenth century, saw the peak of its power in the twelfth through the mid-fourteenth century when it became the chief Slavic kingdom in the Balkans. Overrun by the Turks in the late fourteenth century, by the mid-fifteenth century Serbia became an integral part of the Ottoman Empire. It was controlled by Turkey until the internal decomposition of the Porte made the resurgence of Serbian nationalism possible. The Serbs gained autonomy in 1829 after a series of rebellions against the Turks, and in 1878 Serbia became the first South Slavic state to become fully independent. Imbued with a sense of mission to restore the historic "Greater Serbia," in 1912 and 1913 Serbia fought two Balkan wars against Austria's clients, acquiring parts of Macedonia in the process.

The Croats had a history of independent statehood until the eleventh century, when Croatia fell under Magyar domination and subsequently became a part of the Habsburg realm until the end of World War I. As the Turks pushed into Europe, historically Croatia marked the southern periphery of the Habsburg

Empire, constituting the borderlands between Christian Europe and the Ottoman Empire. After the centuries of confrontation with Turkey, the Croats have formed a strong national myth of Croatia being the *ante muralis* of the West.[2] Dominated by outside powers and frequently overrun by the Tatars and the Turks, the Croats developed a sense of being in a permanent state of siege. Croatian nationalism was also influenced by the resistance to the Habsburg policies of Germanization, which began in the Croatian lands in the seventeenth century. Croatian national identity was thus formed in opposition to the Hungarian, Turkish, Austrian, and Serbian influences.

At the time of the outbreak of World War I, the largest portion of the South Slavic population was Serbian; as of 1910 the Serbs numbered about 6,568,000, of whom 2,911,000 were citizens of independent Serbia; there were 2,789,000 Croats and 1,252,000 Slovenes.[3] Historically, both the Serbs and the Croats had formed important medieval kingdoms, while the Slovenes enjoyed only a brief period of self-rule in the eighth century. The Serbian adherence to Orthodox Christianity and the Croatian adherence to Catholicism were important elements defining their respective national identities. Croatia and Slovenia developed within the Western orbit, while Serbia was for five centuries under the control of the Muslim empire.[4]

Change in the political status of the Serbs and the Croats came in the early nineteenth century as a result of the French Revolution and Napoleonic wars. Serbia achieved autonomous status in the 1830s; in Croatia the Illyrian movement established Croatian national goals. Serbian success was largely due to the weakening of the Ottoman Empire and to Russian support for Serbian nationalists.

During the 1848–1849 revolutions, during which the Hungarian uprising threatened the integrity of the Habsburg Empire, the Croats under the leadership of Josip Jelacic came to the aid of the imperial government. The Croats as well as the Serbs in the Habsburg Empire supported the concept of Austroslavism, that is, the restructuring of the monarchy so as to give the Slavs a greater role in the government.[5] In contrast, the Serbian government was halfhearted in its support for the Habsburgs against the Hungarians.

After the revolutionary upheaval, the nationalist movement in Serbia made considerable strides, with the country achieving complete independence in 1878. Subsequently, the issue of which state, Serbia or a future Croatia, was to control Bosnia-Herzegovina (inhabited by both peoples) led to a clash of two competing nationalisms. Croatian politics were radically altered by the reorganization of the Habsburg Empire into the Dual Monarchy following the *Ausgleich* of 1867. As a result of the reorganization, Croatia and Slavonia were placed under Budapest's control, while Dalmatia and Slovenia were directly controlled from Vienna. Following an 1868 compromise negotiated by the Croats and the Hungarians, Croatia was granted administrative autonomy, an independent judiciary, and its own educational system.[6]

The controversy over Bosnia in 1878 further aggravated the relations between the Serbs and the Croats. Until 1878 Bosnia was under Ottoman control. The crisis in the Balkans from 1875 till 1878, including an uprising in Bosnia and Herzegovina, the war of Serbia and Montenegro against the Ottoman Empire, and finally the Russo-Turkish war of 1877–1878, transformed the Bosnian question into an international issue. At the Conference of Berlin in 1878 the great powers recognized the independence of Serbia, Romania, and Montenegro and created an autonomous Bulgarian state. The two provinces of Bosnia and Herzegovina were placed under Habsburg administration. In Bosnia and Herzegovina the Orthodox people constituted at the time 44 percent, Slavic Muslims 33 percent, and Catholic Croats 22 percent.[7] While the Serbs bitterly denounced Habsburg control over Bosnia and Herzegovina, the majority of the Croats welcomed it as the first step to the future restoration of an independent Croatian state. Relations between the Serbs and Croats continued to deteriorate into the twentieth century.

Slovenia shares with Croatia the experience of being a part of the Habsburg domain. From the fourteenth century until 1918 Slovenia was firmly anchored within the Austrian empire. Montenegro, a poor mountainous region in the southern reaches of the former Yugoslav federation, was until the fourteenth century an independent principality of Zeta within the Serbian empire and was subsequently completely dominated by the Serbs. It shared the fate of Serbia proper during the Ottoman expansion into Europe and reemerged in the late nineteenth century after Turkish power had waned; the 1878 Congress of Berlin formally recognized Montenegro as an independent republic. Montenegro remained dominated by Serbia and subsequently joined the Yugoslav federation.

Macedonia has a historical experience of the Macedonian empires, Roman domination, Serbian and Bulgarian domination, and, from the fourteenth century through 1912, total control by Turkey. One of the principal causes of the 1912 First Balkan War, Macedonian territory was contested by Greece, Serbia, and Bulgaria. After 1918, Macedonia was incorporated into the Yugoslav kingdom and was dominated by the Serbs throughout the duration of the Yugoslav federation. Bosnia-Herzegovina was settled by the Serbs and Croats. In the twelfth century it briefly became a powerful and independent Balkan state, but by the fifteenth century it was conquered by Turkey. As Turkish power waned, Bosnia-Herzegovina was passed in succession to Hungarian, German, and finally Yugoslav control.

The territory of former Yugoslavia is mountainous, with some 70 percent of the area being covered by hills. Historically, the area was a border region between the Habsburg Empire (Slovenia and Croatia) and the Ottoman dominion (Serbia, Montenegro, Macedonia, and Bosnia-Herzegovina). It was also a place where the Romanovs vied for position as a protector of all Slavic peoples. The Yugoslav federation was established as a single state in 1918, when the Croats and the Slovenes joined in the federation with the Serbs. Until its breakdown in 1990, the Yugoslav state consisted of six republics: Serbia, Croatia, Slovenia, Bosnia-Herzegovina, Macedonia, and Montenegro, with the two additional autonomous regions of Vojvodina and Kosovo-Metohija located within Serbia. The country's population before the breakdown was approximately 25 million, the largest nations being the approximately 8 million Serbs, the 4.5 million Croats, and the 2 million Slovenes. Although nominally a federation, the state was controlled by the Serbian majority, while the overall sense of South Slavic kinship could hardly make up for the bitter cultural divisions among the Yugoslav people.

Historically, religious differences have run deep among the Southern Slavs. About 50 percent of the citizens of former Yugoslavia, mainly Serbs, were Eastern Orthodox; about 30 percent were Roman Catholic (mainly Croats and Slovenes); and about 10 percent were Muslim, mostly concentrated in Bosnia-Herzegovina and Kosovo. As elsewhere in central and eastern Europe, this religious division has affected the national distinctions as far back as the Middle Ages. The country's five basic languages were Serbian, Croatian, Slovenian, Albanian, and Macedonian (some scholars treat the Serbian and Croatian as one language with two different transcriptions, classifying it as the Serbo-Croatian or Serbo-Croat language). The Serb and Croatian languages trace their roots to the time when Slavs migrated to the Balkan peninsula. Both the Latin and Cyrillic alphabets have been used to transcribe the languages, with Croats and Slovenes using the Latin characters and the Serbs and Macedonians using the Cyrillics. While the Serb and Croat languages can be written with both the Latin and the Cyrillic characters, Slovenian can be written only in Latin script and Macedonian only in Cyrillics.

THE SERB-CROAT ANTAGONISM: WORLD WAR II AND TITO'S YUGOSLAVIA

The bitter hatred that divides the Serbs and the Croats today is the principal driving force in Balkan politics, fueling in the early 1990s the bloodiest war Europe has seen in half a century. The historical animosity of the two nations was inflamed by Yugoslavia's experience during World War II and by the federal communist experiment. The division within the interwar Yugoslav monarchy ran between the historic "Habsburg Catholic North" (Slovenia and Croatia) and the "Ottoman South" (Serbia, Montenegro, Macedonia, and Bosnia, although the latter had been briefly occupied by Austria after 1878 before being incorporated into Serbia).

German invasion in early 1941, which resulted in a humiliating defeat for the Yugoslavs, gave way to brutal occupation, which in turn bred Yugoslav resistance. The first anti-German guerrillas were the London-supported Serbian Chetniks led by Draza Mihailovic. After the German attack on the Soviet Union in June 1941 Yugoslav communists also rose against the occupier, establishing a second resistance movement, the Partisans led by Josip Broz (Tito), a Yugoslav communist leader since 1937. The third political force was the Ustasa fighters of the newly established Croat state, a puppet of Germany. The political divisions between the Chetniks, the Partisans, and the Ustasa, fueled by the historical Serb-Croat animosity, led to an all-out civil war in addition to the popular resistance to German occupation. For their part, the Germans made Yugoslavia into a site of horrendous atrocities. In some instances, entire communities were wiped out by German punitive operations. The Chetniks and the Partisans, after a brief initial period of cooperation, engaged in merciless warfare against each other throughout the war, with Ustasa forces continuing their nationalist campaign against the Serbs.

The eventual victory of the Partisans was in part due to Tito's leadership qualities (he would dominate Yugoslav politics until his death in 1980) and in part due to the British decision to throw their support behind Tito as a more effective warlord than Mihailovic. Tito, who as a Croat-Slovene was a quintessential Yugoslav, emerged after the war as the proponent of communism and of continued Yugoslav federalism; he declared the creation of a new Yugoslav federal government in 1943. In 1945 Tito formally abolished the monarchy and a year later created the Federal People's Republic of Yugoslavia. Tito's wartime record, his undeniable charisma, and his ability to stand up to the Russians in 1948 to assert Yugoslav independence would allow him to maintain the illusion of unity virtually until his death.

Although initially the Yugoslav economy was subjected to a full-scale communist experiment, the breakup with Stalin in 1948 forced upon Tito the need to reassess policies. Having no other choice but to turn to the West for assistance, Tito restructured the Communist Party, modified the strictly Stalinist economic policy, and pushed for a greater role for Yugoslavia in the nonaligned movement. In 1952 the Communist Party of Yugoslavia was renamed the League of Communists of Yugoslavia. Changes in agriculture included cooperative and private farming, central planning was modified, and a workers' self-management formula was introduced in the industrial sector, with pay tied to workers' productivity. Western assistance became essential to Yugoslavia's survival; as early as the 1950s, Yugoslavia was receiving $3.5 billion of assistance from the West.

IN WAR'S SHADOW: NATION-STATE BUILDING IN THE BALKANS

The Balkan wars of the early 1990s were a direct consequence of the breakup of the Yugoslav federation. They ravaged the region, were condemned by the West, strained the meager resources of the Southern Slavs, and raised questions about the ultimate viability of some of the successor states, especially Bosnia-

Herzegovina. In 1991 the Serb-Croat confrontation, the principal antagonism driving the politics in former Yugoslavia, erupted into an all-out war. The national tensions, submerged during Tito's rule, emerged with full force in the decade following his death.

By 1987 Slobodan Milosevic emerged as the key Serbian politician, riding the tide of Serbian discontent with the structure of the federal system and its alleged discrimination against the Serbs.[8] In Slovenia and Croatia there was a growing tide of discontent with the government-mandated transfer of wealth from the more affluent North to the impoverished South. Politically the Slovenes and the Croats were moving increasingly in the direction of greater pluralism than that of the Serbs. Milosevic and his Socialist Party capitalized on the rising tide of Serbian nationalist grievances, including the Serb demands to reassert control over Vojvodina and especially Kosovo, which the Serbs claim as the medieval cradle of their state and culture and where some two million ethnic Albanians constitute roughly 90 percent of the region's population. The 1991 Serbian constitution restricted significantly the autonomy of the Kosovo Albanians. An open Serbian-Albanian conflict appeared likely after the Kosovo Albanians carried out a 1991 underground referendum and legislative vote in favor of complete independence from Serbia.[9]

The 1990 free elections in Slovenia and Croatia brought about the breakdown of the old communist system in the North, with the installation in Slovenia of a center-right government and a reform-communist president, Milan Kucan. In Croatia a conservative government under General Franjo Tudjman was established. As 1990 progressed, Slovenia and Croatia moved quickly toward complete independence. Belgrade attempted to stop the disintegration of Yugoslavia by resorting to military force. The former federal army—its officer corps heavily dominated by Serbs and Montenegrins—became a tool of Serbian policy in the North. As Slovenia and Croatia declared on June 25, 1991, their determination to proceed with full independence, the federal army attacked selected targets in Slovenia. The fighting, referred to by the Slovenes as their "ten-day war for independence," failed to break Ljubljana's resolve to secede. Confronted with determined Slovenian resistance, the campaign proved largely ineffective. On July 18, 1991, the federal army signed an agreement with Slovenia that provided for the evacuation of army bases and freed Slovenia from federal control.[10]

The Balkan conflict became much more involved when fighting shifted from Slovenia to Croatia. Whereas Slovenia was the only ethnically homogeneous Yugoslav republic, Croatia has a large Serbian minority interspersed throughout its territory. Fighting between the Croat militia and the Serbian irregulars supported by the federal army in the Krajina and eastern Slavonia regions escalated quickly, with Croatia determined to achieve full independence and Serbia equally committed to holding on to the ethnically Serbian areas. The Ustasa-Chetnik hatred of World War II came again to life, as each side charged the other with premeditated aggression. By the end of 1991, 550,000 people were displaced in various parts of Yugoslavia because of the conflict; 40,000 had fled to Hungary, 6,000 had been killed, and 15,000 wounded.[11]

In 1992 the Serb-Croat fighting spread to Bosnia-Herzegovina, bringing in a third group, the Bosnian Muslims. Although internationally recognized as an independent state, Bosnia-Herzegovina was divided up in the course of the fighting into Serbian, Croat, and Muslim enclaves, with the capital of Sarajevo cut off from the rest of the republic and sustained only by U.N. relief assistance. The Bosnian Muslims were decimated and pushed out of their historical areas, a Serbian policy that gained international notoriety as "ethnic cleansing." The U.N. relief operations averted the threat of starvation in Bosnia-Herzegovina, but they failed to arrest the escalation of fighting. As 1993 progressed, reports of widespread human rights abuses, concentration camps run by the Serbs, and the "ethnic cleansing" of entire villages of their Muslim population called into question the very viability of continued U.N. operations. The diplomatic initiative conducted by the U.N. mission under Cyrus Vance and Lord Owen proved irrelevant, while the continued U.N. embargo on weapons sales to the Bosnians, imposed in the name of limiting bloodshed, maintained the dramatically uneven odds in the fighting between the well-armed Serbs and the poorly armed Bosnian militia. Western assistance was limited to U.N. food-and-medicine drops and a NATO-enforced no-flight-zone policy over Bosnia-Herzegovina. The outcome of the crisis was being decided by the combatants on the ground. As 1993 drew to a close, with the peace negotiations deadlocked, partition of Bosnia-Herzegovina between Serbia and Croatia appeared an ever more likely solution.

INDEPENDENT SLOVENIA

Slovenia's road to independence began in 1989, with the adoption of an amendment to the republican constitution by the Slovene Assembly asserting national control over the republic's economic assets and claiming the sole right for the republic's parliament to introduce the state of emergency. This, in effect, amounted to the separation of Slovenia's economy from the rest of Yugoslavia. The Serbs responded with an economic boycott, but it failed to bring Slovenia back into line. In March 1990 the Slovene Assembly dropped the word "socialist" from the republic's name. A parallel development was the separation between the League of Communists of Yugoslavia and Slovenian communists, who renamed their party the Party of Democratic Renewal.

Demos, Slovenia's most powerful pro-independence organization, was set up in January 1990. It called for full national sovereignty, free elections, and a national referendum on the republic's future. The first free elections were held in April 1990, with *Demos* winning 126 of the 240 seats in the parliament. The new parliament then declared the republic sovereign. The referendum held on

December 23, 1990, with more than 88 percent of registered voters taking part, expressed an overwhelming popular support for independence. The declaration of independence, on June 25, 1991, was followed by a brief period of intense fighting, the "ten-day war for independence," as Belgrade attempted to reassert its control. The failure of the Yugoslav army to bring Slovenia back into the federation marked the beginning of Slovenia's fully independent existence. The cause of Slovenian independence was helped by the early offer of full diplomatic recognition to the new state from the European Community and the United States.[12]

Postcommunist Slovenia has emerged as one of the smallest European countries, with a population of only about two million. On October 7, 1991, the Assembly of the Republic of Slovenia declared the country's formal separation from Yugoslavia; the last unit of the Yugoslav National Army left Slovenia later that month. On January 15, 1992, the European Community formally recognized Slovenia as an independent state; on the same day Germany and Austria established diplomatic relations with Slovenia.

The new Slovenian constitution was adopted on December 23, 1991, one year after the referendum.[13] It provides for a two-chamber parliament: the National Assembly, the highest legislative body in the country, with ninety deputies elected to a four-year term (Article 81), and the National Council, with forty councilors elected to a five-year term as an advisory body to the National Assembly. The National Council may send the legislation back to the National Assembly for reconsideration, may require that a referendum be called, and may call for the establishment of a special parliamentary inquiry commission to investigate key issues of national policy (Articles 97 and 98).

The election of the president of the republic is called by the president of the National Assembly (Article 104). In keeping with the focus of power on the parliament, the president is the Slovenian commander-in-chief and has other representative functions. The president can be brought before the Constitutional Court if the National Assembly files a formal complaint against him for a breach of the constitution or an illegal act. The president can be dismissed from office by a two-thirds majority vote in the Constitutional Court (Article 109).

The president has the first choice in nominating the prime minister, but the parliament has to vote its approval. The cabinet selected by the prime minister must also be approved by the National Assembly (Article 111). The government can be dismissed if a vote of no-confidence passes in the National Assembly. The vote of no-confidence can be initiated by the minimum of ten deputies in the National Assembly (Article 116).

The constitution provides for an independent judiciary, with Supreme Court judges elected by the National Assembly upon the recommendation of the Judicial Council (Article 130). The Slovenian constitution provides a bill of rights and explicit guarantees of minority rights to the Italian and Hungarian ethnic minorities (about 0.5 percent of the total population), including the right to use Italian and Hungarian as the other official languages (Article 11) and full citizenship-rights protection to the minorities (Part IV of the Preamble). The Slovene Italians and Hungarians are also guaranteed representation in the National Assembly.

On December 6, 1992, Slovenia held both the presidential election and the elections to the National Assembly and the National Council. The elections returned seven political parties to the parliament, including the Liberal Democratic Party (LDS), the Christian Democrats (SKD), the Unity (or Associated) List (ZL), the Slovenian National Party (SNS), the Slovenian People's Party (SNS), the Democratic Party (DS), and the Greens of Slovenia (GS). Milan Kucan was reelected as president, winning some 64 percent of the vote. The new coalition government is led by Janez Drnovsek, head of the Liberal Democrats.[14] Drnovsek's LDS (22 seats) coalition government with the Christian Democrats (15 seats), Unity List (14 seats), and the Slovenian National Party (11 seats) gives the new government majority support in the legislature.

Since independence Slovenia has been performing remarkably well economically, especially compared to other republics of former Yugoslavia. In 1992 the country managed to register a trade surplus despite the loss of the Yugoslav market by shifting its trade to the EC and EFTA. The economic policy, which has emphasized the need for currency stability, has contributed to declining inflation. The unemployment rate in 1992 stood at 10.8 percent.[15] The overall goal of Slovenia's economic policy is full membership in the European Union.

Slovenia introduced its currency, the *tolar*, in October 1991. Two 1991 laws, the Law on Foreign Trade Transactions and the Law on Foreign Exchange Business, have laid the foundation for the radical market transformation of the Slovenian economy. In November 1992 these were augmented by the Law on Privatization. The country's economic reform program has been directed at market privatization, price liberalization, and increased foreign trade. The EU has been Slovenia's principal trading partner, accounting for 70 percent of all Slovenian exports and 60 percent of all its imports. The EFTA countries are Slovenia's second most important trading partner, accounting for 9.6 percent of Slovenia's exports and 15 percent of its imports.[16]

Slovenia's traditional industries are ferrous metallurgy, furniture, light industry, and mining. In recent years the country branched into electronics, household appliances, cars, food processing, pharmaceuticals, and chemicals. Finally, tourism has been a traditional foreign exchange earner.

Since independence, Germany, Italy, Austria, and France have been Slovenia's principal trading partners, accounting for over 63 percent of all imports and almost 70 percent of all Slovene exports in 1992.[17] In the first half of 1992 Slovenia registered a trade surplus of $338 million.[18] The country's foreign debt in 1992 stood at approximately $1.7 billion, fairly equally divided between private and government creditors.[19]

In the foreign policy arena, Slovenia won general international recognition in 1992 and became a member of the United Nations the same year. It is committed to full membership in the European Union at the earliest possible date and to pan-European collective security structures, including NATO.

POSTCOMMUNIST CROATIA

Croatia declared independence on June 25, 1991.[20] The declaration was accompanied by a law on Serb and other minority rights in the new state, which prohibited any action detrimental to the "sovereignty, territorial integrity and political independence of the Republic of Croatia."[21] With over 570,000 ethnic Serbs, interspersed amid some 4.7 million Croats and intent on securing their territory for a future Serbian state, the fighting has been intense. The Croats have considered the war as a concerted effort by Belgrade to pursue the policy of building Greater Serbia.[22] In contrast to Slovenia, which paid for independence with only ten days of fighting against the Yugoslav army, Croatia has been struggling to build the foundations of an independent state while fighting a protracted war with Serbia-Montenegro since 1991.

Transition to democracy in Croatia has proceeded haltingly on account of the ongoing conflict with Serbia and the unresolved border and ethnic minority issues. The war in neighboring Bosnia-Herzegovina, during which Croatia initially supported the Bosnian Muslim side before moving effectively to partition the country with Serbia, further retarded the process of political and economic transformation. The constitution of the Republic of Croatia was proclaimed in December 1990.[23] It speaks to Croatia's concern for the well-being of the "parts of the Croatian nation in other states" (Article 10)—a clear reference to Croat ethnic minorities in neighboring Yugoslav republics.

The new constitution provides for a bicameral legislature, the Croatian *Sabor*, consisting of the Chamber of Representatives and the Chamber of *Zupanije* (or Counties) as the supreme legislative body of the country (Article 70). The Chamber of Representatives has the minimum of 100 and the maximum of 160 deputies elected to a four-year term by direct and secret ballot; every *zupanija* elects in the same way three representatives to the Chamber of *Zupanije* (Article 72). The president of Croatia can nominate up to five candidates to the Chamber of *Zupanije* and he himself automatically becomes one of its members upon the expiration of his term as head of state (Article 71).

The Croatian constitution gives the president considerable powers. He is elected to a five-year term, with the term limitation proviso of two consecutive terms (Article 95). The president is the head of state and the commander-in-chief of the Croatian armed forces (Articles 95 and 100). He calls the elections to the *Sabor*, calls national referenda, and appoints and dismisses the prime minister and the government (Article 98). He has the power to pass decrees with the force of law in case of war or national emergency (Article 101), which in the context of the ongoing war has given Franjo Tudjman the prerogative to legislate; however, the decrees must be subsequently approved by the *Sabor*. The president can call government sessions to consider issues he wants placed on the agenda; he presides over such sessions (Article 102). The president also has in effect the power to counter the parliamentary vote of no-confidence in the government and to force the dissolution of the legislature. He can dissolve the Chamber of Representatives "with the countersignature of the prime minister" and "after having consulted with the Chairman of the Chamber" if the Chamber has passed a vote of no-confidence in the government or if it has failed to pass the budget within a month from the date it was proposed (Article 104). In effect, if the president approves of the government the prime minister can continue in office despite the loss of support in the parliament. The president can be impeached by a two-thirds majority vote of all representatives, provided the Constitutional Court concurs with a two-thirds majority vote (Article 105). The constitution also makes the president the key actor in foreign policy, with the government also playing a part in the process (Article 132). In yet another affirmation of strong presidential power, the constitution makes the government responsible to both the president and the legislature (Article 111). The president appoints the government, subject to parliamentary approval (Article 112).

Croatia's independent judiciary includes the Constitutional Court, which consists of eleven judges elected by the Chamber of Representatives on the recommendation of the Chamber of *Zupanije* to an eight-year term.

The first free election since Croatia's independence was held on August 2, 1992. It gave Franjo Tudjman over 56 percent of the popular vote in the presidential election. In the parliamentary election on the same day Tudjman's conservative Croatian Democratic Union (*Hrvatska Demokratska Zajednica*; HDZ) won 42 percent of the vote; the challenger Croatian Social-Liberal Party polled 18 percent.[24] The HDZ emerged with eighty- five of the 138 seats in the parliament, followed by the former communists with fourteen seats and the Social-Liberal Party with eleven seats.[25] The fact that the election took place was in itself remarkable, because it occurred at the time of especially bitter fighting around the southeastern Croatian town of Slavonski Brod.

The war has taken its toll on Croatia in more ways than one, retarding both the development of democratic institutions and the economic reform. After the election the opposition charged that Tudjman and the HDZ were increasingly prone to authoritarian methods in government.[26] The economic reform began to be implemented in earnest only in 1993, with the creation of the Croatian Privatization Fund, a state agency based on the merger of the Agency for Restructuring and Development and the Croatian Development Fund. The Croatian Privatization Fund is charged with the sale of some 300 state-owned enterprises.[27] The country was paying the price of war with high inflation, the decline of industrial output, and the shortages of foreign exchange as its tourism industry stagnated.

Zagreb's most pressing concern remains foreign policy, both the future of the four U.N. "protected areas" within the territory of the former Socialist Republic of Croatia and the future of the Croatian position in Bosnia-Herzegovina, now appearing to be heading for a Serb-Croat partition and an uneasy condominium. In 1992 Croatian relations with Slovenia also soured, with Zagreb charging Ljubljana with betrayal and abandonment to fight the Serbs alone.

"THIRD YUGOSLAVIA" (SERBIA-MONTENEGRO)

The postcommunist Serbia-Montenegro was proclaimed the "Third Yugoslav Federation" by the new constitution adopted on April 27, 1992.[28] Serbia passed its own constitution in September 1990 and Montenegro in October 1992.[29] The passage of the new Yugoslav constitution was the final recognition in Belgrade that Tito's state was indeed a thing of the past. The new basic law established the Federal Assembly consisting of the Chamber of Citizens and the Chamber of Republics. The federal deputies to the Chamber of Citizens are elected in a direct ballot, with one deputy elected for every 65,000 voters, with each republic guaranteed no fewer than thirty deputies. The Chamber of Republics consists of twenty federal deputies elected from each constituent republic (Article 80).[30] All deputies serve a four-year term (Article 81). The Federal Assembly can be dissolved by the president on the initiation of the government, unless the procedure for a no-confidence vote in the government has been initiated in the parliament (Article 83).

The federal president performs the usual representative functions and serves as the commander-in-chief of the armed forces. He nominates the prime minister, recommends the Federal Assembly candidates for justices of the Federal Constitutional Court, justices of the Federal Court, the federal public prosecutor, and the head of the National Bank (Article 96). Unlike the presidents of Serbia and Montenegro who are elected in a direct ballot, the president of the new federation is elected by the parliament. In 1992, Dobrica Cosic became Yugoslavia's first president; he was replaced by Zoran Lilic in 1993. The separate Serbian constitution provides for the one-chamber legislature, the 250-member National Assembly, elected to a four-year term (Articles 73, 74, and 75). The Serbian president is elected to a five-year term (Article 86).

The position of Serbian President Slobodan Milosevic was consolidated as a result of the December 1992 federal, republic, and presidential election, during which he defeated the former prime minister Milan Panic. The election was reported by both Serbian and international media to be "seriously flawed," because of widespread voting irregularities. According to a CSCE monitoring mission, as many as 5 percent of those casting votes (most of them opposition supporters) were not registered.[31] Milan Panic, who had challenged Milosevic in the election, as well as several opposition parties including the Democratic Movement (DE-

POS) and the Democratic Party (DP) accused Milosevic and his ruling Socialists (SPS) of cheating and demanded new elections in ninety days under strict international control. Milosevic dismissed the accusations as unfounded.

The final election results gave Milosevic 56 percent of the vote, with Panic getting slightly over 34 percent. In the new Serbian parliament, the Socialist Party of Serbia (*Socijalisticka Partija Srbije*; SPS) won 101 of the 250 seats in the Serbian National Assembly; the ultranationalist Serbian Radical Party (*Srpska Radikalna Partija*; SRP) won seventy-three seats; DEPOS won forty-nine seats; the Democratic Alliance of Vojvodina Hungarians (*Demokratska Zajednica Vojvodjanskih Madjara*; DZVM) won nine; the Democratic Party (*Demokratska Partija*; DP) won seven; the Citizens' Group–Zeljko Raznjatovic (*Grupa Gradjana–Zeljko Raznjatovic*; GG–ZR) won five; the Farmers' Association of Serbia (*Seljacka Stranka Srbije*; SSS) won three; the Coalition of the Democratic and Reform Democratic Parties of Vojvodina (*Koaliciona Partija Demokratskih i Reformskih Snaga Vojevodine*) won two; and the Muslim Democratic Reform Party (*Muslimanska Demokratska Reformska Partija*; MDRP) won one seat.[32] In Montenegro the ruling Democratic Socialist Party (*Demokratska Partija Socjalista*; DPS) carried the election, with the Liberal Alliance opposition party coming in a distant second.[33]

Milosevic's party and its allies dominated the Federal Assembly as well, with the SPS taking forty-seven seats. The ultranationalist SRP won thirty-four seats, and the Democratic Socialist Party (Montenegro) (*Demokratska Partija Socjalista Crna Gora*) won seventeen seats, thus giving Milosevic a lock on the 138-member Chamber of Citizens of the Federal Assembly. The opposition DEPOS won twenty, with the balance going to smaller parties, two additional parties from Montenegro.[34]

The Third Yugoslavia is today Europe's pariah state. The population of the new Yugoslav state is less than half that of the former federation, over 10.5 million.[35] As a country that has engaged in war against its neighbors since 1991, the new Yugoslavia is internationally isolated, including by U.N.-mandated economic sanctions. The country's economic conditions are disastrous. Unemployment in 1992 ran at about 25 percent with the complete collapse of the currency, the *dinar*. The Yugoslav GDP fell by close to 27 percent in 1992, while personal income declined by 51 percent,[36] with decline continuing throughout 1993. However, economic considerations and international relations seem to have taken the back seat to Belgrade's policy of reconstituting the Serbian state through military force.

FUTURE AREAS OF TURMOIL: MACEDONIA AND KOSOVO

In 1993 Macedonia and Kosovo were increasingly in danger of being drawn into the Balkan war, with the prospect of the fighting spilling for the first time outside the boundaries of the former Yugoslav federation. The dangers of drawing additional states into the Balkan war were clearly demonstrated when Macedonia voted for independence on September 7, 1991; the declaration of independence that followed led to a strong opposition from Greece, which demanded that the new state remove the word "Macedonia" from its official name.[37] In 1992 Greece lobbied successfully against Macedonia's recognition by the European Community and the United States. The Greek pressure contributed to the isolation of Macedonia and denied it desperately needed international economic assistance, while its observance of the U.N. sanctions against Serbia, Macedonia's largest trading partner, led to a severe economic crisis. When Macedonia was finally recognized by the United Nations, its officially accepted name was the "Former Yugoslav Republic of Macedonia."

Macedonia's territory has been historically contested by Serbia, Bulgaria, and Greece. In contrast to Croatia and Slovenia, ethnic Macedonians have a relatively weak sense of separate national identity, which makes the new state vulnerable to outside pressure. Ethnic Macedonians constitute about 65 percent of the country's two million people, with other minorities including Albanians (21 percent), Turks (4.8 percent), Romanis (2.7 percent), Muslims (2.5 percent), and Serbs (2.2 percent).[38] Serbian nationalists have frequently discounted the very existence of a distinct Macedonian nationality, treating it as one of Tito's inventions. The Serbs have frequently asserted a historic right to Macedonian territory, with Serbian nationalists referring to Macedonia as simply "Southern Serbia."

The Macedonians are ethnically Slavic and Orthodox, which puts them in conflict with their Muslim minority as well as the neighboring Albania. The dangers of an explosive confrontation between the ethnic Macedonians and the ethnic Albanians may threaten Macedonia's integrity. Even if Serbia does not exercise direct pressure to bring Macedonia into the new Yugoslavia, Macedonia may be drawn into a war with Serbia if the Bosnian conflict spills into Kosovo. The United Nations has tried to insulate Macedonia from the regional ethnic conflict by stationing a U.N. protection force in Macedonia in 1991–1992 as a deterrent against aggression.

As of 1993, Macedonia has managed to maintain a precarious domestic balance while struggling to survive economically, with President Kiro Gligorov skillfully negotiating among the ethnic groups and the rapidly proliferating political parties. The country is ruled by a four-party coalition government headed by Branko Crvenkovski, including the former communists, now called the Social Democratic Union of Macedonia (SDUM), and the Reformist Forces of Macedonia-Liberal Party (RFM-LP) in cooperation with Albanian parties. The principal opposition party among the eight parties represented in the National Assembly (*Sobranie*) is the right-wing Internal Macedonian Revolutionary Organization (IMRO-DPMNU), while the key ethnic party is the Party for Democratic Prosperity (PDP), which although open to all ethnic groups is dominated by the Albanians. The PDP has twenty-three seats in the National Assembly. According to the Macedonian constitution, the National Assembly of the Republic of Macedonia is a unicameral legislature made up of between 120 and 140 deputies elected to four-year terms. The president of the republic is the center of power in Macedonia and among representative functions is the commander-in-chief of the army and head of the National Security Council.[39]

A possible explosion in the Kosovo region of Serbia, where the Albanian minority has been pushing for complete independence, constitutes another scenario that may broaden the Balkan war. While the Yugoslav army is powerful enough to put down an uprising by the Kosovo Albanians, the flow of refugees into Macedonia among others could break the delicate ethnic balance in Macedonia. Furthermore, while the Macedonian government is committed to steer clear of any conflict in Kosovo, it is likely that Macedonian Albanians would cross into Kosovo to assist their brethren, thus pulling Macedonia into a conflict with Serbia and possibly inviting a direct Serbian attack. Considering that Albania proper is unlikely to remain neutral, the worst-case scenario involves the real danger of the war extending outside the frontiers of former Yugoslavia.

ALBANIA IN HISTORY

Tiny Albania, with a population of just over three million and an area of some eleven thousand square miles, is the poorest and least developed of the Balkan states. The Albanians are descendants of an ancient tribe of Illyrians, a nationality separate from the Slavs, Turks, or Greeks.[40] This in itself has been a source of considerable national pride. Historically, Albania was ruled through a clannish system, the two most powerful clans being the Gegs and the Tosks. It is predominantly an Islamic nation, with Muslims comprising about 70 percent of the total and with the remainder of the population divided between Greek Orthodox and Roman Catholics.[41] As were its neighbors to the north and east, Albania was ruled by the Ottomans from the fifteenth century until the nineteenth century. The country's geostrategic location at the entrance to the Adriatic and only forty miles away from Italy made it an attractive acquisition for any power bent on controlling the Balkan peninsula. In 1913 Austria-Hungary transformed Albania into a sovereign principality in an effort to deny Serbia access to the Adriatic. In 1920 Albania became a fully independent state, although the disastrous economic conditions, political instability, and military weakness made it questionable from the start whether Albania could ever be made viable.

Yugoslavia, Greece, and Italy competed for influence over Albania, in an effort to occupy, control, or dismember it. Initially the Yugoslav monarchy was the most successful in controlling Albania, but by 1930 Albania became dominated by Italy, with the self-proclaimed King Zog (Ahmed Zogu) transformed into Mussolini's client.[42] In 1939 the Italians moved in to occupy the country. In the course of World War II, the Italians were supplanted by the Germans as Mussolini's fortunes declined. Albanian wartime resistance was largely dominated by the communists, owing to their support from Tito and the British. Enver Hoxha, the Albanian leader of the National Liberation Front, the principal communist resistance group, was Tito's wartime client. In 1944 Hoxha established an independent Albanian government in Tirana. True to its history, Albania's Italian tutelage was replaced by Yugoslav domination. Hoxha, who started as Tito's client, would subsequently emerge as his sworn enemy; Albania broke off diplomatic relations with Yugoslavia in 1948.

The post–World War II Albanian politics is the story of Hoxha's personal dictatorship. The 1945 elections were stolen by the communists, who in reality had less than 5 percent of the popular support in the countryside. In January 1946 Albania was declared a People's Republic, with the communists launching a terror campaign to eliminate all opposition. In 1948 the communist party was renamed the Albanian Party of Labor; Hoxha's supremacy as its leader was by then unquestioned.

A committed Stalinist as well as an Albanian nationalist, Hoxha was truly a political survivor, maintaining his independent political position both through the 1948 break between Tito and Stalin and the restoration of Yugoslav-Soviet relations in the mid-1950s. Hoxha was the first to challenge the Soviet claim to supreme authority on matters of communist ideology, even before the Chinese took that position. Albania's open break with the Soviet Union came in 1961, before the Sino-Soviet split became public knowledge. Hoxha's domestic and foreign policy line was hard-line Stalinist dogmatism. At the same time, concern for Albanian national independence led Hoxha to take formal steps to withdraw from the Warsaw Pact after the 1968 Soviet invasion of Czechoslovakia. In addition, Albania shifted its foreign policy toward a firm alignment with China.

Domestically, Hoxha pursued an autarkic economic policy that left the country economically devastated. The government was run in a "mafia style," with Hoxha's relatives holding high-level government jobs. At the same time, the staunchly nationalist foreign policy contributed to the process of Albanian nation building, giving the people a sense of national identity unprecedented in their clannish past. In 1967 Hoxha declared Albania an atheist state and ordered the destruction of some two thousand churches and mosques; others were converted into movie houses, stores, dance halls, garages, and museums.

Chinese assistance to Albania lasted until 1978, when China decided to improve relations with the West. The PRC stopped all economic (about $800 million over the years) and military assistance to Albania and withdrew its experts. Hoxha responded to this foreign policy setback by declaring Albania the only remaining genuine Marxist-Leninist country in the world. Finding itself without a patron, in the 1980s Tirana had no choice but to turn increasingly to Belgrade for assistance, but the problem of Serbian treatment of the Albanian minority in Kosovo remained an intractable obstacle to a genuine rapprochement.

Hoxha died in 1985; he was succeeded by Ramiz Alia, the first secretary of the Albanian Party of Labor, at the time when Gorbachev was preparing to launch his *perestroika* reforms. Alia tried to maintain the autarkic policies of Hoxha but moved also to improve relations with Yugoslavia, as symbolized by the opening of a railroad link between the two countries.

POSTCOMMUNIST ALBANIA

The breakdown of communism in Albania began in December 1990 when Ramiz Alia accepted demands put forth by student demonstrators for a multi-party system. The first multiparty election was scheduled for March 1991. The pent-up pressures of the half-century of communism led to an outburst of popular resentment, manifested by the tearing down of Hoxha's monuments throughout the country. Alia assumed full presidential powers in February 1991, claiming that this was the only way to avoid bloodshed as events accelerated out of control. Mass hysteria in January 1991 led to thousands of Albanian refugees seeking refuge in the neighboring Greece. Sporadic clashes between communists and the opposition continued throughout the election campaign, and in the first week of March neighboring Italy had to cope with the outflow of desperate Albanian boat people fleeing the country as the national crisis of confidence continued to deepen.

The first free Albanian election took place on March 31, 1991, with Western observers present. The election to the 250-seat legislature was judged fair, with a 95 percent voter turnout. The opposition Albanian Democratic Party carried the urban areas, including Tirana, with the Albanian Party of Labor (communists) dominating the countryside, winning two-thirds of the seats in the parliament.[43] In May 1991 Alia was elected the country's president by the new parliament, further strengthening his position as the country's leader.

The first government led by Fatos Nano was appointed in May, but it collapsed a month later as a wave of strikes paralyzed the country. The new communist-dominated coalition government led by Ylli Bufi, a former high-level apparatchik in the Albanian communist *nomenklatura,* was installed in June 1991, while the Albanian communists changed the party's name to the Albanian Socialist Party. However, the Bufi government failed to consolidate its position. The electoral victory of the communists was rejected in the streets, where bloody clashes between the police and the opposition intensified throughout 1991, the most violent rioting taking place in the northern city of Shkoder, a city with a large Roman Catholic population. The opposition demonstrations against the communists continued throughout 1991, until the opposition Albanian Democratic Party forced the government to agree to a new election in early 1992. The elections would prove the first critical step on the road to rejecting communism in Albania.

The March 22, 1992, election gave the Albanian Democratic Party a decisive victory over the socialists, with 62 percent of the votes, which gave the Democrats 92 of the 140 parliamentary seats.[44] In April the leader of the Democratic Party, Sali Berisha, became Albania's first democratically elected president, replacing communist Ramiz Alia. Berisha quickly became the most popular and powerful political figure in the country; the new government established in 1992 has been led by Aleksander Meksi of the Albanian Democratic Party. Meksi's policies concentrated on restoring law and order and addressing Albania's disastrous economic situation.

The economy of postcommunist Albania has collapsed. By the end of 1991 there was a real threat of starvation in the country as Albanian industrial and agricultural outputs were halved, with severe shortages of spare parts and equipment virtually crippling the entire economy.[45] The Meksi government has implemented an IMF-recommended economic austerity program, but as of 1993 there were few positive results to show for it. Unemployment in Albania for 1992 was estimated at 50 percent of the labor force, and the country's foreign debt stood at $600 million.[46]

Albania's decrepit economic base consists chiefly of mining, some food processing, and textiles. Albania has some natural resources, of which chromium is the most important, and it produces some oil, which is sold to Germany, Switzerland, and Romania. Its inefficient agriculture was fully collectivized under communism. General anarchy in the countryside has been accelerated by the breakdown of state authority and the disintegration of the collective farms.

Since the collapse of communism Albania has obtained some pledges of aid from France, Italy, Austria, and Romania, as well as China and Russia, but the amounts received so far have not been sufficient to make a difference. Italy has been effective in providing emergency food relief supplies (in "Operation Pelican," which has been administered by the Italian government), followed by additional food supplies from the G-24 countries. Germany contributed credits and technical assistance valued in 1991 at DM75 million.[47] The Albanian government has attempted to deal with the economic collapse by pushing through a land reform law that distributed private parcels of the land to individual peasant families and by liberalizing price controls.[48]

Since the collapse of communism Albania has had some success in breaking out of the communist-imposed international isolation. In 1991 the country became a full member of the Conference on Security and Cooperation in Europe and established ties to the European Community. It also joined the World Bank and the International Monetary Fund and established diplomatic relations with the Vatican. Albania has made a concerted effort to build better relations with the United States, as symbolized by a June 1991 visit to Tirana by U.S. Secretary of State James Baker. According to Albanian Foreign Minister Muhamet Kapllani, Albania "expected a lot from the United States, especially because of the Albanian-American community."[49] Tirana has hoped that the ethnic Albanian community in the United States would both assist Albania directly and lobby for aid from the U.S. government. So far, the expectations have been largely unfulfilled.

Another new development in Albanian foreign policy has been a greater emphasis on relations with the Islamic world. In December 1992 Albania joined the Organization of the Islamic Conference and has worked since to establish closer ties to Turkey as its best ally in the region in the event of the Balkan war spreading to Kosovo and Macedonia.[50] In January 1993 President Berisha visited Saudi Arabia to explore the possibility of Saudi assistance. Tirana has also applied for help from the Islamic Development Bank to pay for urgently needed infrastructure projects.

The biggest and potentially most destabilizing foreign policy issue for Tirana remains the future of over two million ethnic Albanians in Kosovo in neighboring Yugoslavia. If war spreads across the entire former Yugoslav federation, Albania may find itself drawn into a conflict it is ill-prepared to handle. Albania inherited from the communist era a small army of less than fifty thousand. The military equipment is primitive by Western standards, and the army has a history of being politicized rather than maintaining a high level of professionalism. Should war come, Albania will be no match for the power of Serbia-Montenegro.

NOTES

1. Richard F. Staar, *Communist Regimes in Eastern Europe* (Stanford, Calif.: Hoover Press, 1988), p. 221.

2. *Croatia 1990* (Zagreb: The Presidency of the Republic of Croatia, 1990), p. 9.

3. Charles Jelavich, *South Slav Nationalisms—Textbooks and Yugoslav Union before 1914* (Columbus, Ohio: Ohio State University Press, 1990), pp. 1–2.

4. Ibid., pp. 3–6.

5. Ibid., p. 9.

6. Ibid., p. 12.

7. Ibid., pp. 14–15.

8. Patrick Moore, "Yugoslavia: Ethnic Tension Erupts into Civil War," *RFE/RL Research Report*, January 3, 1992, p. 68.

9. Ibid., p. 69.

10. Ibid., p. 70.

11. Ibid., p. 71.

12. "Reactions from Abroad," *RFE/RL Daily Report*, June 26, 1991.

13. The discussion of the Slovenian constitution is based on *Constitution of the Republic of Slovenia* (Ljubljana: Uradni list Republike Slovenije, 1992).

14. "Coalition Building Begins in Slovenia," *RFE/RL Daily Report*, December 8, 1992.

15. *Slovenia Your Partner* (Ljubljana: The Chamber of Economy of Slovenia, 1992), p. 21.

16. Ibid., p. 7.

17. *Bank of Slovenia*, September 1992.

18. *Slovenia Your Partner*, p. 21.

19. *Foreign Trade Regime of the Republic of Slovenia* (Ljubljana: Republic of Slovenia Ministry of Foreign Affairs, 1992), p. 9.

20. "Constitutional Decision on the Sovereignty and Independence of the Republic of Croatia" and "Declaration on the Establishment of the Sovereign and Independent Republic of Croatia" were published in *Narodne novine*, no. 31, June 25, 1991.

21. "The Charter of the Rights of Serbs and Other Nationalities in the Republic of Croatia," published in *Narodne novine*, no. 31, June 25, 1991, section 3.

22. Dushan Bilandzic, *Croatia between War and Independence* (Zagreb: University of Zagreb, 1991), p. 61.

23. The following discussion of the Croatian constitution is based on *The Constitution of the Republic of Croatia* (Zagreb: The Sabor of the Republic of Croatia, December 22, 1990).

24. "Tudjman Leading in Croatian Elections," *RFE/RL Daily Report*, August 3, 1992.

25. Patrick Moore, "Issues in Croatian Politics," *RFE/RL Research Report*, November 6, 1992, p. 10.

26. Ibid., p. 9.

27. *Croatian Privatization Fund* (Zagreb: Masmedia, 1993), p. 5.

28. "Declaration of the Promulgation of the Constitution of the Federal Republic of Yugoslavia," *Yugoslav Survey*, no. 2, 1992, p. 31.

29. *The Constitution of the Republic of Serbia* (Belgrade: The Secretariat for Information of the Republic of Serbia, 1990) and *Ustav Republike Crne Gore* (Podgorica: Sluzhebni List RCG, 1992).

30. The discussion of the Yugoslav federal constitution is based on *Constitution of the Federal Republic of Yugoslavia* (Belgrade, 1992).

31. "Serbian Elections 'Seriously Flawed,' " *RFE/RL Daily Report*, December 22, 1992.

32. Official election results released by the Republic of Serbia Ministry of Information, January 15, 1993.

33. "Montenegrin Balloting," *RFE/RL Daily Report*, December 22, 1992.

34. Official election results released by the Republic of Serbia Ministry of Information, January 15, 1993.

35. Based on *The Federal Republic of Yugoslavia in Figures* (Belgrade: The Federal Institute of Statistics, 1992).

36. "The Economy of FR Yugoslavia in 1992," *Yugoslav Survey*, no. 4, 1992, pp. 89 and 106.

37. Duncan M. Perry, "The Republic of Macedonia and the Odds for Survival," *RFE/RL Research Report*, November 20, 1992, p. 13.

38. Ibid., p. 17.

39. Duncan M. Perry, "Politics in the Republic of Macedonia: Issues and Parties," *RFE/RL Research Report*, June 4, 1993, pp. 31–37.

40. Anthony Harding, "The Prehistoric Background of Illyrians in Albania," in Tom Winnifrith, ed., *Perspectives on Albania* (New York: St. Martin's Press, 1992), pp. 14–15.

41. Hugh Poulton, *The Balkans: Minorities and States in Conflict* (London: Minority Rights Group Publications, 1991), p. 193.

42. J. F. Brown, *Eastern Europe and Communist Rule* (Durham, N.C.: Duke University Press, 1988), p. 371.

43. Louis Zanga, "Albania: Between Democracy and Chaos," *RFE/RL Research Report*, January 3, 1992, p. 74.

44. Louis Zanga, "Albania: Democratic Revival and Social Upheaval," *RFE/RL Research Report*, January 1, 1993, p. 75.

45. Zanga, "Albania: Between Democracy and Chaos," p. 76.

46. Zanga, "Albania: Democratic Revival and Social Upheaval," p. 75.

47. Zanga, "Albania: Between Democracy and Chaos," p. 75.

48. Ibid., p. 74.
49. "Albania Expects Much from America," *RFE/RL Daily Report*, June 21, 1991.
50. Louis Zanga, "Albania Moves Closer to the Islamic World," *RFE/RL Research Report*, February 12, 1993, p. 28.

III
THE BALTIC RIM

7

LITHUANIA

HISTORICAL LITHUANIA AND THE INTERWAR REPUBLIC

Unlike the other two Baltic states, the restored postcommunist state of Lithuania has a long history of national existence. An independent Lithuanian kingdom was recognized as early as 1251; it accepted Christianity in 1387.[1] During the reign of Grand Duke Algirdas, in the fourteenth century, Lithuania ranked among the largest and strongest European powers, its domain stretching from the Baltic to the Black Sea and including the cities of Kiev and Smolensk.[2]

Lithuania's culture has been shaped by the indigenous Baltic tradition, as well as the influence of Germany, Russia, and most important, Poland, with which Lithuania entered into a dynastic union in the late fourteenth century. This was followed in 1569 by a political union when the Commonwealth of Poland-Lithuania was established. The Polish-Lithuanian state lasted for over two hundred years, until its 1795 partition among Russia, Austria, and Prussia, at which time Lithuania fell principally under Russian rule. It was controlled by Moscow until 1915, when in turn Germany occupied Lithuanian territory in the course of World War I.

In the nineteenth century, a national and cultural renaissance movement swept through Lithuania, laying the foundations for the modern Lithuanian national identity. In contrast to the territories of present-day Estonia and Latvia, where serfdom was abolished in 1816–1819, Lithuanian peasants were not liberated from serfdom until 1861.[3] The problem of Russian and German control was compounded by the continued influence of Polonized Lithuanian gentry and the Poles themselves, who regarded Lithuania as a part of their own state. The "Polish problem" in Lithuania would remain a powerful determinant in Lithuanian politics to this day. Lithuanian national consciousness developed in the precarious environment of Polish-Russian-German rivalry in the Baltic region.

Like other east and central European successor states, Lithuania became independent after World War I because of the collapse of the Russian and German empires. Lithuania became formally an independent state in 1918 following the adoption of the Provisional Constitution of Lithuania by the Lithuanian State Council (*Lietuvos Valstybes Taryba*) led by Antanas Smetona, a well-known writer and the man who would subsequently become Lithuania's interwar dictator. The constitution of Lithuania was adopted on August 1, 1922.

The interwar Republic of Lithuania was predominantly an agricultural economy. Most of Lithuania's trade was with Germany and the United Kingdom. In 1938 Lithuania's exports to Germany constituted 17 percent of its total exports, while exports to the United Kingdom constituted 47 percent. Conversely, that same year Lithuania imported 22 percent of its total imports from Germany and 28 percent of its total imports from the United Kingdom.[4]

Domestically, Lithuania failed to consolidate its nascent democratic system sufficiently to resist authoritarian pressures. Following a series of weak governments, a military coup, staged by a small group of army officers on the night of December 16–17, 1926, succeeded in dispersing the parliament (*Seimas*) and forced the resignation of the government and the president. The coup leaders then ordered the reconvened parliament to elect Antanas Smetona as the president of the republic.[5] In April of 1927 Smetona dissolved the parliament and effectively established himself as dictator. On May 26, 1928, he introduced a new constitution by presidential decree, in which he provided for the election of the president by an electoral college for a term of seven years. A brief interlude of Lithuanian democracy was over.

Lithuania remained internationally isolated during the interwar period, with no diplomatic relations with Poland after the Polish occupation of the city of Vilnius. After the rise of Hitler in 1933 the Germans worked to recover Memelland in western Lithuania, organizing an anti-Lithuanian movement among the Klaipeda Germans. Following the German annexation of Austria and Czechoslovakia, in March 1938, the Lithuanians accepted the German ultimatum for an immediate return of Memelland to Germany.

During World War II, Lithuania was subject to three successive military invasions that finally resulted in Soviet occupation. Once again, caught between Russia and Germany, Lithuania found itself helplessly struggling against overwhelming odds. After the German invasion of Poland on September 1, 1939, and the Soviet invasion of Poland on September 17, Lithuania was forced on October 10 to accept a Soviet-Lithuanian pact of mutual assistance. In return for the reincorporation of the city of Vilnius into Lithuania, Kaunas agreed to the stationing of Soviet troops on Lithuanian territory "for the duration of the European war."[6]

What followed constituted a predictable pattern of communist subversion and control. All political parties were outlawed, a communist party was created, the parliament was dissolved, and elections for a new parliament were ordered. Secret-police terror against all potential sources of opposition followed. Rigged elections to the parliament took place in 1940 and predictably returned a 100 percent communist-controlled legislature. The new *Seimas* decreed unanimously on July 21, 1940, to petition for the incorporation of Lithuania into the Soviet Union. It also decreed the nationalization of property and the amalgamation of the Lithuanian armed forces with the Red Army. The country's independence thus formally ended for the next half-century.

LITHUANIA UNDER COMMUNIST CONTROL

The Lithuanian Soviet Socialist Republic became subjected to Soviet-style economic transformation, including collectivization of agriculture, the nationalization of industry, and the abolition of private property. Two new waves of mass deportations of Lithuanians to the Soviet interior followed in 1948 and 1949.[7] The total number of Lithuanian deportees to the Soviet interior for the period 1941–1952 was set at 29,923 families, totaling 120,000 for the period, with the total for all Lithuanian deportees during Soviet occupation estimated to approach 300,000.[8] Armed resistance to Soviet occupation continued in Lithuania through 1953.

The survivors of those deportations, as well as those from the 1941 wave of deportations, returned to Lithuania only in the late 1950s and early 1960s. Only one out of eight deportees survived the Siberian labor camps.[9] The condition for their return was that they never discuss their experience in Siberia. In the 1950s the Soviets banned the singing of the Lithuanian national anthem, the displaying of the Lithuanian tricolor (yellow-green-red), and the symbol of a knight on horseback—Lithuania's national emblem. The Soviets introduced a program of bilingual education in Lithuanian schools, which in effect meant imposing Russian as the language of instruction.

From the early 1950s through the 1970s Moscow implemented a radical industrialization program in Lithuania, with the goal of transforming the republic from an agriculturally based economy into an industrial-agricultural area strongly integrated into the Soviet Union's centrally run economy. The Soviets expanded the existing light, food processing, and timber industries, while constructing new machine-building, metalworking, and power plants. Lithuania became the site of heavily polluting chemical and petrochemical industries built on the basis of inefficient Soviet technologies. Concurrently with forced industrialization, Lithuania experienced a rapid urbanization process, with the urban population rising from 39 percent of the total in 1959 to 68 percent of the total in 1989.[10]

As elsewhere in the U.S.S.R., agriculture paid the price of bolshevik social engineering. Forced collectivization was completed between 1949 and 1952 and all private land ownership was abolished. The decline of agricultural output was reversed by the heavy reliance on chemical fertilizers, which in addition to pervasive industrial pollution contributed to an ecological devastation of the countryside.

Finally, Soviet occupation and the crash industrialization program encouraged migration of non-Lithuanians, predominantly Russians, into Lithuania. By 1990, 20 percent of Lithuania's population was ethnically non-Lithuanian. The percentage of non-Lithuanians was considerably higher in the cities than in the countryside.

All political power in Lithuania remained in the hands of the Lithuanian Communist Party, which was integrated with the Communist Party of the Soviet Union. Initially, the Lithuanian Communist Party was dominated by the Russians and other non-Lithuanians, with Lithuanian communists constituting only 18 percent of the total in 1947. Gradually, new indigenous communist cadres were prepared, and by 1986 70 percent of the 197,000 communist party members in Lithuania were Lithuanian.[11]

THE RESTORATION OF INDEPENDENCE: *SAJUDIS*

In the late 1980s Lithuania experienced an upsurge in the national independence movement, spurred on by the loosening of Soviet secret-police terror in the wake of Mikhail Gorbachev's *perestroika*. Lithuanian dissidents were also encouraged by the success of the national self-determination movement in Poland led by the Solidarity trade union. In June of 1988 the Lithuanian Reform Movement *Sajudis* (*Lietuvos persitvarkymo sajudis*), led by Vytautas Landsbergis (a music and art historian by training), was established.[12] The founding group consisted of thirty-six intellectuals, who were elected at a meeting of some five hundred intellectuals convened in the Academy of Sciences Presidium Hall in Vilnius.[13] The movement's stated primary goal was to work to support *perestroika*, while the real objective became the restoration to the Lithuanian people of their true national history by demolishing the propaganda spread for decades by the Soviets. Soon, the program became radicalized into demanding the restoration of national independence. Other anticommunist organizations soon proliferated.

The regime gradually gave in to the popular pressure for change. On August 17, 1988, Lithuania's national tricolor flag and the country's national anthem were legalized.[14] Next, the communists officially admitted the existence of the secret protocol to the Ribbentrop-Molotov Pact of 1939 and condemned the official distortions of the historical record. By 1988 there was an effective duality of political power, with *Sajudis* increasingly assuming the role of a political party, all its claims to the contrary notwithstanding. Lithuanian resistance to the Soviet military draft increased exponentially.

Increasingly, the Lithuanian national independence movement began to enjoy support within the Lithuanian Communist Party (LCP). With *Sajudis's* support, Algirdas Brazauskas was elected the LCP's new first secretary, and a year later he led the party in its separation from the Communist Party of the Soviet Union (CPSU). On December 7, 1989, the Lithuanian Supreme Soviet passed a resolution by a vote of 243 to 1 that abolished the Communist Party's exclusive right to rule.[15] In 1990 Brazauskas's Communist Party renamed itself the Lithuanian Democratic Labor Party, while the remaining hard-line communists in Lithuania continued under the Lithuanian Communist Party banner.

A qualitative change in Lithuania's struggle for independence, as well as that of the entire region, came on May 13–14, 1989, when the Baltic Assembly of Independence Movements in the three Baltic states held its first meeting in Tallinn, Estonia. The meeting addressed an appeal to the U.S.S.R. Supreme Soviet, the CSCE leadership, and the U.N. secretary general outlining the desire of the three nations to regain independence in a neutral demilitarized zone of Europe, referred to as "Baltoscandia"—the term originally coined by Swedish geographer Sten de Geer to describe the region that includes the Scandinavian countries and the Baltic states as a geographic unit distinct from the Great Russian plains.[16] The "Declaration of the Rights of the Baltic Nations" also called for the "right to self-determination and free determination of their political status."[17] In addition, the Baltic Assembly expressed its commitment to continue close cooperation between the Estonian Popular Front, the Latvian Popular Front, and the Lithuanian Reform Movement *Sajudis*. The three organizations at the conclusion of the Tallinn session created the Baltic Council and decided to hold Baltic Assembly meetings on an annual basis, setting the date of the next meeting for May 1990 in Riga.[18] On September 9, 1989, the Baltic Council of the Latvian Popular Front, the Estonian Popular Front, and the Lithuanian Reform Movement *Sajudis* issued a declaration following a meeting in Panevezys, Lithuania, on September 8, to work jointly toward the expansion and integration of the Baltic economies.[19]

A critical turning point in Lithuania's struggle for independence came in February 1990, when a new Lithuanian Supreme Soviet was elected in free direct elections, giving *Sajudis* an overwhelming majority. On March 11, the parliament, led by *Sajudis*, voted to restore the Republic of Lithuania as an independent, sovereign state.[20] The legislature used the 1989 denunciation of the Ribbentrop-Molotov Pact by the U.S.S.R. Congress of People's Deputies as the legal foundation of its action. The denunciation constituted an indirect repudiation of Lithuania's incorporation in the Soviet Union. The legislature also elected the leader of *Sajudis,* Vytautas Landsbergis, as the country's president; Kazimiera Prunskiene, an economist, became the country's prime minister (until January 1991). The March 11 parliament meeting adopted a new provisional constitution of the state and a number of new bylaws.[21]

Gorbachev denounced the declaration of Lithuanian independence as illegal and warned the new government not to attempt to set up its own military and border units. Moscow tried to force Lithuania back into the union by imposing economic sanctions. The cost of the Soviet economic blockade was estimated at 338 billion rubles in 1990.[22] Attempts at intimidation through a display of military force followed throughout the summer and winter of 1990, leading on January 11–13, 1991, to an aborted military crackdown in Lithuania and Latvia following an ultimatum from the Soviet military to Gorbachev that demanded an end to the secession movements in the U.S.S.R.[23] The aborted crackdown, during which the Soviet troops occupied a number of government buildings, left fourteen dead and close to 700 injured. The parliament moved to assert its legitimacy in the eyes of international public opinion by calling a national referendum on February 9, 1991, on the future of the country. About 76 percent of all eligible voters responded, of which 90.5 percent voted for complete independence and the introduction of democracy in Lithuania. The final push for independence came after the aborted coup in the U.S.S.R. in August 1991, when the new Soviet Supreme Council recognized all three Baltic states as independent.

POSTCOMMUNIST POLITICS: FROM *SAJUDIS* TO LDDP

The popularity of *Sajudis* began to decline rapidly once economic hardships associated with the transition to the market became an everyday reality of Lithuanian politics. The growing dissatisfaction with the Landsbergis presidency was accompanied by the rise of support for the postcommunist Lithuanian Democratic Labor Party (LDDP) and its leader Algirdas Brazauskas, the republic's former Communist Party boss.

The early parliamentary election, scheduled for October and November 1992, was contested by three principal political groupings: (1) the *Sajudis* coalition (consisting of the Lithuanian Green Party, the Citizens' Charter, and the Union of Political Prisoners) aligned with the Coalition for a Democratic Lithuania (a combination of the Lithuanian Christian Democratic Party, the Union of Lithuanian Political Prisoners and Deportees, the Lithuanian Democratic Party, the National Union of Lithuania, and the Independence Party); (2) Brazauskas's Lithuanian Democratic Labor Party; and (3) the centrist coalition, including the Lithuanian Social Democratic Party, the Lithuanian Liberal Union, the Center Movement, the Moderate Movement, and the National Progress Movement.[24]

The first free parliamentary elections on October 25, 1992, demonstrated that Lithuanians were voting their pocketbook. Unlike minorities in the other Baltic states, the 19 percent Russian, Polish, and other minorities were allowed to vote in the election and reportedly voted predominantly for the LDDP.[25] The Brazauskas party captured forty-four seats outright in the first round of balloting. In the runoffs of the first free election to the parliament (*Seimas*) on November 15, 1992, for the remaining sixty-one of the 141 seats, the LDDP captured thirty-five seats.[26] After the final count the LDDP received seventy-three of the 141 seats, with only thirty seats going to the *Sajudis* coalition.[27] During the elections the voters also approved the country's new constitution, providing for a directly elected president.[28]

In the aftermath of the election, Landsbergis charged that Moscow had influenced the outcome by tightening its economic pressure on Lithuania, including the transition to hard-currency settlements for oil and gas deliveries from Russia. Landsbergis also accused Russia of slowing down the critical gas supplies to Lithuanian hospitals and of infiltrating Lithuania with "brainwashing experts" from Russian security.[29] Although Russia's real and potential impact on Lithuania must have been a factor in the election, the defeat of *Sajudis* was chiefly a result of the movement's internal fragmentation and its failure to form an effective political party, not a result of outside influence. The strong personality of Landsbergis, who was at times accused of authoritarianism, contributed to the gridlock within the movement. The ultimate reason for *Sajudis*'s reversal was the dismal state of Lithuania's economy. In 1992 industrial output and wages in Lithuania were cut in half, while inflation hit 1,700 percent.[30] Plagued by fuel shortages, skyrocketing inflation, and rising unemployment, the Lithuanian electorate turned away from the center-right coalition that had brought about the country's independence from Russia.

The October 25 and November 15, 1992, *Seimas* election was a stunning reversal of the February and March 1990 elections to the Supreme Soviet that had brought *Sajudis* to power and taken Lithuania out of the Soviet Union. In 1990 *Sajudis* drew its strength and unity from its members' commitment to Lithuania's independence, political differences within the movement notwithstanding. Having achieved that goal it shared the fate of Poland's Solidarity movement, that is, internal fragmentation and the emergence of competing political programs and parties. The divisions within *Sajudis* effectively paralyzed the Supreme Soviet, fueling the rising disillusionment of the electorate with the new political elite. Hence, although it had been elected to a five-year term, on July 9, 1992, the Supreme Soviet called for a new parliamentary election as the only solution to the deadlock of Lithuanian democracy.[31]

The rejection of *Sajudis* in the parliamentary vote was also a sign that the Lithuanian electorate was increasingly uncomfortable with the extreme nationalism that had become the hallmark of the Landsbergis government.[32] This popular sentiment would be reconfirmed several months later in the first free presidential election. Still, *Sajudis* could claim significant accomplishments, the most important among them being the passage of a new democratic constitution and the finalized agreement on Russian troop withdrawal.

In the following presidential elections, on February 14, 1993, Algirdas Brazauskas won 60 percent of the vote, thus becoming Lithuania's first democratically elected president since the collapse of communism.[33] The challenger, Stasys Lozoraitis, an emigre Lithuanian politician widely considered a living symbol of the interwar independent Lithuanian state and a close advisor to Landsbergis, was attacked as a "prince from abroad" out of touch with the common man.[34] Brazauskas, who repeatedly renounced his communist past, campaigned on a social-democratic platform. He promised to establish a *litas* committee, which would supervise the introduction of a national currency as the first step on the road to reform. Brazauskas also insisted that at home economic reforms would continue, while in foreign relations he would work to establish close relations with Russia, Belarus, and Poland.

Shortly after his victory, Brazauskas appointed Adolfas Slezevicius as the new prime minister. Slezevicius, a former Communist Party Central Committee official and a minor member of the *Sajudis* government of Gediminas Vagnorius, has also had experience in business as head of the milk-producers association and one of the Lithuanian-Norwegian joint ventures.[35] Vytautas Landsbergis moved after the election to form a conservative opposition political party, charging that the West once again had turned its back on the Baltic states, effectively conceding them to Russia.[36]

DOMESTIC POLITICS

The Lithuanian constitution, passed by the Supreme Soviet on October 13, 1992, and approved by the voters on October 25, 1992, the parliamentary election reflects a compromise between the proponents of a strong presidential rule and those favoring an all-powerful parliament.[37] An earlier referendum on the new constitution, held on May 25, 1992, had failed because it did not win the support of the majority of all eligible voters. The new basic law accepted in October reflects a compromise negotiated in the Supreme Soviet. It divides power in Lithuania among the *Seimas*, the president of the republic and the government, and the judiciary (Article 5).

The new constitution establishes Lithuanian as the official state language (Article 14) while it also guarantees the rights of ethnic minorities to "foster their language, culture, and customs" (Article 37). It guarantees property rights (Article 23) and private ownership (Article 46). Chapter 2 of the Lithuanian constitution, "The Individual and the State," is a mixture of the bill of rights, with guarantees of free speech (Article 26) and freedom of assembly (Article 36), as well as an expressed prohibition of censorship (Article 44) and a set of constitutionally guaranteed social welfare policies. Article 41 guarantees every citizen free education from elementary through university levels. The constitution also guarantees "the right to adequate, safe and healthy working conditions, adequate compensation for work, and social security in the event of unemployment" (Article 48). Rest and leisure time and annual paid holidays are a constitutional right of the Lithuanian citizen (Article 49), as are retirement or disability pensions and health care (Articles 52 and 53).

The *Seimas*, elected to a four-year term with 141 seats, is the principal legislative body in Lithuania (Article 55). It convenes for two regular sessions, spring and fall, but extraordinary sessions may be called by the chairperson of the *Seimas* or by the president (Article 64). The prime minister is proposed by the president, while the *Seimas* has the prerogative either to approve or to reject the nominee. The *Seimas* also approves or rejects the government's program and appoints judges to the Constitutional Court and the Supreme Court, as well as the state controller and the chairman of the board of the Bank of Lithuania; it ratifies state treaties, levies state taxes, decides on the use of the military forces, and declares martial law (Article 66). Although the right of legislative initiative belongs to the *Seimas* members, the president, and the government, Lithuanian citizens can initiate laws directly, provided 50,000 signatures are gathered in support of the proposed law, which then must be considered by the *Seimas* (Article 68). The *Seimas* can also impeach the president, judges of the Supreme and Constitutional Courts, and members of the legislature; a three-fifths majority vote is required to remove an impeached official (Article 74).

The president is the head of the Lithuanian state; he is elected by a direct vote to a five-year term, with the limitation of two consecutive terms (Article 77). The president has broad prerogatives on foreign policy and defense matters; subject to the *Seimas* approval he appoints the prime minister and makes key ministerial appointments, including the commander-in-chief of the army and the head of the Lithuanian Security Service. He can impose martial law and order military mobilization subject to approval of the subsequent *Seimas* (Article 84). The prime minister is appointed by the president, upon the *Seimas*'s approval; he must present his program to the parliament within fifteen days of confirmation (Article 92).

The Constitutional Court consists of nine judges appointed by the *Seimas* to a nine-year term, with one-third of the judges being replaced every three years. The *Seimas* selects three candidates from the candidates nominated by the president, three candidates from the pool of candidates nominated by the chairperson of the *Seimas*, and three candidates from those nominated by the chairperson of the Supreme Court (Article 103). The *Seimas* also appoints the Supreme Court judges and judges of the Court of Appeals upon recommendation of the president (Article 112).

The Lithuanian Democratic Labor Party, the reformist wing of the former Lithuanian Communist Party, has an absolute majority in the parliament, with seventy-three seats; *Sajudis* is the second-largest party with thirty deputies. The Lithuanian Christian Democratic Party has nine seats, the Lithuanian Social Democratic Party has eight seats, and the Union of Lithuanian Political Prisoners and Deportees has five seats. Parties with fewer than five seats include the Lithuanian Democratic Party, the Union of Poles, the National Union of

Lithuania, the Center Movement of Lithuania, the Coalition for a United Lithuania, and the Independence Party.[38]

The LDDP political program is careful to emphasize a clear break with its communist past.[39] On matters of domestic politics it declares itself committed to the constitution and the division of powers, while emphasizing the overall supervisory authority of the *Seimas*. The LDDP has also declared its unequivocal support for an independent judiciary and an independent press.

ECONOMIC POLICY

Economic reform, especially the return of property to its former owners and the right to acquire property freely, has become a central part of the Lithuanian reform program. The privatization process began with the February 28, 1991, Law on the Initial Privatization of State Property, which provided for investment vouchers of between 1,000 and 5,000 rubles, which could be used to purchase stock in state-owned enterprises. On May 28, 1991, the Law on the Privatization of Apartments was passed to allow tenants to purchase their apartments, with up to 80 percent of the cost of the units redeemable in investment vouchers.[40] On January 14, 1992, the Lithuanian parliament extended the right to reclaim property down to the level of grandchildren of the prewar owners.[41]

Another important avenue of Lithuania's economic transformation has been the changeover to a new currency to replace the "coupons" (*talonas*) introduced on October 1, 1992, after Lithuania had left the ruble zone. The new currency, the *litas*, was introduced in the summer of 1993, with one *litas* replacing 100 coupons.[42] In early 1994, Lithuania considered pegging the *litas* to a hard currency, most likely the U.S. dollar. The introduction of the new currency is essential to the future of the country's twenty-seven fledgling commercial banks. As part of the banking reform, these commercial banks will have no choice but to merge if they are to meet the new minimum capital base requirement mandated by the central bank of 500 million *talonas* (US $1 million); the previous threshold for commercial banks was 40 million *talonas* (US $80,000).[43]

Still, inflation in Lithuania remains the highest among the three Baltic states, running at 12.7 percent in May 1993.[44] The Council of Europe meeting in Helsinki on June 4, 1993, placed Lithuania together with Romania, Bulgaria, and Albania among the postcommunist countries yet to reverse their economic decline.[45] As of June 1993, the average monthly salary in Lithuania amounted to about $30, with the average family spending 64.4 percent of its income on food.[46] The dramatic decline in the level of consumption since independence prompted some Lithuanian observers to argue that by the end of 1992 close to 80 percent of the population found itself below the poverty line.[47] With the average monthly wage in Lithuania pegged at the equivalent of US $30, the minimum monthly earnings in Lithuania stand at about US $5.[48]

As part of the movement to a market economy, the government opened the National Stock Exchange of Lithuania on September 30, 1992, by pooling two privately owned commodity exchanges, *Lietuvos Birza* and *Bltijos Birza*, with the Ministry of Finance and the Lithuanian Investment Bank. The operations of the National Stock Exchange are supervised by the State Securities Commission, which also issues licenses to stockbrokers. Although still at the organizational stage and lacking appropriate computer equipment, the National Stock Exchange will be an important part of the privatization program as a means for buying and selling the government privatization vouchers.[49]

Like the other successor states to the U.S.S.R., Lithuania is in the process of restructuring its economy to reverse its complete dependence on Russia. The legacy of complete past integration in the Soviet economy is the greatest weakness and the greatest challenge facing Lithuania's economic reformers. Although Lithuania's infrastructure is much better than Russia's (Lithuania's highway system was arguably the best in all of the former Soviet Union), it is still inadequate by Western standards.

The potentially strongest part of Lithuania's economy remains its agriculture, which was by far more productive than Russian agriculture; during Soviet domination Lithuania exported 50 percent of its agricultural output to the rest of the Soviet Union.[50] Still, in the past Lithuania's agriculture relied heavily on animal fodder supplied centrally by Moscow, which is no longer available.[51] As part of the privatization campaign, in 1991 the government gave the collective farms the status of state enterprises as the first step toward their liquidation and privatization. Furthermore, the dissolution of the Soviet collective farm system has proceeded in a haphazard way. The breakdown of the administrative structures of collective farms has often led to the virtual abandonment of land. At least a quarter of all arable land in Lithuania was left unplowed in the fall of 1992.[52]

Lithuania has no significant natural resources, and its industry is completely dependent on imported materials. For energy the country depends in part on nuclear power plants, built during the Soviet period, that are seriously deficient in terms of safety.[53] Lithuania has to import oil, natural gas, and coal, which since independence has put a serious strain on the country's economy.

Lithuania's industrial base needs to be modernized if the country's wares are to be competitive in Western markets. Considering that in 1990 42 percent of Lithuania's labor force was employed in the industrial and construction sector, modernization of the country's industrial base is imperative to limit unemployment.[54] The Lithuanian Association of Industrialists, set up in mid-1989 and representing 80 percent of Lithuania's industry, has as its goal reforming the industrial plants to meet Western standards. Lithuania lacks capital to modernize its industrial base, while the *Sajudis* government was hesitant about foreign investment in the country; while foreign investors can acquire Lithuanian factories, they can only lease the land on which these plants are sited. As a result, over the last two years Lithuania has received consistently less foreign investment than Estonia and Latvia.[55] Prime Minister Adolfas Slezevicius has moved to reverse the pattern in an effort to convince both the foreign investors and the IMF that his government is keen to change. A notable success of the new policy was the March 1993 investment of US $12.5 million by Philip Morris to purchase 65.5 percent of the Klaipeda tobacco factory, with the proviso that the Americans would invest an additional US $40 million to modernize the plant.[56]

Although the economic decline has continued after Brazauskas's electoral victory, Lithuania has begun to make some progress. In a televised speech on June 3, 1993, which marked his first one hundred days in office, Brazauskas claimed that Lithuania's exports to the West had gone up by 60 percent since December 1992 to constitute one-third of all the country's exports.[57] The government also moved to establish free trade zones on former Soviet military bases and airports in Vilnius, Kaunas, Siauliai, and Kedainiai, as well as two sites in Kaunas and Klaipeda. A decree of March 12, 1993, stated that at free trade zones "all commercial activities barring retail trade will be exempt from taxes as well as quantity, price and transport restrictions."[58] The program has run into bureaucratic snags, however, as the Lithuanian Defense Ministry pushed for the transfer of all former Soviet bases for the use of Lithuania's armed forces.

The most disturbing part of Brazauskas's economic program remains his insistence on gradualism in the country's transition to a market economy. Upon taking office Brazauskas spoke strongly against the privatization and market pricing program recommended for Lithuania's agriculture by the International Monetary Fund, comparing it to a "Faustian deal of selling the country's soul to Mephistopheles."[59]

FOREIGN POLICY, SECURITY POLICY, AND RELATIONS WITH RUSSIA

The foreign policy program of the Lithuanian government is effectively the foreign policy agenda of the ruling LDDP. This includes eventual full membership in the European Union, with a near-term associate membership agreement, close cooperation with the Baltic states, Scandinavia, and Germany, as well as closer ties to Western Europe, the United States, and NATO. In a departure from the *Sajudis* policies, the LDDP emphasizes its willingness to negotiate with the International Monetary Fund only on the condition that the agreements "correspond to the conditions and abilities of Lithuania."[60]

Lithuania's principal foreign policy objective is to increase its ties to Europe. During his June 15, 1993, visit to France, Lithuanian President Algirdas Brazauskas pushed for greater economic and cultural cooperation with France and asked French President Francois Mitterrand to help Lithuania become an associate member of the European Community.[61] As a step in that direction, the

Council of Europe at a February 4, 1993, meeting in Strasbourg agreed to bring Lithuania into the Council of Europe on May 14, 1993.[62]

At the same time, Lithuania has made an effort to initiate cooperation with Latvia and Estonia in the area of national security. In June 1992, the defense ministers of the three Baltic states signed an agreement in Parnu, in western Estonia, which has laid the foundations for pooling the infrastructure and training resources.[63] Although short of a formal alliance, the Parnu Agreement does lay the foundations of a better future common deterrent against aggression and a mechanism for regional crisis management.

The security policy espoused by the LDDP calls for broader contacts with neighboring countries, to include in addition to the other Baltic states also Poland, Belarus, and Russia. The party is committed to a pan-European security system including strengthening the CSCE, increasing Lithuania's ties to NATO, and building a collective security system on the continent.[64] The LDDP has called specifically for signing, with Russia, a treaty on good neighborly relations that would resolve the question of Russian access to the Kaliningrad District, establishment of full diplomatic relations including exchange of ambassadors, full implementation of Russian troop withdrawal from Lithuania, and the implementation of bilateral trade agreements with Russia, Ukraine, Belarus, and other Commonwealth of Independent States (CIS) member states with the goal of securing their raw material supplies for Lithuanian industry.

The emphasis on the need for better relations with Russia constitutes a departure from the policies of the *Sajudis* government, which viewed Russia as the principal threat to Lithuania's continued independence. In addition, the decision to improve relations with Poland is an effort to overcome the legacy of mistrust that governed the policies of the previous government. The LDDP considers rapprochement with Poland a prerequisite for greater cooperation with the Visegrad Group as another conduit for Lithuania's improved relations with Europe.

Another major regional initiative in which Lithuania has played an important role has been negotiations on a free trade agreement among the three Baltic states. On April 17, 1993, during a Vilnius summit of the three prime ministers, Lithuania signed a free trade agreement with Latvia and made substantial progress in the negotiations to bring Estonia into the agreement. During the summit the three prime ministers agreed to set up a working commission to prepare the pan-Baltic free trade treaty, which is to be preceded by a bilateral trade agreement between Lithuania and Estonia.[65] Estonia and Latvia also made an offer to assist Lithuania in the changeover to the national currency.

At the core of Lithuanian relations with Russia has been the withdrawal of the remaining Russian troops as well as Lithuania's continued dependence on Russia for its energy. In August of 1990 the Supreme Soviet of Lithuania set up a commission to negotiate with Moscow the procedures for solving the outstanding issues between the two parties. An official communique of the

Lithuanian government, published on December 18, 1992, summarized the results of the negotiations and outlined the framework for future relations between the two states. The position of the Lithuanian government in the course of the talks with Russia has been that Lithuania was never a part of the U.S.S.R., but only a "state occupied by the U.S.S.R."; hence, the withdrawal of the remaining Russian troops simply meant "liquidating the remaining effects of an international crime."[66] From the start Vilnius took the position that negotiations were not about whether the troops were to be withdrawn, but solely about the withdrawal's timetable and procedure. Likewise, it rejected the Russian offers for a joint use of military installations in Lithuania as part of a new framework for security cooperation between the two states.

Formal negotiations on the Russian troop withdrawal started in January 1992 and were concluded by the two governments on September 8, 1992, although Russia agreed to sign only three points of the agreement, those dealing with the withdrawal timetable, the order in which units were to be withdrawn, and organizational-technical issues concerning the withdrawal.[67] The four remaining points of the treaty that Moscow refused to sign dealt with, among other things, the issue of Lithuanian claims to residual Soviet military property as well as the primacy of Lithuanian laws in governing the behavior of the Russian troops as long as they remained on Lithuanian territory.

The Lithuanian-Russian agreement called for the completion of troop withdrawal by August 31, 1993.[68] Immediately after the October 1992 parliamentary elections, Brazauskas called upon Moscow to honor the timetable agreement to withdraw its 20,000 troops. While calling for an improved relationship with Russia, Brazauskas also insisted that Lithuania would never become a member of the CIS. The Lithuanian Foreign Ministry announced in June of 1993 that the Russian troop withdrawal from the Baltics would be carried out under the supervision of a U.N. observer team, which would then submit a report to the U.N. General Assembly session on September 27, 1993.[69] As part of the Russian troop withdrawal, Lithuania agreed to assist with housing construction for Russian troops in the Kaliningrad District. Still, tensions between Russia and Lithuania over the issue of troop withdrawal remained high. The Lithuanians complained that the Russians continued to ignore the Lithuanian authorities; in the first week of June 1993 alone, Lithuanian border guards reported eighty-two unsanctioned flights by Russian air-force planes in Lithuania and the unauthorized movement of twelve Russian army trains through Lithuanian territory.[70] Still, in April 1993, Russian President Boris Yeltsin reaffirmed his commitment to the troop withdrawal agreement with Lithuania in contrast to the troop withdrawal negotiations with Latvia and Estonia where, as Yeltsin put it, "Russian minorities were being persecuted."[71] The last Russian army units left Lithuania on August 31, 1993.

Lithuania has also asked to be compensated for the expense incurred in connection with the movement of Russian troops from Germany across Lithuanian territory. Already in July 1992 Vilnius announced that it would approach Moscow with a request for compensation.[72]

FUTURE PROSPECTS

In contrast to former Soviet satellites in eastern and central Europe that had retained basic state institutions during the communist period, Lithuania faces a formidable task of rebuilding itself as a state virtually from the ground up. Considering the vastness of the task at hand, Lithuania has a considerable record of achievement in this regard, including the passage of a new constitution, a freely elected parliament and president (the return of the former communists to power notwithstanding), the 1993 withdrawal of the remaining Russian troops, and the foundations of a market economy.

Economic vulnerability will likely remain the gravest challenge facing the Lithuanian state in the foreseeable future, with the need for a stable currency being at the center of the country's economic woes. Changes in the policies of the Bank of Lithuania, including the replacement of Vilis Baldisis, a man notorious for his inflationary policies during his tenure as the bank's chairman, may finally end the continued inflationary pressures. The introduction of the *litas* in place of the coupon system as part of an IMF-supported currency stabilization plan may be the solution to this problem, provided inflationary pressure can be kept down.[73] The legacy of dependence on the Russian market and supplies will continue to bedevil the Lithuanian economy until the economy has been restructured to make its exports competitive in the West. In the interim, the government moved to remedy the desperate supply situation by signing on February 9, 1993, a free trade agreement with resource-rich Kazakhstan. As a result Lithuania will receive Central Asian cotton, wool, metal, and tobacco in return for Lithuanian consumer goods such as electronics and textiles. In addition to the treaty with Kazakhstan Lithuania has signed similar agreements with Uzbekistan and Kyrgyzstan, while negotiations are under way with Tadjikistan and Turkmenistan.[74]

Living standards in Lithuania continue to decline as the average monthly wage, equivalent to US $30, is less than half of what it is in Estonia. While skyrocketing interest rates reach 50 percent,[75] the danger of social unrest remains high. Inflation continues to erode living standards in Lithuania, as well as making the prospects for regional cooperation among the Baltic three uncertain, as Lithuania lags further behind its Estonian and Latvian partners. The growing disparity in the level of economic development between Lithuania and the two other Baltic states raises questions about the effectiveness of the Baltic-area free trade agreement. So far Lithuania has had a poor record of putting the limited foreign assistance it has received to good use. Most of the loans the country received in 1992 were used to purchase food and pay for energy to heat apartment buildings.

Continued energy shortage is a second key challenge facing the newly independent Lithuanian state. Lithuania desperately needs fuel for its power stations, transportation, and heating. Lithuania was the only Baltic state to join a March 1, 1993, meeting in Surgut in western Siberia of eleven former Soviet republics in creating an oil union to coordinate energy policies.[76] Although Lithuania did not sign the final Surgut agreement, its participation in the meeting was a significant sign of a changing climate in relations between Vilnius and Moscow.

In order to diversify its oil-supply sources Lithuania plans to build an oil terminal north of the city of Klaipeda on the Baltic coast. The cold days of the fall of 1992 with persistent energy shortages were a grim reminder to the voters of how vulnerable Lithuania has become and influenced the shift among the electorate away from *Sajudis* toward the former communists led by Brazauskas. Even more disturbing appears to be the waning of the initial popular enthusiasm for market capitalism after the bitter experiences during the ineffective *Sajudis* government. According to a poll conducted by the Institute of Philosophy, Sociology, and Justice in Vilnius in April 1993, only 20 percent of the Lithuanians now favored radical economic reform, while 68 percent preferred a gradualist approach to market reform.[77] Emphasis on the need for a gradual transition to the market has become a part of the LDDP platform.[78]

Finally, there is the issue of minority rights in the country where Lithuanians constitute 80 percent of the population. In December 1991, Lithuania adopted a new citizenship law which grants citizenship to all pre-1940 citizens as well as those who were granted citizenship under the provisional citizenship law of 1989–1991. Others must satisfy a ten-year residency requirement, demonstrate their ability to speak and read Lithuanian, and show means of support.[79] The law has been challenged by the minorities as discriminatory against their national and cultural heritage. The minority issue, which is largely the old "Polish problem," is likely to remain a concern in relations between Vilnius and Warsaw.

NOTES

1. Leonard Geron, "Roads to Baltic Independence," *The World Today*, August/September 1991, p. 136.

2. Leonard Geron, "The Baltic Challenge," *The World Today*, March 1990, p. 40.

3. Thomas G. Chase, *The Story of Lithuania* (New York: Stratford House, 1946), pp. 221–222.

4. Gregory Meiksnis, *The Baltic Riddle* (New York: L. B. Fischer, 1943), p. 88.

5. Chase, *Story of Lithuania*, p. 291.

6. Ibid., p. 296.

7. Alfred Erich Senn, *Lithuania Awakening* (Berkeley, Calif.: University of California Press, 1990), p. 5.

8. *The Baltic States: A Reference Book* (Tallinn: Estonian Encyclopedia Publishers, 1991), pp. 180–181.

9. Senn, *Lithuania Awakening*, p. 45.

10. *Baltic States*, p. 181.

11. Ibid.

12. Senn, *Lithuania Awakening*, p. 2.

13. *Lithuanian Way 1* (Vilnius: Lithuanian Reform Movement *Sajudis*, 1990), p. 23. "Baltic States" Collection, Hoover Institution Archives, Stanford, California.

14. Senn, *Lithuania Awakening*, pp. 113–114.

15. Geron, "The Baltic Challenge," p. 40.

16. Alfred Bilmanis, *A History of Latvia* (Princeton, N.J.: Princeton University Press, 1951), pp. 8–9.

17. "Declaration of the Rights of the Baltic Nations," included in the Documents of the Baltic Council section of *Lithuanian Way 1*, p. 95.

18. "Resolution" of May 14, 1989, Documents of Baltic Assembly, *Lithuanian Way 1*, p. 101.

19. "Resolution on Cooperation in the Sphere of Economy," in Documents of the Baltic Council, *Lithuanian Way 1*, pp. 107–108.

20. Senn, *Lithuanian Awakening*, pp. 256–257.

21. *Baltic States*, p. 178.

22. Ibid., p. 182.

23. Zhores Medvedev, "Before the Coup: The Plot inside the Kremlin," *Washington Post*, September 1, 1991.

24. Saulius Girnius, "The Parliamentary Elections in Lithuania," *RFE/RL Research Report*, December 4, 1992, p. 7.

25. Celestine Bohlen, "A New Democracy Votes Communist," *New York Times*, November 4, 1992.

26. Steven Erlanger, "Lithuanians Oust Governing Party," *New York Times*, November 17, 1992.

27. "Good-by Sajudis?" *Moscow News*, November 22, 1992, p. 7.

28. Serge Schememann, "Ex-Communists Ahead in Lithuanian Elections," *New York Times*, October 27, 1992, p. A10.

29. Bohlen, "A New Democracy Votes Communist."

30. Barry Newman, "Communists Find New Life in Lithuania," *Wall Street Journal*, April 15, 1993, p. A10.

31. For an extensive discussion of the Lithuanian 1992 parliamentary elections see Girnius, "The Parliamentary Elections in Lithuania."

32. Newman, "Communists Find New Life in Lithuania."

33. "Brazauskas Storms into Office," *The Baltic Independent*, February 19–25, 1993.

34. Matthias Lufens, "Lozoraitis Campaign Takes the High Road," *The Baltic Independent*, February 12–18, 1993, p. 8.

35. Edward Lucas, "Brazauskas Picks New PM," *The Baltic Independent*, February 26–March 4, 1993, p. 1.

36. "Vitautas Landsbergis: neyzheto Evropa vnov' ustupit Baltiyskiye strany Rossii?" *Ekho Litvy*, February 14, 1992, p. 1.

37. The discussion of the constitutional division of power in Lithuania contained in this section is based on *The Draft Constitution of the Republic of Lithuania* and *Law on Elections to the Seimas* (Vilnius: Supreme Council of the Republic of Lithuania, no. I–2965, October 13, 1992). This is the document that was approved by the popular referendum accompanying the October 1992 election and that constitutes the basic law of Lithuania.

38. *Lietuvos rytas*, November 24, 1992, as quoted in Girnius, "The Parliamentary Elections in Lithuania."

39. The discussion of the LDDP's political program is based on "Nekotoryye politicheskiye printsipy DPTL," *Ekho Litvy*, February 18, 1992, p. 4.

40. Saulius Girnius, "Lithuania: A Bloody Struggle," *RFE/RL Research Report*, January 3, 1992, p. 59.

41. *Baltic Chronology: Estonia, Latvia, Lithuania* (New York: Baltic Appeal to the United Nations BATUN, January 1992), p. 4.

42. "Lithuania Introduces Its Currency Next Week," *RFE/RL Daily Report*, June 18, 1993.

43. Andrius Uzkalnis, "Lithuanian Banks Still Await Breakthrough," *The Baltic Independent*, June 11–17, 1993, p. B4.

44. "Statistics: Inflation," *The Baltic Independent*, June 11–17, 1993, p. B2.

45. "First Signs of Recovery," *The Baltic Independent*, June 11–17, 1993, p. B3.

46. "Lithuania May Liberalize Exports," *The Baltic Independent*, June 11–17, 1993, p. B3; and Uzkalnis, "Lithuanian Banks Still Await Breakthrough."

47. "Cherta bednosti?" *Golos Litvy*, December 16–22, 1992, p. 4.

48. "Statistics," *The Baltic Independent*, February 12–18, 1993, p. 4.

49. Andrius Uzkalnis, "Sellers Sought as Lithuania's Stock Markets Emerge," *The Baltic Independent*, June 11–17, 1993, p. B2.

50. Geron, "The Baltic Challenge," p. 41.

51. "The Baltic Republics: Free at Last," *Economist*, August 31, 1991, p. 40.

52. Arunas Brazauskas, "Lithuanian Farmers Braced for a Bleak Spring," *The Baltic Independent*, April 2–8, 1993, p. 6.

53. *The World Factbook 1992* (Washington, D.C.: Central Intelligence Agency, 1992), p. 203.

54. *Handbook of International Economic Statistics 1992* (Washington, D.C.: Central Intelligence Agency, 1992), p. 118.

55. Girnius, "Lithuania: A Bloody Struggle."

56. "Philip Morris Rolls into Klaipeda," *The Baltic Independent*, April 9–15, 1993, p. 7.

57. Andrius Uzkalnis, "Brazauskas Optimistic after First 100 Days," *The Baltic Independent*, June 11–17, 1993, p. 6.

58. Daiva Vilkelyte, "Free Trade Zone Plan Sparks Military Row," *The Baltic Independent*, March 19–25, 1993, p. 7.

59. "Pro Sibir, kolkhozy i oruzhiye," *Lietuvos rytas*, February 13–20, 1992, p. 1.

60. "Nekotoryye politicheskiye printsipy DPTL."

61. "Brazauskas Meets Mitterand," *RFE/RL Daily Report*, June 17, 1993.

62. "Lithuania and Council of Europe," *RFE/RL Daily Report*, February 8, 1993.

63. Bruno Kelpsas, "Baltic Military Co-operation—Theory Beats Practice," *The Baltic Independent*, April 16–22, 1993, p. 3.

64. "Nekotoryye politicheskiye printsipy DPTL."

65. Andrzej Jezioranski, "Summit Brings Baltic Free Trade Closer," *The Baltic Independent*, April 23–29, 1993.

66. "Soobshcheniye gosudarstvennoy delegatsii Litvy po peregovoram s Rossiyey," *Ekho Litvy*, December 18, 1992, p. 3.

67. Ibid.

68. Bohlen, "A New Democracy Votes Communist."

69. "UN to Observe Troop Withdrawals in Baltic," *RFE/RL Daily Report*, June 17, 1993.

70. "Troop Watch," *The Baltic Independent*, June 11–17, 1993, p. 3.

71. "Troop Watch," *The Baltic Independent*, April 16–22, 1993, p. 3.

72. "Litva Transit," *ITAR–TASS* press release, July 29, 1992.

73. Andrew Clark, "Lithuania Grapples with Money Matters," *The Baltic Independent*, March 19–25, 1993, p. 5.

74. "Lithuania Rebuilds Central Asia Ties," *The Baltic Independent*, February 12–18, 1993, p. 5.

75. "Interest Rates Rocket in Lithuania," *The Baltic Independent*, February 12–18, 1993, p. 4.

76. Stephen Wolgast, "Vilnius Discusses CIS Energy Plan," *The Baltic Independent*, March 5–11, 1993, p. 6.

77. "Lithuanians Prefer Slower Change," *The Baltic Independent*, April 23–29, 1993, p. B3.

78. "Nekotoryye politicheskiye printsipy DPTL."

79. *Baltic Chronology*, December 1991, p. 2.

8

LATVIA

THE NATION AND THE STATE

Like Lithuania, the course of Latvia's history has been determined by the struggle between Germany, Russia, Sweden, and Poland for control of the Baltic Sea rim and the trade routes to the East. Known in the Middle Ages as "Livonia,"* the territory of present-day Latvia was controlled by the German Order of Livonian Knights through the sixteenth century, becoming in the seventeenth and eighteenth centuries the arena of a series of Polish-Russian, Polish-Swedish, and Swedish-Russian wars for the control of the Baltic coast. Present-day Latvia has historically been the key to controlling the Baltic area.

Anthropologically, the Latvians form an east Baltic group related to the Scandinavians together with the Finns, Estonians, and Lithuanians. Like their Lithuanian cousins, the Latvians are descendants of the aboriginal Balts, while the Finns and Estonians are of Finno-Ugric extraction. Latvia's capital, Riga, was founded at the mouth of the Daugava River in the second century A.D. Settled and occupied by the Vikings in the early Middle Ages, Riga fell under German influence becoming a thriving Hanseatic town.[1] In the wake of Sweden's rise to preeminence in the Baltic in the mid-seventeenth century, Riga passed under Swedish control, followed by Russian domination as the Romanovs asserted their authority along the Baltic Rim. Riga became the leading port of the Baltic provinces, connected with the Russian interior by railroad.

---

*Latvian territories, referred to by the Germans as *Livonia* or *Lievland*, became in the eleventh century a target of both German commercial expansion and German efforts to spread Christianity eastward. The term *Livonia* was eventually used to describe both the Latvian and the Estonian lands.

The freeing of the peasantry in the late nineteenth century and the gradual industrialization of Latvia, especially in Riga, began slowly to change the traditional social structure. The nineteenth century also saw the growing national and cultural awareness among the Latvians. The rise of national consciousness was accompanied by improvements in education that built upon the reforms introduced during the Swedish suzerainty. The first generation of educated and nationally conscious Latvians sprang from among the Latvian peasantry in the late nineteenth century. Increasingly, the Latvians were beginning to take part in the region's economic and cultural life. This was accompanied by a rising tide of European romanticism and the renewed interest in tradition and folklore. An important role was also played by the groundbreaking work of Latvian philologists, who established the roots of the language and contributed to the standardization of Latvian grammar. The Latvian cultural renaissance of the late nineteenth century played a similar role in the creation of an independent Latvian state after World War I as the cultural revival in the 1980s played in the restoration of Latvia's independence after the fall of communism in the Soviet Union.

World War I and the collapse of both Russia and Germany made it possible for an independent Latvia to rise. The 1917 meeting of various Latvian organizations, including the Latvian Refugees' Committee, the Latvian Farmers' Association, the Radical Democrats, the National Democrats, the Provincial Council of Kurzeme and Latgale, the National Union of Latvian Warriors, and the Central Association of Agriculturists, called for the convocation of a Latvian national assembly. The meeting created the Latvian Provisional National Council (LPNC), which declared Latvian independence.

After a period of fighting against the Russians and the Germans, the Latvian Constituent Assembly convened on May 1, 1920; Janis Cakste, the president of the National Council, was elected president of the assembly and of the Latvian Republic. Karlis Ulmanis continued as prime minister. The new government attempted, largely unsuccessfully, to tackle the country's economic and political problems.

Interwar Latvia was a weak agricultural state, with a population of 1,950,000, of which 75 percent were ethnic Latvians.[2] The economy was based on dairy farming which became an ever more important part of agriculture. Butter and meat became Latvia's major exports to the West, in particular to Great Britain and Germany. Latvia's economy in the interwar period was characterized by a relatively strong agriculture and rapidly emerging industry. Latvia's struggling commodities-based economy was devastated by the onset of the Great Depression. The government of Karlis Ulmanis reacted by imposing contingency quotas on imports to protect the economy, but which in fact further aggravated the crisis. Faced with a strong opposition from the left-wing parties in the parliament to his demands for constitutional changes that would give him greater executive powers, on May 15, 1934, Ulmanis staged a coup and established an authoritarian regime and placed the country under martial law.[3] Two years later, Ulmanis issued a decree making the president the supreme commander of the armed forces and transferred that office to himself to be held indefinitely. The promised new constitution was never implemented. In 1938, when martial law formally lapsed, it was replaced by a new Law for the Defense of the State that increased police controls and censorship further.[4]

SOVIET OCCUPATION AND COMMUNIST LEGACY

The Ribbentrop-Molotov Pact of August 23, 1939, doomed the three Baltic states, despite their efforts to stay out of the conflict and to maintain strict neutrality. After the fall of Poland, the Soviets moved to take over the Baltic states. On October 2–3, 1939, Latvian Foreign Minister V. Munters was summoned to Moscow to receive the Soviet demands for access to Latvian harbors, including the transit routes. With sixteen Soviet divisions poised on its border, Latvia signed on October 5, 1939, a Pact of Mutual Assistance with the U.S.S.R., which gave the Soviets control over the Gulf of Riga through ten-year leases on bases in Liepaja and Ventspils. In June 1940, Moscow presented the Latvian government with an ultimatum demanding the establishment of a communist government and the introduction of additional Soviet troops into Latvia, and Riga accepted the inevitable.

Latvia was swiftly occupied by Soviet troops, and a Latvian People's Government was formed, which then organized rigged elections. On July 21, 1940, the Soviet-controlled *Saeima* declared the establishment of Soviet power in Latvia and petitioned for the formal inclusion of Latvia into the U.S.S.R.; the sham procedure was concluded on August 5, 1940, when the U.S.S.R. Supreme Soviet formally admitted the Latvian Soviet Socialist Republic into the union. Police terror, including the deportation of 15,000 Latvians to the Soviet interior, followed. The Soviets reoccupied Latvia in July 1944–May 1945 and reestablished the communist regime. The complete collectivization of Latvian agriculture followed in 1949; it was accompanied by the deportation of 42,000 Latvian peasants.[5] Latvia was also subjected to Soviet-style industrialization.

Prior to the communist takeover, the Latvian economy was based on thriving agriculture, with dairy and pig farming being the two primary occupations of Latvian peasants. Agricultural exports constituted 53.5 percent of all Latvian exports in 1939. Latvia also had a substantial wood-processing industry, with timber exports making 35.5 percent of all exports in 1939.[6] Manufacturing was weak, although Latvia managed to produce some high-technology goods, such as radios and cameras. By 1930, industry employed only 13.5 percent of the labor force, the largest industrial sectors being manufacturing, woodworking, food processing, and textiles.[7] Latvia's exports of manufactured goods were limited in the interwar period to bicycles and simple radio receivers; both constituted only 1.4 percent of Latvia's sales abroad. Most of Latvian trade in the interwar period was with the West, with the Soviet Union accounting in 1938 for only 3 percent of Latvian exports and 3.5 percent of Latvian imports.[8] The country's currency, the *lats*, was fully convertible, because of the government's stringent fiscal and monetary policies.

Because of the communist path of autarkic economic development pursued by the Soviets, the harbor at Riga and Latvian waterways, which had been a major trade route into Russia for Western merchants, lost its previous significance as a result of the collapse of the Russian trade. Half a century of Soviet control brought about a dramatic restructuring of the country's economy. Efficient private farming was destroyed during the collectivization drive of 1949 and the 1950 consolidation of the *kolkhozes* into larger units. By 1951 98 percent of Latvian farms were collectivized.[9] Agricultural output plummeted. Increasingly, Latvia had to import grain feed from the rest of the U.S.S.R., while exporting meat and dairy products. It is estimated that, in the process of Sovietization, Latvia lost about 30 percent of its prewar population. In addition to Russification, Latvia was a target of large-scale Russian immigration policies, with an estimated 535,000 Russians arriving in the first decade after the war alone.[10] The continued migration of non-Latvian, chiefly Russian, administrators and laborers dramatically altered the ethnic composition of Latvia, raising concerns about the nation's ability to survive.

Soviet central planners targeted Latvia for investment in machine building and metal working, electrical engineering, and chemical and petrochemical plants. A large portion of Soviet high-technology industry was also located in Latvia (and in the Baltics in general) to take advantage of the higher level of skill of the population. The largest industrial centers of those obsolete and severely polluting industries are Riga, Liepaja, Ventspils, Valmiera, and Daugavpils. A portion of Baltic industry was devoted to military production. According to a 1991 estimate, less than 10 percent of all of Latvia's industrial output was competitive on world markets; these were food and timber products.[11] The railroads, the highway network, telephone and communication systems, and housing are inadequate by Western standards. Still, relative to the rest of the Soviet Union, the Baltic economies were much more developed and the agricultural output was above the average level throughout the U.S.S.R. The level of national consumption and GNP (or national income) per capita in the Baltics was substantially higher than the U.S.S.R. average, especially in Latvia and Estonia.

INDEPENDENCE MOVEMENT

The revival of a national independence movement in Latvia came on the heels of Gorbachev's *perestroika* reforms in the second half of the 1980s. Compared to the powerful surge of nationalist sentiment in Lithuania, pressure for national independence in Latvia was more restrained. In June 1987 the dissident human rights group Helsinki 76 put forth a demand for Latvian independence. In June 1988 the National Independence Movement of Latvia (*Latvijas Nacionalas Neatkaribas Kustiba*; LNNK) was formed with a membership of several thousand. In the same month the Latvian Writers' Union demanded democratization and national sovereignty.[12]

The Popular Front of Latvia (*Latvijas Tautas Fronte*; LTF) was established in October 1988 demanding sovereignty and democratic change in Latvia. Shortly thereafter the Latvian language was made the official language of the republic, and the Latvian national flag was relegalized. A portion of the Russian-speaking population responded to what it saw as the threat of Latvian nationalism by forming the International Front of Latvian Working People (*Interfront*). The Latvian Communist Party continued to lead the opposition to the independence movement while relying on the support of senior officers of the Soviet Baltic Military District.

In 1989, as conflict with Moscow grew over the proposed new constitution that would severely hamper the republics' rights to secede, the Citizenship Committee (*Pilsonu komiteja*), set up by the LNNK in cooperation with the environmental group VAX and the Helsinki 76 group, began registering Latvian "nationals" as citizens. The outpouring of popular support for the idea radicalized the Popular Front of Latvia, which shifted its demands from autonomy to complete independence. During its second congress in October 1989, the Popular Front of Latvia adopted independence as its goal.[13]

A landmark in Latvia's drive for independence was the Latvian Supreme Council's decision of December 1989, following Lithuania's example, to abolish the Communist Party's monopoly on political power in the country. In the aftermath of the decision, some thirty independent political parties sprang up, organized in the Popular Front of Latvia. The key political parties established in the fall/winter of 1989/1990 included the Latvian Social Democratic Workers Party (established in 1905 and the largest party during Latvia's independence), the Latvian Green Party, the Liberal Party of Latvia, the Agricultural Union, the Republican Party of Latvia (RPL), and pro-Moscow *Interfront*.[14] In April 1990, the Latvian Communist Party split, with the reform-minded communists forming their independent party.

On March 18, 1990, the first competitive and free parliamentary elections since 1940 were held in Latvia for the candidates to the newly reconstituted Latvian Supreme Council The Popular Front of Latvia, representing a wide range of pro-independence forces, won 116 of the 170 seats in the first round of voting and an additional five in runoff races on March 25 and April 1, 1990.[15] At the same time, a reform faction of the Latvian Communist Party called for its complete independence from the Communitst Party of the Soviet Union (CPSU).

The Supreme Council was Latvia's transitory parliament preceding the *Saeima* elected in 1993. It had 201 deputies elected on March 18, 1990, to five-year terms. Approximately two-thirds of the deputies belonged to the Popular Front of Latvia, and the rest represented the Equal Rights faction, including *Interfront* and Communist Party deputies. The Supreme Council established fifteen permanent commissions, including the Commission on the Economy. Prime Minister Godmanis was appointed from within the Popular Front after the 1990 election; Anatolijs Gorbunovs, the chairman of the parliament, became the country's president.[16]

Latvia's drive for independence was not as strong as in Estonia and especially Lithuania on account of the high proportion of non-Latvians living in the republic, who constitute approximately 50 percent of the population; Russians constitute about 34 percent, and the remainder includes Byelorussians, Poles, Lithuanians, Ukrainians, and Jews. However, polls taken in 1990 indicated that 53 percent of Russian speakers and 96 percent of native Latvians supported the full restoration of independence.[17] The 1990 elections to the Supreme Council accelerated the process.

On May 4, 1990, the Declaration on the Renewal of the Independence of the Republic of Latvia was adopted following the Lithuanian example, in an effort to preempt Moscow's constitutional changes that would make it virtually impossible for the republic to leave the Soviet Union. The bloody crackdown in Vilnius and Riga, in January 1991, catalyzed the Latvians and non-Latvians alike to push for complete national independence. A public-opinion poll conducted on March 3, 1991, indicated that 73.7 percent of all citizens of Latvia (with 87.6 percent of the registered electorate voting), regardless of their ethnic origin, supported independence.[18]

The final act in Latvia's movement toward independence came in the wake of the aborted Soviet coup on August 21, 1991; the Latvian Supreme Council declared the state an independent republic and restored its 1922 constitution, thus formally severing all ties to the Soviet Union. The first to recognize independent Latvia were Lithuania, Estonia, and Russia. Iceland became the first Western country to extend formal diplomatic recognition to Latvia, with Denmark and the European Community extending diplomatic recognition to the Baltics on August 27, 1991. The United States recognized the Baltic states on September 2, with the U.S.S.R. following two days later.[19] By December Latvia was an internationally recognized member of the United Nations.

DOMESTIC POLITICS AFTER COMMUNISM

Rather than drafting a new constitution, the newly independent Latvian state restored the 1922 constitution as its basic law, specifically Articles 1, 2, 3, and 6, which define the principles of state independence, sovereignty, territorial integrity, and the supreme authority of the *Saeima*. It is expected, however, that a new document will be drafted to modify or replace the current document, as provided in the independence declaration of May 4, 1990.[20] A special commission for revising the constitution was set up in 1990.

The 1922 constitution[21] provides for the 100-member legislature *Saeima* (Article 5), which elects the country's president by a simple majority vote (fifty-one votes) to a three-year term (Article 35), with a two-term limitation provision (Article 39). The president is the supreme commander of the armed forces (Article 42) and has the power to dissolve the parliament, provided that a popular referendum on the issue is held and returns a simple majority in favor of such action (Article 49); if he fails to win the simple majority, the president is then obliged to resign and the *Saeima* elects a new president (Article 50). The *Saeima* may also dismiss the president with a two-thirds majority vote in the parliament (Article 51). The president designates the prime minister and the cabinet ministers, whom the *Saeima* must approve (Article 56). The government can impose a state of emergency, provided the *Saeima* is notified within twenty-four hours and concurs. The parliament is in sole control of the budget and has the sole right of legislation, although the president and the prime minister can initiate legislation (Articles 64, 65, and 66), and it ratifies all international treaties (Article 68). The 1922 constitution also provides for an independent judiciary (Articles 82 through 83) and a State Control Department (Articles 87 and 88).

The 1922 constitution vests the *Saeima* with powers exceeding by far those of the president and the government. The revisions of the basic law currently under consideration are likely to strengthen the executive to provide for more effective government. The July 6, 1993, meeting of the Fifth *Saeima* elected its chairman, the state president, and approved the government.

Political parties in Latvia are still in the process of development and consolidation. The June 1993 parliamentary election has greatly accelerated the process. After the 1991 formal declaration of independence, the Latvian political spectrum began to diversify, laying the foundations of nascent political parties. During the transition period Latvian domestic politics had been defined by two political camps: one pro-Soviet, led by the Latvian Communist Party and its affiliate organizations, and the other pro-independence, represented by the Popular Front of Latvia.

On June 5 and 6, 1993, Latvia held its first free election since the 1991 restoration of independence to choose deputies to the Fifth *Saeima* (parliament). As reported by the Electoral Commission, 87 percent (1,119,390) of Latvian citizens turned out to vote.[22] Of the twenty-three political parties, organizations, and coalitions that contested the seats in the parliament, only eight gained representation in the *Saeima*.[23] In order to gain representation in the *Saeima*, the party had to receive over 4 percent of the popular vote.

Only about 30 percent of the former members of the Supreme Council were reelected to the new parliament. A number of the deputies are "newcomers to Latvia," that is, Latvians who, until independence, had lived in the West.[24]

The most powerful political force in Latvian politics today is the Latvia's Way coalition (*Latvijas Cels*; LC), a broad spectrum coalition of center-right politicians including the country's current president, Anatolijs Gorbunovs. Set up in January 1993, Latvia's Way is widely recognized in the country as well as in the emigre community, and it is arguably the most politically heterogenous organization to enter the parliament.[25] Since Latvia's Way hosted the new government and lacks a parliamentary majority, its ability to enter into lasting coalitions with other parties will go a long way in determining the stability of the democratically elected government.

The second-most powerful organization in the parliament, the National Independence Movement of Latvia (*Latvijas Nacionalas Neatkaribas Kustiba*) has since 1988 played a key role in Latvia's struggle for independence. Together with For the Fatherland and Freedom (*Tevzemei un Brivibai*), the LNNK represents the conservative movement in Latvia's politics today. Other conservative organizations in the parliament include Latvia's Farmers' Union (*Latvijas Zemnieku Savieniba*) and Latvia's Christian Democratic Union (*Latvijas Kristigo Demokratu Savieniba*).

The moderate left in Latvian politics today is represented by Harmony for Latvia-Rebirth of the Economy (*Saskana Latvijai-Atdzimsana Tautsaimniecibai*) and the Democratic Center Party (*Demokratiska Centra Partija*) and Equal Rights (*Lidztiesiba*). The three include former communist intellectuals and are committed to preservation of minority rights for non-Latvians; Equal Rights in particular is committed to the protection of ethnic Russians living in Latvia.[26]

In the new *Saeima*, Latvia's Way won thirty-six seats, followed by National Independence Movement of Lativa (fifteen seats), Harmony for Latvia-Rebirth of the Economy (thirteen seats), Latvia's Farmers' Union (twelve), Equal Rights (seven), For the Fatherland and Freedom (six), Latvia's Christian Democratic Union (six), and the Democratic Center Party (five).[27]

Immediately after the election, the Russians living in Latvia, who represented 34 percent of the population but were not allowed to vote, complained that the new parliament is unlikely to represent their political interests, as only two parties, Equal Rights (seven deputies) and Harmony for Latvia (thirteen deputies), ran on the platform of representing "all the people who live in Latvia."[28] Only 52 percent of Latvia's 2.6 million people are ethnic Latvians, and the June election did not grant the non-Latvians the right to vote.

As none of the parties has a majority in the parliament (the largest party, Latvia's Way, has approximately 33 percent of the seats), the new Latvian government is a coalition led by Valdis Birkavs of Latvia's Way; his cabinet was approved by the *Saeima* on July 20, 1993. The Birkavs coalition includes Latvia's Way, the Farmers' Union, and the Christian Democrats. The far-right opposition in the parliament consists of the National Independence Movement and For the Fatherland and Freedom (twenty-one deputies in total). The left-of-center groups in the *Saeima* include Harmony for Latvia, Equal Rights, and the Democratic Center Party; however, the three are not likely to cooperate as a bloc in the parliament because the Democratic Center Party wants to distance itself from the two postcommunist parties.[29]

On July 6, 1993, during the first session of the newly elected *Saeima*, the reestablishment of the 1922 constitution was confirmed. Anatolijs Gorbunovs of Latvia's Way was elected *Saeima* chairman, defeating Maris Grinbalts sixty-five to twenty-five, with Andrejs Krastins of the National Independence Movement of Latvia and Aivars Berkis of the Farmers' Union as his deputies and Imants Daudiss as secretary.[30] On July 7 Guntis Ulmanis of the Farmers' Union, a great-nephew of the last president of independent Latvia, was elected president on the third ballot.[31]

As can be expected in a nation occupied for almost half a century, the Latvian domestic political scene is constantly evolving. The political parties remain relatively weak and disorganized, which weakens their effectiveness. The parliamentary experience in the democratically elected *Saeima* ought to accelerate the process of consolidation of domestic politics.

The question of citizenship rights for non-Latvians remains at the core of the country's domestic politics. Because only those who were citizens of Latvia in the interwar period, or their descendants, were allowed to vote in the 1993 parliamentary elections, about one-third of the population was effectively disenfranchised.[32] The majority of those excluded in the 1993 election were Russians or other Slavs who settled in Latvia after World War II.

The question of Latvian citizenship is likely to remain the most heatedly debated issue facing the newly elected *Saeima*. On February 6, 1991, the government created a Department of Nationalities with ministerial status whose task was to study the nationalities question and report to the prime minister on possible solutions to the problem, including a new law on national minorities to be submitted to the parliament.[33] On December 5, 1991, a new draft citizenship law called for a sixteen-year residence and fluency in Latvia, while excluding Latvian Communist Party apparatchiks who settled in Latvia after 1940.[34] Prior to the elections, the government indicated that it was considering various proposals, including the "0-variant" or "0–5 variant," that is, granting citizenship to either all presently living in Latvia or those who could prove they had lived in Latvia for the last five years. The more extreme nationalists, however, called for granting Latvian citizenship only to those who held Latvian citizenship prior to 1940 and their descendants. That was, in fact, the criterion used in the 1993 elections. The draft law does not explicitly deny citizenship to ethnic Russians, but it refuses naturalization rights to anyone who settled in Latvia after being discharged from the Soviet army and security services in the wake of the republic's annexation by the Soviet Union in 1940.

More important, there is a considerable imbalance in terms of ethnic concentration between the countryside and the cities: in the rural areas the Latvians comprise close to 71.5 percent of the total population, while in cities they make up only 44 percent of the population on average. In Riga, the nation's capital, the numbers are truly dramatic: 36.5 percent is Latvian and 47.3 percent is Russian—in effect, from the ethnic point of view, Riga is more a Russian city than Latvian. In southeastern Latvia the situation is even less favorable to ethnic Latvians; for example, the city of Daugavpils is 58.3 percent Russian, while Latvians constitute only 13 percent of the population.[35]

ECONOMIC POLICY

Despite the lack of raw materials, the Soviets developed in Latvia a sizeable heavy industry, which in 1989 constituted close to 55 percent of Latvia's industrial sector. During the communist period Latvia produced radios and telecommunication equipment, industrial machinery, minibuses, and engines. The largest share of the industry consists of machine building and metalworking, as well as chemical, wood, and construction materials industry. Light industry, especially textiles, shoes, and leather, represents about one-fifth and the food-processing industry about one-fourth of the total of Latvia's industrial output.[36] In short, Latvia's industry is critically dependent on raw materials imported from Russia (minerals) and Uzbekistan, Kazakhstan, and Georgia (cotton and wool). Latvia's energy dependence is almost total; in 1990, 90 percent of heating fuel, 100 percent of oil, and 50 percent of all consumed electricity were imported from the Soviet Union.[37] In July 1993, amid growing concern that Russia might cut off gas supplies to Latvia, the Latvian government paid off using as foreign credit the outstanding $4.5 million debt to the St. Petersburg concern Lentransgaz for past gas supplies. The Russians continued to demand an additional $12 million in late-payment penalties.[38]

The key goals of Latvia's economic policy since independence have been to extricate itself from total dependence on Russia and to transform the command economy into a working market system. Since independence from the U.S.S.R., Latvia has reaffirmed its commitment to privatize both agriculture and industry. The economic program currently in place has been recommended and approved by the International Monetary Fund. The Latvian government expects to privatize land ownership fully within the next twelve to fifteen years; it estimates that by then 75 percent of all agricultural land will be privately owned.[39] Riga is committed to making the transition to a market economy; it is often argued that cultural values in Latvia favor such reforms, in particular its residual Protestant work ethic and individualism.

Since independence Latvia has pursued an economic austerity program, including a tight monetary policy and a balanced budget. On January 2, 1992, Latvia ended all price controls.[40] On July 20, 1992, Latvia announced that it would introduce its own currency, the *lats*, in place of the inflated Latvian ruble. In the summer of 1993, all planned denominations of the new currency (1 *lats* = 100 *santimi*) were introduced in the country.

Privatization has proceeded the fastest in agriculture. A land reprivatization law, introduced in July 1991, which provides for the return of collectivized land as restitution, has already resulted in the creation of over 50,000 private farmers in Latvia. However, foreign citizens are still not allowed to purchase and own land, which has raised the question of the guarantees foreign investors have to offset the risk of doing business in Latvia.[41] A law on the privatization of small-scale businesses was passed in November 1991, but the small-scale industrial reprivatization has proven to be less successful than the privatization effort in agriculture.

On March 3, 1992, the Supreme Council adopted four general privatization laws, which include (1) a voucher privatization scheme along the lines of similar solutions applied elsewhere in east central Europe, (2) new guidelines for the management of the remaining state property, (3) a new law on the assessment of state property values, and (4) a law on the transformation of large state enterprises into joint stock companies. A list of twenty-three large enterprises to be sold to foreign investors was drawn up. In addition, a bankruptcy law was passed in December 1991.[42]

Privatization in Latvia also extended to real estate. In 1992 approximately 10,000 apartments were privatized; in addition, 2,026 buildings were returned to their former owners. In early 1993, the government received 50,879 applications for the return of land in Latvian towns. The total proceeds from the 1992 sale of shops and service establishments in Latvia amounted to 269.9 million Latvian rubles (US $1.8 million).[43] Still, the privatization process in 1992 proceeded more slowly than had been anticipated, leading to calls by some Supreme Council deputies for the replacement of the Commission for Denationalization in charge of privatization.[44]

In 1992 the Latvian government introduced a progressive income tax, with top rates of 35 percent and a value-added tax of 12 percent.[45] On March 1, 1993, Latvian Prime Minister Ivars Godmanis announced that the government intended to introduce the new national currency, the *lats*. The new currency will gradually replace Latvia's transitory currency, the Latvian ruble, introduced in May 1992 to shield Latvia from Russian inflation. The exchange of the Latvian rubles into the *lats* was conducted gradually. First, on March 5, the government introduced only the five-*lats* note, to be followed by the ten-*lats* note and other denominations. On the day of introduction the five-*lats* note was worth 1,000 rubles or US $6.67.[46] During the transition period the *lats* circulated alongside the ruble and foreign currencies. The government planned to phase the Latvian ruble out completely by the end of the summer.

In April 1993 Latvia lifted import duties from most industrial goods and spare parts.[47] Prices have been liberalized and most of the state subsidies cut, which by 1993 contributed to a gradual economic upturn. Latvia has cooperated closely with the International Monetary Fund and the World Bank, both of which have strongly endorsed Riga's economic reform program. After the August 1992 visit to Latvia by Michel Camdessus, managing director of the IMF, the fund assessed the financing gap for the period between July 1992 and June 1993 at $350 million, with $300 million earmarked to cover the projected balance of payments deficits and $50 million to be added to Latvia's national currency reserves. Most of the funds were to be provided by the European Community ($115 million), the IMF ($81 million), and the World Bank ($40 million); in addition, the European Bank for Reconstruction and Development and the governments of Sweden and Denmark would provide money to make up the difference.[48] In exchange for the IMF-sponsored loans and grants package, Riga pledged to accept all the recommendations on economic reform presented by the fund.

Despite continued decline in the real GDP growth, pegged at minus 30 percent for 1992, Latvia has managed to improve its foreign trade performance dramatically by focusing on the CIS countries, rather than the West, which has been the principal target of the other two Baltic states. In the first quarter of 1993 relative to the average for 1992, Latvia's exports went up 50 percent, reaching $171 million. The first-quarter exports in 1993 were roughly evenly divided between the West and the East (the CIS and the Baltics). In contrast to 1992, in the first quarter of 1993 Latvia maintained a trade surplus with both the East and the West.[49]

Still, the country faces a formidable economic task ahead. Since independence Latvia's terms of trade have deteriorated by 40 percent and in 1992 the country's GNP fell by 30 percent.[50] During the campaign leading up to the June 1993 parliamentary election, Latvia's Way presented its blueprint for dealing with the economic crisis. The program "Latvia-2000" sets the membership in the European Union as the ultimate objective of Latvia's economic strategy. The plan calls for a complete overhaul of the administrative structure to do away with the residual vestiges of the Soviet system. It reaffirms the state's commitment to complete the transition to a market economy by the turn of the century.[51] The relative success of the economic program, rather than foreign policy decisions, will ultimately decide how successful Latvia's transition to democracy is going to be.

RELATIONS WITH RUSSIA, FOREIGN POLICY, AND NATIONAL SECURITY

Relations with Russia are bound to remain high on the agenda of Latvia's new, democratically elected government. In 1993 about 27,000 Russian soldiers still remained on Latvian territory, with no final agreement on Russian troop withdrawal in sight. At the core of the dispute lies Moscow's insistence that the withdrawal of Russian soldiers be linked to the issue of citizenship rights for Latvia's Russian minority, as well as the demand for control of some of the remaining naval facilities in Latvia which the Russians consider essential to their security position in the Baltic. Transfer of the Russian military installations to Latvian control is viewed by Riga as both a symbol of national sovereignty and independence and the removal of a serious security threat posed by the continued presence of heavily armed foreign troops on Latvia's territory.

Latvia's wariness of Russia's intention in relations to the Baltic states reflects half a century of Soviet domination. Riga considers official Russian charges that the Latvian Russian minority is being denied its basic human and civil rights as a thinly veiled attempt to manipulate the country's domestic politics. Moscow questioned repeatedly specific pieces of new Latvian legislation as discriminating against Russians. For example, Moscow pointed to the 1990 language law which requires that, since January 1, 1992, those employed in administration and health services have sufficient knowledge of Latvian for professional purposes. Although the law has not yet been strictly enforced, for lack of teachers and textbooks, it has created considerable unease among non-Latvians. The government is also preparing a new curriculum for the Latvian schools and university, which will give preferential treatment to Latvians and will make Latvian mandatory from first grade on even in Russian-language schools.[52]

In April 1993 Russian President Boris Yeltsin halted the bilateral Latvian-Russian talks on Russian troop withdrawal and charged Latvia with pursuing a policy of "ethnic cleansing" against the noncitizen population, especially the Russians.[53] Yeltsin's accusation followed the Latvian parliament's decision to grant a temporary one-year residency permit to members of the Russian occupation force and their dependents.

Although the talks resumed a month later, in May 1993, Sergei Zotov, the head of the Russian delegation to the Latvian-Russian talks in Jurmala, asserted that Russia could complete the evacuation of its military sites in Latvia no sooner than in five to ten years.[54] The United Nations moved to investigate the validity of Moscow's charges of discrimination against ethnic Russians. The chairman of the U.N. General Assembly, Stoyan Ganev, paid a three-day visit to Riga from July 1 to 3, 1993, where he held talks with Latvian parliament chairman Anatolijs Gorbunovs and other high officials, as well as the commander of the Northwestern Group of Forces, Leonid Mayorov, and the Russian ambassador to Latvia, Aleksandr Rannikh. After the visit Ganev noted that Russia was failing to comply with the November 25, 1992 U.N. resolution calling for the complete, early, and orderly withdrawal of its troops from the Baltic states. He also asserted that there was no policy of discrimination against minorities in Latvia and that any violations could be handled at the local level.[55] A similar position on the Russian troop withdrawal from Latvia was taken by NATO. The director of NATO's Political Directorate, John Kriendler, stated during his visit to Riga in late June 1993 that the Russian troop withdrawal from the Baltics should be unconditionally completed.

The current tense relationship between Latvia and its former imperial hegemon is bound to remain throughout the current period of economic and political transition in the Baltic Rim, especially if the Russians continue to stall on the troop withdrawal issue. It has made the task of creating an army an issue symbolic of Latvia's assertion of national sovereignty. The Latvian defense forces are important in asserting national control over Latvia's borders, with each Latvian soldier being in effect a border guard.[56] The defense doctrine of Latvia emphasizes the defense of the national territory and borders. Latvia's insistence that no other power has the right to use its territory to station troops or for other military-related purposes underlies the conflict with Moscow over the withdrawal of Russian troops. Latvia is committed to the principle of collective security and to cooperation with its neighbors to foster stability in the region.

In light of the country's limited human and material resources, Latvia has rejected the principle of neutrality as a viable security option. Latvian defense planners speak of two principal "sources of threat" to the country's independence: (1) the internal forces hostile to Latvia's independence and (2) instability in the former Soviet Union, especially in the Russian Federation. Hence, Latvia's defense planners envision a three-pronged approach to ensure the nation's security: the regular national defense forces, the emergency volunteer corps (*Zemessardze*), and the security service of the Ministry of Internal Affairs.[57] The army has returned to the prewar national uniform and has redrawn the training plans to conform with the national heritage and national military tradition. Latvia's national defense plan drafted by the Ministry of Defense was presented at the meeting of the State Defense Council following the inauguration of the new government. Reportedly, the new strategy emphasizes regional cooperation with the other Baltic states, as symbolized by the 1992 Parnu Agreement. More important, Latvia looks to NATO and other existing security structures in Europe to bring it into the evolving pan-European security system; full membership in NATO is Latvia's long-term objective.

According to Latvia's minister of defense, the lack of an effective air defense network remains the most urgent problem of the nation's military preparedness. According to the Latvian Ministry of Defense, in 1992 over 130 unauthorized flights by the Russian air force violated the country's air space.[58] Another significant problem is the weakness of Latvia's coastal defenses. The Latvian navy needs both equipment and training, both of which the government hopes to obtain from the West. As of 1993, Latvian naval forces consisted of three patrol boats, and Riga hoped to obtain six additional vessels from the West to improve its ability to patrol the Baltic coastline.[59] In June 1993, the U.S. Coast Guard cutter *Gallatin* visited the port of Liepaja, with a mission to provide information about coastal defense in the United States. The visit of the American warship to Liepaja was the first in the past seventy years and was hailed in Riga as a visible sign of new ties developing with Western naval forces.[60]

THE TASK OF REBUILDING A NATION

The newly independent Latvian state faces a formidable task of building a cohesive nation-state under conditions where close to 50 percent of the population is non-Latvian. The ethnic imbalance is viewed by many in Latvia as a threat to national survival, especially considering the low birthrate of ethnic Latvians and the historically slow pattern of the immigrants' cultural assimilation, as symbolized by their failure to learn the Latvian language. In the 1989 census, 66 percent of Latvians reported fluency in Russian as a second language, while only 21 percent of Russians reported fluency in Latvian.[61]

The pattern of Russian and other immigration ought to be noted as well. Most of the immigration was directly related to the industrialization process in Latvia, and hence it consists predominantly of a blue-collar labor force; only 36 percent of blue-collar labor in Latvia is Latvian; in railroad and waterway transport the percentage of Latvians in the labor force is even lower: 26 percent and 11 percent, respectively. At the same time, the administrative apparatus was 56 percent Latvian (as of 1987), while the cultural and art field was 75 percent Latvian dominated.[62] The ethnic dilemmas facing independent Latvia in the wake of the imminent dislocations caused by economic reform, especially in the heavy state-owned industrial sector, has an immediate socioeconomic dimension. Put simply, workers' resentment at the close of inefficient factories may easily acquire a nationalist dimension by pitting the Latvian-dominated administration against the Russian-dominated labor force.

According to the official 1989 census, the ethnic Latvians constitute barely a majority of the country's 2.6 million people. This is a dramatic population shift relative to the interwar period, when non-Latvians constituted no more than 25 percent of the total population. According to the current citizenship law as outlined in the restored 1919 citizenship law, Latvian citizenship can be claimed by proof of ethnicity. The current law does not outline the naturalization requirements and procedures; this issue is to be addressed in a new citizenship law to be drafted by the country's first democratically elected *Saeima*. Under the 1919 law, non-Latvians cannot vote, hold government office, serve in the armed forces, or own land.[63] Following an early 1992 registration of prospective citizens, chairman of the Supreme Council Anatolijs Gorbunovs confirmed that only approximately 60 percent of the people currently living in Latvia have a realistic prospect of acquiring Latvian citizenship.[64]

Riga has made a concerted effort to change the ethnic balance decisively in favor of ethnic Latvians. In 1990 the government curtailed immigration into Latvia to the point that in 1990, for the first time in its postwar history, the country had negative migration, largely because of the departure of some Russians and other nationalities. The challenge of rebuilding the Latvian nation-state around the Latvian ethnic core is bound to put Latvia on a collision course with Russia, whose insistence that the rights of the Russian minority in Latvia be protected will likely result in powerful pressure on the Latvian government.

NOTES

1. Alfred Bilmanis, *A History of Latvia* (Princeton, N.J.: Princeton University Press, 1951), p. 15.

2. *Economic Survey of the Baltic Republics: A study undertaken by an independent team of experts on the initiative of the Swedish Ministry for Foreign Affairs in collaboration with the government authorities of Estonia, Latvia, and Lithuania* (Stockholm, June 1991), p. 74 (available at Hoover Institution Library, Stanford, California). Hereafter referred to as *Economic Survey (Swedish)*.

3. Bilmanis, *History of Latvia*, pp. 358–359.

4. Ibid., p. 361.

5. *Baltic States: A Reference Book* (Tallinn: Estonian Encyclopedia Publishers, 1991), p. 95.

6. *Baltic States*, p. 96.

7. *Economic Survey (Swedish)*, p. 75.

8. Ibid.

9. Ibid., p. 76.

10. Ibid.

11. *Baltic States*, p. 97.

12. *Economic Survey (Swedish)*, p. 78.

13. Ibid.

14. *Elections in the Baltic States and Soviet Republics: A Compendium Report on Parliamentary Elections Held in 1990* (Washington, D.C.: Commission on Security and Cooperation in Europe, December 1990), pp. 58–59.

15. Ibid., p. 51.

16. *Economic Survey (Swedish)*, p. 87.

17. *Elections in the Baltic States*, p. 53.

18. *Baltic States*, p. 95.

19. Dzintra Bungs, "Latvia: Laying New Foundations," *RFE/RL Research Report*, January 3, 1992, p. 63.

20. "Declaration of the Supreme Soviet of the Latvian SSSR on the Renewal of the Independence of the Republic of Latvia" (Riga: The Supreme Soviet of the Latvian SSSR, May 4, 1990), p. 2.

21. References to the 1922 constitution are drawn from "The Constitution of the Latvia Republic Adopted by the Latvian Constituent Assembly Plenary Session of February 15, 1992," *Latvian-Russian Relations* (Washington, D.C.: The Latvian Legation, 1944).

22. Based on data released by the Embassy of Latvia, June 8, 1993.

23. Dzintra Bungs, "The Moderate Right Wins in Latvian Parliamentary Elections," *RFE/RL Research Institute*, June 18, 1993, p. 1.

24. Ibid.

25. Dzintra Bungs, "Latvia Holds Successful Parliamentary Elections," *RFE/RL Research Report*, June 7, 1993, p. 1.

26. Ibid.

27. Data released by the Embassy of Latvia, Washington, D.C., June 8, 1993.

28. Bungs, "The Moderate Right Wins," p. 1.
29. Ibid., p. 2.
30. "New Latvian Parliament Meets," *RFE/RL Daily Report*, July 7, 1993.
31. *RFE/RL Daily Report*, July 8, 1993.
32. Bungs, "Latvia Holds Successful Parliamentary Elections," p. 1.
33. *Economic Survey (Swedish)*, p. 92.
34. *Baltic Chronology: Estonia, Latvia, Lithuania* (New York: Baltic Appeal to the United Nations BATUN, December 1991), p. 2.
35. *Economic Survey (Swedish)*, p. 91.
36. Ibid., p. 81.
37. Ibid., p. 82.
38. "Latvia Pays Gas Debt to Russia," *RFE/RL Daily Report*, July 6, 1993.
39. *Economic Survey (Swedish)*, p. 83.
40. *Baltic Chronology*, January 1992, p. 1.
41. "Innostrantsam zemlya poka prodavat'sya ne budet," *Diena*, February 25, 1992, p. 1.
42. Anders Aslund, "Latvia: A Successful Currency Reform," *Ostekonomisk Rapport* (Stockholm: Ostekonomiska Institutet, September 24, 1992), 4(10): 2.
43. "Privatization in Latvia," *The Baltic Independent*, March 5–11, 1993, p. 4.
44. "Danatsionalizatsiya provoditsya medlenno," *Diena*, February 25, 1992, p. 6.
45. Aslund, "Latvia: A Successful Currency Reform," p. 2.
46. Peter Morris, "Lats Hits the Streets," *The Baltic Independent*, March 5–11, 1993, p. 1.
47. "Latvia Lifts Customs Duties," *The Baltic Independent*, April 30–May 6, 1993, p. B3.
48. Aslund, "Latvia: A Successful Currency Reform," p. 7.
49. "Latvia Turns to the East for Trade," *The Baltic Independent*, June 25–July 1, 1993, p. B6.
50. Aslund, "Latvia: A Successful Currency Reform," p. 1.
51. "Latvian Way Presents Economic Program," *The Baltic Observer*, May 21–27, 1993, p. 5.
52. *Economic Survey (Swedish)*, p. 92.
53. Maris Ozols, "Latvia Stands Firm against Yeltsin Blast," *The Baltic Independent*, April 30–May 6, 1993, p. 1.
54. "Latvian Talks Resume, but Old Problems Remain," *The Baltic Observer*, May 21–27, 1993, p. 4.
55. "UN General Assembly Chairman Visit to Baltic States," *RFE/RL Daily Report*, July 5, 1993.
56. "V mukakh rozhdennaya armiya," *Rigas Balls*, December 12, 1992, p. 4.
57. Ibid.
58. Ibid.
59. Ibid.
60. "Foreign Warship Visits Latvia," *Diena Chronicle*, June 13–18, 1993.
61. *Economic Survey (Swedish)*, p. 91.
62. Ibid.
63. Latvian Embassy Brief #1, June 8, 1993, p. 3.
64. "Vremya rabotayet protv nas," *Diena*, February 26, 1992, p. 2.

9

ESTONIA

THE NATION AND THE INTERWAR STATE

Estonia, the smallest of the three Baltic states, has shared a common history with Latvia and Lithuania in this century. However, it has a distinct language and culture of its own. The name of the country (*Eesti* in Estonian) is probably derived from the old German *Aisti* used by ancient Germans to describe the peoples living northeast of the Vistula River. The first written record of the *Aisti* dates back to the first century A.D. Estonians, along with the Finns and Hungarians, belonging to the Baltic-Finnic group of the Finno-Ugric peoples, arrived on the territory of present-day Estonia in the third century B.C.1 The country's geographic boundaries are delineated by the Narva River, Lake Peipsi (Peipus), the Gulf of Finland, and the Baltic Sea; the only frontier that is geographically undefined lies to the south. In this southern area a branch of the Estonian race, the Livs, have fought incessant wars with the Letts or Latvians.[2]

An important element of Estonia's development was its relative isolation. The great trade route between the Baltic and the Mediterranean lay further south, along the Dvina (Daugava) River in Latvian territory. Estonia was repeatedly overrun by waves of invaders, from the Vikings to the Slavs. The Danes brought Christianity to the Estonians and took over northwest Estonia and the islands of Hiiumaa (Dago) and Saaremaa (Osel) as Danish provinces.[3] German control over Estonia, as well as all of the Baltic region, was asserted only after the arrival of the Teutonic Knights in Prussia and the merger of the Livonian Knights with the much more powerful Teutons. Under the joint authority of the Teutons and the Knights of the Sword, northern Latvia and southern Estonia constituted the so-called Land of the Virgin (St. Mary's Land).

Under German control, four Estonian towns became members of the Hanseatic League, including Tallinn. The Reformation, which reached Estonia in the mid-sixteenth century, brought Lutheranism to its people, with Protestantism becoming the dominant religion. As Ivan IV the Terrible continued to threaten the region, in the mid-sixteenth century northern Estonia submitted to Swedish rule, while southern Estonia fell under Polish control. By the seventeenth century the Russians were forced out of Estonia, and in the early seventeenth century the whole territory of Estonia was conquered by the Swedes.

The period of Swedish control, often referred to by Estonians as the "good Swedish rule" or the "good old Swedish days," witnessed the substantial weakening of serfdom, the introduction of the rule of law, a reform of land administration that for the first time clearly spelled out the peasant's obligations as well as his rights, and the promotion of education. Tartu University (*Academia Gustaviana*) was founded by Swedish King Gustav Adolf's decree in 1632, as were a number of Estonian-language schools. Among the eight chairs originally established at Tartu University was a professorship in the Estonian language. The university was demolished in the course of the Northern War, but it was reformed and generously endowed by Tsar Alexander in 1802, when the school was rebuilt as *Universitas Dorpatensis*.[4] The university became a premier institution of German-Balt education; most of the faculty was German, and henceforth instruction was conducted in German. Only in 1919, after Estonia became an independent state, was Tartu University rebuilt as the Estonian National University, with Tartu becoming the cultural capital of the new state.[5]

Estonia passed to Russian rule after the defeat of Sweden by Peter the Great in the Northern War of 1710 and remained under Russian control until independence. Like elsewhere along the Baltic Rim, the nineteenth century was a period of national awakening in Estonia. The rising national consciousness, strengthened by the complete elimination of illiteracy, led to a growing popular resistance to both the German-Baltic barons and the Russians. An increased interest in Estonian folklore and myths and the rising tide of books and newspapers in Estonian marked the emergence of Estonian nationalism. Folk-music festivals were organized that featured Estonian choirs; new fully Estonian secondary schools were established. Among the rising generation of new leaders was Konstantin Pats, the son of a peasant and building contractor; he was a lawyer, educated at Tartu, and the future president of the Estonian Republic.

Estonia emerged as an independent state after World War I and the attendant collapse of the Russian empire. In 1917 the nationalists in Estonia held elections to the Land Council, with the Estonian Agrarian League led by Pats winning the largest number of seats.[6] In 1919 Konstantin Pats, who had been imprisoned in Germany, returned to become prime minister and the minister of war. By the end of 1919 Estonia was finally free of German and Russian military occupation. For the first time since the twelfth century, Estonia became an independent state. The power of nascent nationalism, the collapse of Germany and Russia, and a moderate assistance from the West (a British naval presence in Tallinn contributed to the Estonian victory) combined to create the new republic.

Estonia entered the period of independence with an economy devastated by war. The 1920s were also a period of national consolidation or, rather, of nation building. The parliamentary system proved incapable of establishing stable governments. The economy, still largely based on agriculture, began to recover and until the Great Depression experienced some growth, but then collapsed. The task of creating a working democracy under conditions of economic crisis proved overwhelming. Estonian democracy collapsed because of the dislocations and pressures generated by the Great Depression and the rising tide of fascism. On March 12, 1934, Pats declared a state of emergency and proclaimed martial law, thus transforming the government into his personal dictatorship. An authoritarian system was introduced, with martial law and limits on civil and political rights that would last in Estonia until World War II.

SOVIET OCCUPATION

The Soviet Union forced Estonia in the fall of 1939 to allow it to station troops on Estonian territory. On September 28, 1939, the Estonian government yielded to the Soviet demands. After the Soviet victory over Finland a rigged election was staged in Estonia in 1940, which brought to power a puppet communist regime and a formal petition from Estonia to join the U.S.S.R. The imposition of Soviet rule was followed by mass arrests and deportations of all potential opposition to the government. The U.S.S.R. Supreme Soviet completed the farce on August 6, 1940, when it formally admitted Estonia into the Soviet Union.

The Germans occupied all of Estonia by October 1941. The Estonians, whom the Nazis regarded as racially superior to the Slavs, were to be subjected to a program of Germanization. In February 1944 a general mobilization of Estonians was imposed to assist the Wehrmacht on the eastern front. As the tide of the war turned, the Russians reoccupied Estonia in October 1944, with 70,000 Estonians fleeing before the approaching Soviet army.[7]

Again, mass deportations of Estonians to the Soviet interior followed, including Pats and other key Estonian military and political leaders. By the early 1950s the principal elements of the Soviet political and economic system were firmly in place. There was a marked shift to heavy industry and growing dependence on Soviet industry as a whole. The Estonian Communist Party (ECP) was purged of native Estonians, who were replaced by "Russian Estonians," whom Stalin was willing to entrust with the administration of the country. Large-scale immigration of labor, especially from Russia, which accompanied the industrialization drive, dramatically altered the ethnic composition of Estonia; the ethnic Estonians declined from 75 percent of the population in 1959 to 65 percent in 1979.[8] This change was accompanied by strong efforts at Russification, especially at the level of culture and administration, and was especially pronounced in the 1970s.

The most important natural resources of Estonia are oil shale and phosphate, found in the areas of the country stretching from Tallinn eastward. The Soviets used the shale for fuel in two large power stations in Narva, and it is also refined in the chemical industry to produce oils, sulphur, phenols, and other products. Phosphate was used in the production of fertilizer in newly built chemical plants. Since the mid-1970s about twenty-five million tons of oil shale has been mined.

In addition to rapid industrialization, the changed ethnic structure of Estonia would prove to be the principal Soviet legacy. Large numbers of non-Estonians migrated to Tallinn and to northeastern Estonia. After fifty years of Russian immigration policies, in Tallinn only 47 percent of the population was Estonian; in Narva only 4 percent, in Sillamae only 3 percent, and in Kohtla-Jarve only 21 percent were ethnic Estonians.[9] Estonia lost a quarter of its population in the war, then the Soviet rule claimed 60,000 deported in 1940–1941, 50,000 to 60,000 deported immediately after the war, and 20,000 at the height of deportations in March of 1949. In addition, about 72,000 Estonians have become permanent refugees since the war. The migration of the Russians after the war completed the change. Between 1945 and 1958 about 283,500 Russian speakers moved in, and the net inflow thereafter averaged about 7,000 people per year until 1987.[10]

ANTICOMMUNIST INDEPENDENCE MOVEMENT

Prior to 1987 there was very little political opposition in Estonia. A small dissident movement was successfully contained by the Soviet secret police. In 1987, however, the Estonian population was galvanized to action in opposition to the Soviet plan to develop on a large scale the phosphate deposits in northcentral Estonia, which could lead to serious environmental problems and would accelerate the rate of non-Estonian immigration. Also on August 23, 1987, a group of former political prisoners organized in Tallinn a rally to commemorate the Ribbentrop-Molotov Pact and demanded that the secret protocols be made public. The dissident activity polarized the Communist Party and led to the emergence of a reform movement ("loyal opposition") called the Estonian Popular Front, organized on the initiative of Edgar Savisaar, the country's future prime minister. The movement's original goal was to work toward greater Estonian autonomy within the U.S.S.R. On November 16, 1988, the Estonian Supreme Soviet adopted a declaration of sovereignty. On January

18, 1989, a Law on the Language made Estonian the official "state language."[11] Moscow's quiet acceptance of the sovereignty declaration was superseded by a radicalization of nationalist movement in Estonia, culminating in the August 23, 1989, Baltic Way demonstration. The Baltic Way was to become a formula for complete national independence for the three Baltic states and a search for "national self-determination and . . . honest solutions between the East and the West."[12] Moscow's harsh reaction to this demonstration further radicalized the movement, and by the end of 1989 the former demand for economic independence was replaced with an agenda of complete national independence. The election on March 18, 1990, returned a pro-independence Supreme Soviet (now called Supreme Council) in Estonia, which declared a transitional period for restoring the independent Republic of Estonia, during which the necessary state institutions would be restored and a final settlement with Moscow would be reached.[13]

The principal political organization that took part in the March 1990 elections was the Estonian Popular Front, whose activists became key players in the Social Democratic Party and the Liberal Democratic Party (both created in 1990). The second key grouping called itself "Free Estonia" (*Vaba Eesti*) and claimed national independence as its most important goal. Much of its leadership came from the previous Estonian Communist Party and enterprise managers. The "Free Estonia" movement was led by former prime minister Indrek Toome. Most of the support for the movement came from non-Estonians, despite the dominating position of Estonians in the leadership. The third group were the "national radicals" with ties to the former dissident movement. Prominent leaders included the conservative leader Kaido Kama and the Christian Democrats Mart Laar and Illar Hallaste. This group had no representatives in the government at the time and only reluctantly participated in the work of the Supreme Council because it questioned the very legitimacy of this body. Instead, Laar and others chose to work through the Congress of Estonia, a non-Soviet parliament built up from the grass-roots in 1989–1990. The Congress of Estonia was elected by those who had been citizens of the Republic of Estonia at the time of the Soviet occupation and by their descendants.

The Congress of Estonia was the product of the Estonian Citizens Committee, an opposition movement established in February 1989 by the Estonian National Independence Party, the Estonian Heritage Society, and the Estonian Christian Union.[14] The elections to the Congress of Estonia took place from February 24, 1990, to March 1, 1990, with the deputies calling for complete national independence.[15] The Congress of Estonia convened in March 1990.[16] It was a 499-member alternative parliament. The delegates elected an eleven-member board and a seventy-eight-member "Committee of Estonia" as a standing executive body. Relations between the Estonian Supreme Council and the Congress of Estonia were strained, although on March 28, 1990, the Congress of Estonia handed over its authority temporarily to the Supreme Council in preparation for the Supreme Council's suspension of Soviet military authority in Estonia. The Congress of Estonia played a pioneering role, however, by developing the first mass-supported representative body based on the rejection of Soviet institutions and an alternative forum for the independence movement. The Estonian Supreme Council recognized the Congress of Estonia as "the representative body of the citizens of the Republic of Estonia" and as "the restorer of state power of the Republic of Estonia."[17]

Another important movement was the Union of Labor Collectives of Estonia, committed to independence as the ultimate goal, in preparation for the convening of the Constituent Assembly of the future Estonian Republic. The Green Movement, which has given way to the Green Party, is committed to ecological reconstruction, the search for a "third way" (neither capitalist nor communist economy), and a neutral demilitarized Estonia.[18] The last significant group was the Russian-dominated Intermovement, which was opposed to Estonian independence as well as to any reform in general. Intermovement staged a notorious attack on the parliament building on May 15, 1990; most of the Intermovement members were hard-line communists faithful to Moscow after the ECP split in 1990. The new independent Communist Party had little significance in Estonian politics. After the March 1990 election, the 105-member Supreme Council was divided as follows: "Free Estonia" had 28 percent, Intermovement and allied groups 26 percent, Popular Front 24 percent, and "national radicals" 22 percent.[19] The groups continued to fragment, with twelve "factions" (embryonic parties) registered by mid-1991. The government was dominated by the Popular Front, but it lacked a parliamentary majority.

The period of transition to independence lasted from May 1990 through August 1991, when the Estonian Supreme Council was moved to declare full independence in the wake of the aborted Soviet coup in order to put Estonia on the same legal footing as Lithuania.[20] On August 20, 1991, Estonia formally reestablished its independence from the U.S.S.R. Following the Soviet Union's September 6, 1991, decision to recognize the Baltic states' independence, Estonia entered a series of disengagement talks with Moscow.

DOMESTIC POLITICS OF INDEPENDENT ESTONIA

In the aftermath of the failed August putsch the Estonian transition government of Edgar Savisaar moved against the coup supporters, arresting the key leaders and outlawing the Russian-nationalist Intermovement.[21] After Savisaar's resignation in January 1992, following the loss of parliamentary support, Premier Tiit Vahi formed a caretaker government until the new parliamentary elections in the fall.

The first open and democratic parliamentary and presidential elections were held in Estonia on September 20, 1992. The Pro Patria, or Fatherland (*Isamaa*), coalition of five free-market-oriented parties (subsequently consolidated into one) won twenty-nine or one-third of the 101 parliamentary seats. The reform communist Left Opportunity movement failed to clear the required 5 percent of the popular vote and did not get a single seat in the State Assembly. The most surprising development was the poor showing of the Popular Front, which only two years before was the principal political force in the country.

The current parliament has been elected to a two-and-a-half-year term, rather than the prescribed four years, with the proviso that the next election scheduled for early 1995 will elect deputies to a four-year parliament. The majority of the seats in the current Estonian State Assembly are held by Pro Patria (*Isamaa*), which has twenty-nine mandates, followed by the Secure Home (*Kindel Kodu*) with seventeen seats, the Popular Front with fifteen seats, the Moderates with twelve seats, the Estonian National Independence Party (ENIP) with ten seats, the Estonian Citizen Coalition with eight seats, the Independent Royalists with eight seats, and the Estonian Entrepreneurs' Party and the Green Party with one seat each.[22]

After the elections Pro Patria formed a narrow parliamentary majority with the Estonian National Independence Movement and with the Moderates.[23] In the presidential election, Supreme Council chairman Arnold Ruutel, nominated by the Secure Home (*Kindel Kodu*) coalition, won 48 percent of the vote, with Lennart Meri of the Pro Patria coalition, coming in second with 28.8 percent of the popular vote.[24] Since none of the presidential candidates won over 50 percent of the popular vote, the choice of the president was decided in the parliament, with Ruutel and Meri contending for the office. The presidential election in the State Assembly was won on October 6, 1992, by Lennart Meri, a novelist and filmmaker who had served briefly as Estonia's foreign minister in the Savisaar government and was subsequently the country's ambassador to Finland. Meri received fifty-nine of the votes, and thirty-one votes went to Ruutel.[25] On President Meri's recommendation, Pro Patria's thirty-two-year-old chairman Mart Laar became Estonia's new prime minister. Laar formed his cabinet in coalition with ENIP and Moderates.

The election of Meri as president and the appointments to the Laar cabinet took place according to a new constitution, adopted in 1992. The declaration of Estonia's independence had been followed by the establishment of a sixty-member Constituent Assembly jointly by the Supreme Council and the Congress of Estonia. The Estonian Constituent Assembly then presented the new draft constitution to the nation in a national referendum on June 28, 1992, which approved the new basic law by 91 percent of the 67 percent eligible voters despite considerable pressure from the right to reinstate the 1938 constitution instead.[26]

The 1992 constitution[27] provides for a unicameral State Assembly (*Riigikogu*) made up of 101 deputies (Articles 59 and 60). The parliament is elected to a four-year term and holds most of the powers, including legislative powers, the right to elect the president of the republic, and the power to approve and dismiss the government, and appoint the chairman of the National Court and its judges, the chairman of the Bank of Estonia, the auditor-general, the legal chancellor, and the commander-in-chief of the defense forces (Article 65).

In contrast to the extensive powers of the parliament, the Estonian presidency is restricted and largely ceremonial. The president is elected to a five-year term, with a limit of two consecutive terms in office (Article 80). The assembly decided that the first election of the president would be done by popular vote, while thereafter the president would be elected by the parliament.[28] The election of the president is done by secret ballot in the parliament (Article 79).

The prime minister is nominated by the president and approved by the *Riigikogu*; if the presidential candidate is rejected by the parliament, the legislature then agrees on its own choice for the prime minister (Article 89). Once parliamentary approval is granted, the prime minister then proceeds to form the government. The government can be removed by the parliament through a no-confidence vote (Article 92). The division of political power in Estonia, as determined by the 1992 constitution, provides for a parliamentary system with a weak presidency.

ECONOMIC POLICY

During Soviet rule, Estonia was frequently a test bed for a number of Soviet economic reforms, including the reorganization of agriculture into agroindustrial complexes, modifications of the plan, and private initiative in small-scale businesses in the service sector. However, substantive reform had to await national independence.

In 1991 the Estonian government gave priority to price, wage, and tax reform and progressive disengagement from the Soviet economy. In order to break its complete dependence on Russia for energy, Estonia moved to diversify its sources of fuel. On March 22, 1993, a new oil terminal at the Muuga port east of Tallinn was placed in operation to handle fuel supplied by Finland. The Muuga storage facility, run jointly by Estonian Fuel and the Finnish company Neste (which holds 55 percent of the shares), will allow Estonia to buy fuel from virtually any source on the world market.[29] In mid-1993 Neste considered a plan to build a gas pipeline from Finland to Estonia. The project would involve the entire Baltic region by bringing natural gas from Norway through Sweden to all the Baltic states, and possibly for other European countries; if implemented, it would further reduce Estonia's dependence on Russia for natural gas.[30]

Customs barriers and immigration quotas were introduced. Privatization became the highest priority of the government's reform program, as well as the creation of an effective banking system, reintroduction of the *kroon* as Estonian currency, and land reform. Estonia moved the fastest of the three Baltic states to rebuild the economy and attract foreign investment; by the end of 1991 foreign investment accounted for 3 percent of Estonia's gross national product.[31] In October 1992, when the Estonian Privatization Agency, modeled after

Germany's *Treuhandanstalt,* announced the first round of privatization of large state-owned enterprises, German, Finnish, and Swedish buyers led a new wave of foreign investment.[32] Estonian privatization law was ratified on May 11, 1993.[33] The inflow of foreign capital into Estonia has been accelerated by the government's decision to allow for foreign land ownership. The first land sale to foreign investors was finalized on June 22, 1993, when sixty-four hectares that had once served as a Soviet missile base were sold to AS Baltic Spoon, owned by the U.S.-based Atlantic Veneer Corporation and several private investors.[34] Privatization has been accelerated through a voucher scheme that allows the citizens to turn in their government vouchers for corporate stocks. The Estonian Privatization Agency is expected to find private owners for all enterprises in Estonia valued at over 600,000 *kroons* ($45,000).[35]

On December 19, 1991, the Estonian parliament passed a land reform bill authorizing the return of confiscated real estate (as distinct from dwellings) to its former rightful owners.[36] The land reform was accompanied by a government program approved on April 1, 1993, to make a 50 million *kroon* ($3.8 million) credit available to Estonian farmers in the form of short-term loans to buy seed, fuel, and fertilizer.[37] A Law on Prices had been adopted in December 1989, and it was followed by a decree spelling out the details; it brought about a partial decontrolling of prices already in 1990; on October 15, 1990, government subsidies for meat and milk products were abolished. This shock therapy led to considerable hardship, including the 400 percent increase in the cost of living in 1991 relative to 1990.[38] Still, by mid-1993 there were signs that Estonia's economic decline had bottomed out and that the country was poised for economic recovery. According to a Word Bank study released in 1993, Estonia had good prospects for economic recovery by the end of the year, while the European Bank for Reconstruction and Development asserted that the drop in Estonia's GDP in 1993 should slow to around 5 percent.[39]

Despite some misgivings on the part of the IMF official advising Tallinn on currency reform, on January 6, 1992, the Estonian government approved a plan to seek a $150 million loan to introduce and stabilize the new currency, the *kroon.* The country's industry and its gold reserves were put up as collateral.[40] As part of the currency reform, the government also asked for the return of twelve tons of gold that Estonia had deposited in the United Kingdom, Switzerland, Sweden, and the United States in the 1930s to be used to back the *kroon.*[41] The *kroon* was introduced on June 20, 1992. It is backed by a $120 million stabilization fund and pegged to the Deutsche mark at eight to one. Today the Estonian currency is fully convertible and, by the IMF's own admission, remains the key factor in Estonia's economic success.

In 1993 inflation was no longer the urgent problem it had been a year before. Between January 1992 and April 1992, prices went up in Estonia by 676 percent on average.[42] However, by mid-1993 inflation fell to 1.7 percent per month. The government's goal for 1993 was to keep inflation at a 10 percent annual rate.[43] Overall, Estonia's economic development has surpassed that of the other Baltic States, leading a European Parliament commission to consider the country a strong prospect for joining European organizations and becoming an associate member of the European Union.[44]

In a sign of the country's improved economic performance, in 1993 the average monthly wage in Estonia stood at $70, which was over three times the rate in Lithuania, where the average monthly wage stood at $20.[45]

FOREIGN AND SECURITY POLICY

The principal objective of Estonia's foreign policy is, in the words of President Lennart Meri, to be "a part of Europe."[46] The policy is to ensure that the remaining vestiges of former dependency on Russia are removed and the country's sovereignty maintained. During his first visit to Germany, on June 28, 1993, Premier Mart Laar discussed Estonia's integration into Europe with German Chancellor Helmut Kohl. Another important topic on the agenda was the withdrawal of Russian troops from Estonia. Laar also opened the Estonian embassy in Bonn.[47] Subsequently, the German side expressed support for Estonia's position on the Russian troop withdrawals; reportedly, the issue was raised by Chancellor Kohl during his July 10 meeting with Russian President Boris Yeltsin.

The ongoing negotiations on the withdrawal of the remaining Russian troops is considered by the Estonian government one of the highest foreign policy objectives. Even after the Russian troops have departed, the Estonian government will have to deal with environmental hazards existing at the former Soviet bases, among the most serious being the nuclear reactors at the Russian naval base in Paldiski. Tallinn hopes to obtain assistance from the European Bank for Reconstruction and Development to dismantle the reactors and to move them out of Estonia.[48]

Relations between Russia and Estonia remain strained, with Russian President Boris Yeltsin charging continued discrimination against ethnic Russians in Estonia and Estonian President Lennart Meri accusing Russia of developing a "Monroe doctrine" in the Baltics.[49] The level of tension between Moscow and Tallinn increased further on June 18, 1993, when an official statement of the Russian Foreign Ministry denounced Estonia for "aggressive nationalism" that threatened "serious consequences" and "an interethnic explosion."[50] On May 14, 1993, when Estonia was formally admitted to the Council of Europe as a full member, Russian Foreign Minister Andrey Kozyrev refused to attend the session of the Committee of Ministers in protest of the council's action.[51]

The Estonian side rejected Russian allegations as unfounded. On June 18, in response to the Russian Foreign Ministry statement, Estonian Prime Minister Mart Laar described the charges of discrimination against Russians as "absolute fiction."[52]

The new Estonian basic law establishes the defense forces headed by the *Riigikogu*-appointed commander (Article 127). Among the most controversial issues in Estonia's defense policy was the selection of Aleksander Einseln, a retired U.S. army colonel, as the commander-in-chief of the Estonian forces.[53] Despite objections from the U.S. State Department, Einseln took office on May 4, 1993, following the 82-0 vote in the parliament in favor of the appointment. He formally assumed his post on June 17, when President Meri awarded him the rank of major general of the Estonian defense forces.[54]

According to Hain Rebas, the Estonian minister of defense, the Estonian defense forces will consist of three motorized infantry battalions and a communications company. The existing forces will be increased in case of emergency through general mobilization. The government decided that the small size of the defense forces can be sustained provided they are equipped with the most up-to-date military hardware. The forces have been supplied with new uniforms thanks to assistance from Finland, Sweden, and Norway, as well as Germany and France.[55] Although all of the weapons and equipment will be purchased abroad, the government plans to build weapons repair shops and an ammunition plant.

The greatest security threat facing Estonia today is the potential for instability in Russia and the threat of the rise of hard-line antidemocratic forces in Moscow intent on restoring its past influence in the region. Should this take place, Estonian Defense Minister Hain Rebas sees no alternative for his country but to strengthen the defense of the border with Russia; however, Estonia harbors few illusions about its ability to defend itself against an all-out Russian aggression. Should such a scenario come about, Estonia would do its utmost to resist while turning to the international community for assistance.[56] NATO membership is a long-term prospect that Tallinn considers important to the country's security.

Estonia has moved to reequip its defense forces with weapons purchased from Israel. The $50 million deal with Israel included among other things Uzi submachine guns, Galil rifles, and antitank weapons.[57] More than the basic equipment, the Estonian armed forces need sophisticated radar equipment to monitor their air space and the Baltic Sea coast.[58] In late 1992 Tallinn turned to French, Italian, and Japanese companies with a request for proposals to install a new radar system to monitor the country's seacoast and its air space. The French company Thomson presented a winning proposal to set up a chain of fourteen radars to cover the coast and the coastal air space. In December 1992 the Estonian government moved to secure international funding for the implementation of the project.[59] In 1993 Estonia received some defense-related assistance from Finland, which promised to transfer several patrol boats to Estonian border guards.[60]

In 1993 the most substantial military aid to Estonia came from Sweden. During a May 18 visit to Tallinn, Swedish Defense Minister Anders Bjorck announced a comprehensive grant aid package for Estonia and Latvia. According to Bjorck, by the fall of 1993 Sweden would provide Estonia with armored personnel carriers, radar systems, coastal patrol boats, and equipment for field hospitals. The most important element of the Swedish assistance package would be state-of-the-art electronic surveillance equipment badly needed to ensure control over Estonia's borders. Estonian Defense Minister Hain Rebas welcomed the Swedish offer of military assistance as "a great relief for Estonia."[61]

STRIVING TO PRESERVE NATIONAL IDENTITY

Like Latvia, Estonia faces the challenge of fostering a cohesive nation while preserving nascent democratic institutions. At the beginning of the 1990s Estonia's population stood at 1,576,000, with very low birthrates.[62] Hence, the issue of preserving national identity after years of foreign occupation ranks high on the government's agenda. In November 1991 Estonia reinstated the 1938 citizenship law, and in February 1992 the Supreme Council passed enabling legislation to implement it. The laws grant citizenship rights to all the citizens of the interwar republic and their descendants, regardless of their ethnic origin. Estonian residents who do not qualify for citizenship under the above provisions can become naturalized citizens provided they can prove a two-years' residence starting on March 30, 1990, and have a minimal competence in the Estonian language of about 1,500 words; naturalization would become effective following a one-year waiting period.[63] Estonia has also made a concerted effort to bring home those former citizens or their descendants who had been scattered throughout the former Soviet Union. For instance, in early 1992 the government organized special flights to Abkhazia to repatriate Estonians resettled in the Transcaucasus.[64]

The Estonian law on citizenship, approved by the Estonian Supreme Council on February 26, 1992, will grant Estonian citizenship to all prewar citizens and their descendants. Others will be able to become naturalized citizens after a period of three years, calculated retroactively from March 30, 1990.[65] On July 8, 1993 a special session of the Estonian parliament approved, by a vote of 69 to 1, with two abstentions, twenty amendments to the law on aliens as recommended by the CSCE and Council of Europe. An article was added retaining for noncitizens who had arrived before July 1, 1990, all the rights and responsibilities laid down in previous laws. Residence permits will still be refused to former military and security personnel.[66]

Non-Estonian residents may opt for Russian citizenship. In 1992 some twenty-two thousand Russians chose the Russian citizenship by registering at the embassy of the Russian Federation in Tallinn.[67] The new Alien Law introduced on July 12, 1993, requires that noncitizens register with the government as resident aliens.[68] It allows the resident aliens to vote in local elections but limits the right to stand for office to Estonian citizens. The promulgation of the law was denounced by Russia and increased tension in relations between Moscow and Tallinn. The Russian government accused Estonia of flagrantly violating the basic human rights of its Russian minority. The Estonian side rejected the charges, insisting that it was exercising its sovereign rights within legal guidelines commonly accepted in Europe.

The problem of minority rights in Estonia is bound to remain an issue for some time, especially as Estonia's economy continues to improve, making it an attractive place to live. The rising demands in the northeastern areas for greater autonomy, especially in and around the heavily Russian city of Narva, will continue to strain Estonia's relations with Russia. The Estonian government may find it difficult at times to navigate between the justifiable desire for retribution for fifty years of Russian oppression and the need to maintain democratic standards commonly recognized in the West.

NOTES

1. *The Baltic States: A Reference Book* (Tallinn: Estonian Encyclopedia Publishers, 1991), p. 13.

2. J. Hampden Jackson, *Estonia* (London: George Allen and Unwin, 1948), p. 38.

3. Ibid., p. 43.

4. Ibid., p. 88.

5. Ibid., p. 171.

6. Ibid., p. 129.

7. *Economic Survey of the Baltic Republics: A study undertaken by an independent team of experts on the initiative of the Swedish Ministry for Foreign Affairs in collaboration with the government authorities of Estonia, Latvia, and Lithuania* (Stockholm, June 1991), p. 99 (available at Hoover Institution Library, Stanford, California). Hereafter referred to as *Economic Survey (Swedish)*.

8. Ibid., p. 99.

9. Ibid., p. 102.

10. Ibid., p. 102.

11. *Zakon o yazyke* (Tallinn: Olion, 1990), p. 8. "Baltic States" Collection, Hoover Institution Archives, Stanford, California.

12. *Mati Hint, Balti Tee* (The Baltic Way) (Tallinn: Valgus, 1989), pp. 23–24. "Baltic States" Collection, Hoover Institution Archives, Stanford, California.

13. *Economic Survey (Swedish)*, p. 104.

14. *Elections in the Baltic States and Soviet Republics: A Compendium of Reports on Parliamentary Elections Held in 1990* (Washington, D.C.: Commission on Security and Cooperation in Europe, December 1990), p. 38.

15. "Deklaratsya o 71-y godovshchine Estonskoy Respubliki," *Kongress Estonii: Spetsyal' nyy vypusk glavnogo komiteta grazhdan Estonskoy Respubliki*, February 24, 1990, p. 2. In "Baltic States" Collection, Hoover Institution Archives, Stanford, California.

16. *Elections in the Baltic States and Soviet Republics*, p. 36.

17. Ibid., p. 46.

18. Ibid., p. 37.

19. *Economic Survey (Swedish)*, p. 105.

20. Riina Kionka, "Estonia: A Break with the Past," *RFE/RL Research Report*, January 3, 1992, p. 65.

21. Ibid., p. 66.

22. Riika Kionka, "Free-Market Coalition Assumes Power in Estonia," *RFE/RL Research Report*, November 20, 1992, p. 9.

23. Riina Kionka, "Estonia: A Difficult Transition," *RFE/RL Research Report*, January 1, 1993, p. 89.

24. Kionka, "Free-Market Coalition Assumes Power in Estonia."

25. Ibid.

26. Riina Kionka, "Drafting New Constitutions: Estonia," *RFE/RL Daily Report*, July 3, 1992, p. 57.

27. The discussion of the constitutional framework of Estonia is based on *Republic of Estonia Constitution*, an unofficial translation of the basic law provided by the Estonian Embassy in the United States.

28. *Baltic Chronology: Estonia, Latvia, Lithuania* (New York: Baltic Appeal to the United Nations BATUN, April 1992), p. 4.

29. "Tallinn Gets New Oil Terminal," *The Baltic Independent*, March 26–April 1, 1993, p. 6.

30. "Pipeline May Join Estonia and Finland," *The Baltic Independent*, June 25–July 1, 1993, p. B7.

31. Kionka, "Estonia: A Break with the Past," p. 66.

32. Kionka, "Estonia: A Difficult Transition," p. 91.

33. "Privatization Law Ratified," *The Baltic Independent*, May 21–27, 1993, p., 5.

34. "Investors Land Deals," *The Baltic Independent*, July 2–8, 1993, p. B1.

35. "Estonian Privatization Makes Halting Progress," *The Baltic Independent*, February 19–25, 1993, p. 6.

36. *Baltic Chronology,* December 1991, p. 5.

37. "Farm Aid," *The Baltic Independent*, April 9–15, 1993, p. 7.

38. Kionka, "Estonia: A Break with the Past," p. 66.

39. "World Bank: Growth in Sight for Estonia, Latvia," *The Baltic Independent*, April 30–May 6, 1993, p. B4.

40. *Baltic Chronology*, January 1992, p. 2.

41. Kionka, "Estonia: A Break with the Past," p. 67.

42. *Baltic Chronology*, April 1992, p. 2.

43. "Hard Currency Brings Economic Rebound," *The Baltic Independent*, June 25–July 1, 1993, p. B3.

44. "Estonia Pleases Eurocrats," *The Baltic Independent*, May 14–20, 1993, p. 4.

45. Michael Tarm, "Estonia-Kroon," *Associated Press*, June 23, 1993, p. 2.

46. Excerpts from a speech by Estonian President Lennart Meri delivered on Estonia's Independence Day, February 24, 1993, *The Baltic Independent*, March 5–11, 1993, p. 9.

47. "Estonian Prime Minister in Germany," *RFE/RL Daily Report: Baltic Related Items*, June 30, 1993.

48. "Troop Watch," *The Baltic Independent*, March 12–18, 1993, p. 3.

49. "Meri Blasts Moscow's 'Monroe Doctrine,' "*The Baltic Independent*, May 14–20, 1993, p. 3.

50. Tarmu Tammerk, "Russia Slams Estonia's 'Aggressive Nationalism,' "*The Baltic Independent*, June 25–July 1, 1993, p. 1.

51. "Estonia Joins EC in Spite of Russia," *The Baltic Observer*, May 21–27, 1993, p. 1.

52. "Foreign Relations with Russia and the CIS," *Eesti Ringvaade: A Weekly Review of Estonian News* (Internet Edition), June 28, 1993.

53. "New Commander Goes Ahead in Spite of US Objection," *The Baltic Independent*, May 14–20, 1993, p. 4.

54. "Meri Approves Einseln as Major General of Estonia's Defence Forces," *Eesti Ringvaade: A Weekly Review of Estonian News* (Internet Edition), June 28, 1993.

55. "My ne podnimem oruzhiye protiv russkogo naroda," *Estonia*, December 4, 1992, p. 2.

56. Ibid.

57. Hennart Arismaa, "Estonia Discloses Cost of Israeli Arms Deals," *The Baltic Independent*, June 25–July 1, 1993, p. 4.

58. "Granitsu zashchityat ne pushki, a informatsiya," *Kurier*, February 25, 1992, p. I3.

59. "Frantsuzskiye radary dlya okhrany nashikh granits," *Vecherniy Kur'yer*, December 3, 1992, p. 1.

60. "Finland Postpones Transfer of Boats to Estonia," *RFE/RL Daily Report: Baltic Related Items*, June 16, 1993.

61. "Sweden Announces Military Aid Package for Estonia and Latvia," *The Baltic Independent*, May 21–27, 1993, pp. 1 and 3.

62. *Baltic States,* p. 16.

63. Kionka, "Drafting New Constitutions: Estonia," p. 68.

64. "V Estoniyu dostablena uzhe tret'ya gruppa zakabkazskikh estontsev," *Kurier*, February 24, 1992, p. 5.

65. *Baltic Chronology*, February 1992, p. 7.

66. "Estonian Parliament Amends Law on Aliens," *RFE/RL Daily Report*, July 9, 1993.

67. "22 tysyachi zhiteley Estonii prinyali rossiyskoye grazhdanstvo," *Vecherniy Kur'yer*, December 3, 1992, p. 1.

68. "Estonian President Signs Alien Law," *RFE/RL Daily Report*, July 13, 1993.

IV

EAST EUROPEAN PERIPHERY

10

BELARUS

THE BELORUSSIANS AND THE BELORUSSIAN SSR

Belarus (Belorussia) is a new postcommunist successor state with no prewar history of independent statehood. Until recently, Belorussia or White Russia was known in the West simply as a province of Russia. A variety of theories have been advanced to explain the origin of the name "Belorussia,"* some seeing the root of the name in the white clothing worn by the peasant inhabitants, some in the white snow cover of the region in the winter, some in the rivers Belaja and Belianka; some in the towns of Bela, Beloveza, and Belostok. Most likely, the name dates back to the time of the Mongol conquest. Under the khan's administration the "white lands" were exempt from taxation, while "black lands" bore the full burden of Tatar taxes.[1]

Belorussian nationalists consider their people to be the oldest and purest branch of the Slav family, tracing their origins to the ancient Slavic tribes of the Krivici, Dregovici, and Radimici that lived in the upper reaches of the Western Dvina and the Dnieper and along the banks of the rivers Pripet and Sozh. The Belorussian language contains both its own unique idiom and distinct influences of Polish, Russian, and Ukrainian. It shows strong regional characteristics, with up to twenty dialects. The Belorussian language did not begin to

*The use of the term "Belorussian" in its English translation "White Russian" became even more confusing after the 1917 Bolshevik revolution, when the forces that fought against the communists were known as the "White Russians." Hence after World War I the Latin term "Ruthenia" was accepted by the League of Nations, and the Belorussians became the "White Ruthenians." After World War II the United Nations reverted to "Belorussia." The terms currently in circulation distinguish the Belorussians (White Russians) from the Great Russians and the Ukrainians (Little Russians).

evolve a common literary standard until the publication of the first Belorussian grammar in 1918. Historically, Belorussians used both the Latin and the Cyrillic alphabets to transliterate the phonetics of their vernacular, settling for the Cyrillic after 1918, with the Russian spelling ultimately prevailing over the whole territory of the Belorussian Soviet Socialist Republic (SSR).

That weak sense of national identity, assertions to the contrary by Belorussian nationalists notwithstanding, remains a key political factor in present-day Belarus. The Belorussian peasantry never called itself "Belorussians" until the name was imposed on them by the Polish and Russian scholarship and administration. Until the twentieth century the peasants had a strictly regional identity; when asked about his nationality, the Belorussian peasant would answer that he was neither Polish nor Russian, but *tuteyshi* or *tutashni* (local), that is, one of the natives.[2] At the end of the nineteenth century, the Belorussian ethnic group was defined only geographically, as the area where local dialects were used, and sociologically, as the lower strata of the native population.

Historically, the upper strata of Belorussians considered themselves either Polish or Russian, as these two states controlled the region for centuries. The Polish influence was solidified by the Brest Church Union, which brought the Lithuanian (Ukrainian and Belorussian) Orthodox Christians under the authority of the pope as the so-called Uniates in 1595, thus ensuring for the time being the dominant position of Roman Catholicism in the region.

The movement for Belorussian self-determination began late in the nineteenth century. The process was retarded by the lack of Belorussian literary tradition and the lack of even a unified written form for the Belorussian vernacular. The middle class, which was only beginning to emerge in the Russian empire, was all but nonexistent in Belorussia. Paradoxically, the concept of Belorussia as a nation came first from Polish and Russian scholars conducting ethnographic studies rather than Belorussians themselves. Afterwards, the development of Belorussian national identity followed a conventional route from ethnic to literary, to cultural, and finally to political nationalism.

Political debates and arguments over national programs remained confined to the intelligentsia, with the Belorussian peasant demonstratively indifferent to them. The peasantry remained faithful to its language and tradition but showed little comprehension of or enthusiasm for nationalist ideals.

The ten years between 1906 and 1917 are known as the *Adradzhen'nye*, or the Revival, and are considered to be the formative period of Belorussian political nationalism. It was the time during which the national memory was organized and the demands for national self-determination were fostered. During the decade the national goal was articulated in terms of general culture and practical policies, and a generation of leaders capable of assuming the national leadership in Belorussia was educated.[3] Nevertheless, while Belorussian leadership was ready to move in the direction of independent statehood, the peasant masses in Belorussia remained passive and largely uninterested in the national idea.

An independent Belorussian state under Austro-German tutelage came briefly into existence at the end of World War I. On March 25, 1918, the self-appointed Minsk government issued a declaration of independence and announced the creation of the Belorussian National Republic (*Belaruskaya Narodnaya Respublika*)** and repudiated the Brest-Litovsk Treaty. The new republic claimed all of the territory where people spoke Belorussian; its birth was announced and a national flag of three horizontal stripes—white, red, white—was adopted.[4] The German military command sanctioned the creation of the new government.

Although still an occupied country, Belarus witnessed a revival of national life. The first Belorussian grammar was published, and the country saw the mushrooming of newspapers and journals in the Belorussian language. Still, the weak and divided government was able to maintain its control over the territory only as long as the German army of occupation remained in place. With the defeat of the Central Powers and the subsequent German evacuation, the Minsk government collapsed. The Reds occupied Minsk, and on January 1, 1919, the Belorussian Soviet Socialist Republic was formed. In February 1919 the Polish army occupied Bialystok and Grodno, thus effectively eliminating the last vestiges of Belorussian independence.[5]

Independence lasted in Belorussia ten months. It was never sanctioned by popular election and was in large part brought about by a self-appointed government maintained by the Austro-German occupation forces and lacking the necessary prerequisites for international recognition. Still, the brief existence of the Belorussian National Republic gave birth to a national myth of Belorussian statehood; March 25, 1918, is celebrated by Belorussian nationalists as independence day.[6]

The Belorussian Soviet Socialist Republic gave the administrative framework to the Belorussian state. The territory of Soviet Belorussia covered 49,022 square miles, with a population of 5,567,976, of which 80 percent were Belorussians, with the Jews and the Russians constituting the two largest minorities. Soviet support for the idea of a Belorussian republic integrated with the U.S.S.R. was to serve the purpose of bringing Belorussian nationalism to the side of communist ideology. In a more general sense, it was a direct consequence of the Soviet attempt to integrate nationalism with world revolutionary forces and then to use it to explode from within the existing social order in the West. Finally, it was a means of "selling communism" to those who showed little enthusiasm for the idea itself. Hence, the initial period of aggressive Belorussification in East Belorussia was treated by Moscow as an accept-

---

**The term *narodnaya* can also be translated as "people's"; however, considering the connotation given the term by the communists, it is translated here as "national" to reflect the political makeup of the Provisional Government.

able price to pay for the larger goal. In effect, Belorussian nationalism and communism became almost identical in the first years after World War I in East Belorussia. As a result, between 1925 and 1929 a number of political emigres returned to Belorussia and, with few exceptions, the officials of the government in exile recognized the Belorussian SSR as an inheritor of the Belorussian National Republic.[7]

As the Soviets shifted their policy from world revolution to "socialism in one country," Belorussian nationalism became a target of repression in the name of state consolidation. By the fall of 1929 the whole Belorussian nationalist leadership was arrested and imprisoned. The country's elite was either liquidated in Belorussian jails or deported to Siberia. The purge proved to be immeasurably more ruthless than anything the Poles had ever administered in western Belorussia.[8] The Belorussian literary and cultural heritage was altered to reflect the "socialist content" demanded by Stalin. The history of Belorussia was rewritten on Moscow's orders to reflect the common development of the nations constituting the Soviet Union. The horrors of forced collectivization accompanied by peasant revolts and thousands of deaths from starvation, as well as the purge of the Belorussian Communist Party, completed the process of Sovietization. In order to speed up Russification, the Belorussian language was ordered changed to reflect the Russian, and in 1938 the teaching of Russian became compulsory in all national republics.

During World War II and German occupation, the largely positive attitude toward the Germans changed once the Wehrmacht moved east and was replaced by a civilian German administration intent only on exploiting the region. In addition to the German civilian and military administration, both of which treated Belorussia as a colony, a rudimentary local Belorussian administration was set up, complete with German-controlled Belorussian police. The mass extermination of the Jews, the arbitrary arrests, the preservation of the collective farms, and the draft of laborers to be shipped to Germany worked to change the initial positive reaction of the Belorussians toward the Germans to one of fear and hostility. The small number of Nazi collaborators among the Belorussians, some of them with strong fascist convictions of their own, was more than offset by the growing number of anti-German guerrilla bands roaming Belorussian forests. The belated German attempts to win the population over by allowing at least in theory private land ownership in 1943 and then, in 1944, setting up the Belorussian Central Council (*Belaruskaya Tsentralnaya Rada*), a new national convention, and the embryonic national Belorussian army known as Country's Defense (*Krayeva Abarona*) with the white-red-white national insignia on their caps came too late to change the popular mood and amount to much.[9]

The return of Soviets in the wake of German defeat was followed by yet more devastation, purges, and deportations of real and suspected German collaborators. Although the symbol of Belorussian national identity was retained, its content was subjected to an even more complete restructuring to reflect the Russian imperial design.

The Belorussian industrial base grew substantially during the years of Soviet power. Lacking a significant natural resource base, Belorussia became known as an "assembly-line republic," which supplied a range of products from tractors and heavy equipment to electronics and consumer goods to the rest of the U.S.S.R. Collectivized agriculture of the republic was productive enough to provide for self-sufficiency in basic grain production and to meet a substantial portion of its demand for meat, although the republic still needed to import some food.

Until the arrival of Mikhail Gorbachev's *perestroika* reforms, Belorussian nationalism in the traditional sense was predominantly a prerogative of the Belorussian emigre community scattered throughout the globe. It is a dubious tribute to the success of Soviet assimilation policies that Belarus today, although formally an independent state within the CIS, has accepted substantial constraints on its state sovereignty, including the permission for Moscow to station troops on its territory. The contrast between rebellious nationalist Ukraine and docile Belorussia could not be greater. Even the 1986 Chernobyl nuclear power plant disaster, which left most of Belorussia contaminated with radioactive debris, failed to rouse Belorussian nationalist passions.

The weak national movement in Belorussia was organized into several clubs, dissident organizations, and youth associations. The organizational consolidation came late relative to dissident and nationalist movements in other republics, when in June 1989 the Belorussian Popular Front was established. In a telling display of listlessness at home, the Belorussian Popular Front was set up in Vilnius in Lithuania, because of the pressure against independence exercised by the Russians at home.

POSTCOMMUNIST BELARUS: THE "RELUCTANT REPUBLIC"

Independence came to Belorussia not as a result of a domestic upheaval but as a byproduct of nationalist activism along its periphery; more specifically, on account of Russian President Boris Yeltsin's decision to dissolve the U.S.S.R. As late as March 17, 1991, in a national referendum on the future of the republic, 83 percent of Belorussians voted for the preservation of the union, substantially exceeding the all-union average of 76.4 percent.[10] The rise of national discontent came late, with a wave of work stoppages in April 1991 on account of the projected steep price increases caused by union-wide inflation. The protest action escalated by April 23 to a general strike in factories in Minsk, Orsha, Gomel, and Saligorski.[11] The strikers' agenda evolved from demands for wage compensation to calls for multiparty parliamentary elections, Belorussian independence and sovereignty, and an end to the communist monopoly of political power. However, the government quickly defused the situation by granting across-the-board wage increases and by relying on the official trade unions to calm the workers. By the end of May 1991, the Belorussian Communist Party was again firmly in control, while the Supreme Soviet of the Republic of Belarus (*Vyarkhoyny Savet Respubliki Belarus'*) rejected the demands for sovereignty as unconstitutional. Likewise, the Belorussian communists came out strongly in support of the aborted August 1991 coup.

The collapse of the coup forced the Belorussian communists to accept the notion of sovereignty. On August 25 the Supreme Soviet declared Belorussia's political and economic independence, with the understanding that the goal was to preserve communist power. On September 19, 1991, the name "Belorussian Soviet Socialist Republic" was dropped in favor of the "Republic of Belarus." The Supreme Soviet also removed from the constitution all references to "Soviet" and "socialist" and adopted the national flag and national emblem. In October 1991 the Supreme Soviet elected Stanislau Shushkevich, a moderate democrat, as its chairman and passed a law on Belorussian citizenship.

The declaration of sovereignty led to increased political activism in Belarus. In 1991 two new political parties were registered, the Peasant Party and the Social Democratic Society.[12] Still, the key positions of power, with the notable exception of Shushkevich, remained firmly in the hands of the former communist *nomenklatura*, including the country's prime minister Vyacheslau Kebich.

On December 7 and 8, 1991 Shushkevich met with Russian President Boris Yeltsin and Ukrainian President Leonid Kravchuk to establish the Commonwealth of Independent States, with Minsk serving as the coordinating center for the new association. The meeting marked the final step toward the dissolution of the U.S.S.R. On December 10, 1991, the Belorussian Supreme Soviet accepted Shushkevich's argument that the union treaty was dead and it nullified the validity of all Soviet laws. In effect, independence was foisted on Belarus by the rising tide of nationalism in Ukraine and Yeltsin's decision after the failed coup to dissolve the union.

DOMESTIC POLITICS

Although with some hesitation, in 1992 Belarus began to move toward building an independent state. The preparations of a new constitution have been a landmark development on the road to full state sovereignty. Although a Supreme Soviet commission on constitutional reform had been set up in the summer of 1990, the July 27, 1990, Declaration of State Sovereignty served as a de facto constitution; after the failed August 1991 putsch, it was officially given the status of a law on the constitution.[13]

The first draft of the constitution was approved by the Supreme Soviet and published in November 1991. The second draft, with amended versions of 100 articles, was published on August 22, 1992. The second draft is currently being debated for possible adoption as the state's basic law. If approved, the new constitution will create a relatively weak parliament, while strengthening substantially the executive offices of the president and the chairman of the government.

In the second draft the term "Supreme Soviet" to describe the parliament is dropped in favor of the old Belorussian term *Soim*. The new parliament would have 160 deputies elected to a four-year term, half the number of the present Supreme Soviet deputies.[14] The *Soim* has among other things the powers to adopt, amend, and interpret the constitution and laws, call referendums and elections, pass legislation, approve the state budget, set taxes, declare war, and ratify international treaties. It elects the chairman of the government and, on his recommendation, the deputy chairmen, and ministers of foreign affairs, defense, and internal affairs. The *Soim* also elects the Constitutional Court, the Supreme Court, the Supreme Economic Court, and the chairman of the KGB. Finally, it appoints the prosecutor general and the chairman of the Belorussian National Bank.[15]

The second draft of the constitution adds the institution of the presidency. The idea of introducing the office of state president has been opposed in the parliament on the grounds that Belarus's weak parliamentary tradition will make the system susceptible to manipulation by a strong executive. According to the second draft, the president is elected by direct vote to a five-year term, with a limit of two consecutive terms. The president is the head of state, with the power to nominate the chairman of the government, the Supreme Court, the Supreme Economic Court, and the prosecutor general. He signs laws and has the right to veto legislation. He can dissolve the parliament if it fails to approve a government within a six-month period or if it fails to hold a compulsory vote of confidence twice a year. The president, however, does not have control over the armed forces; this power belongs to the chairman of the government.

The chairman of the government is the commander-in-chief of the armed forces in the event of martial law. He appoints his cabinet ministers, with the exception of those who require parliamentary approval. He has the right to veto decisions taken by local councils and can initiate the process of amending the constitution.

The principal opposition movement confronting the entrenched power of the former communists is the Belorussian Popular Front, founded in 1989 in Vilnius, Lithuania, because of the government's refusal to allow its headquarters in Belorussia. Over the two years of national independence, opposition in the Belorussian Supreme Soviet began to solidify and gain strength. After two years of operations directed from Lithuania, the Popular Front headquarters finally moved to Belorussia. In February 1992 the principal opposition force in the parliament, the Belorussian Popular Front headed by Zyanon Paznyak, began to ask for new parliamentary elections to provide for a truly representative legislature. A national movement, *Novaya Belarus*, led by Paznyak and unifying a number of opposition political parties called for a national referendum to determine whether the Belorussians were in favor of an early election.[18] By August 1992, Paznyak's group had collected the required 350,000 signatures to hold the national referendum; however, the government moved to invalidate the petition drive on procedural grounds.[16] The chairman of the Supreme Soviet, Stanislau Shushkevich, rejected the referendum idea as a ploy by the Popular Front to seize power.[17] The opposition refused to give in.

In 1992–1993 noncommunist political parties in Belarus were clearly at an initial stage of development. The existing small organizations, some of which were not well known or recognized in the republic, included the Social Democratic Party (moderate nationalist), the United Democratic Party (liberal), the National Democratic Party (moderately nationalist), the Christian Democratic Union, and the People's Accord Party (left-leaning, with a considerable number of former communists).[19] The apparent weakness of the nascent political parties in Belarus is largely due to the lack of a new constitutional framework and, most important, the absence of genuine electoral experience and the continued influence of the communists.

Arguably, the key problem facing Belarus today is the weak national identity of its people. The problem is cultural, rather than ethnic, with russification having been most successful in Belarus, among all non-Russian republics. The Belarus population today is 80 percent Belorussian, but 30 percent of the Belorussian ethnics speak only Russian; 60 percent speak both Russian and Belorussian; 10 percent of the ethnic Belorussians speak only Belorussian. More important, the political and administrative elite is thoroughly russified, and it is interesting that even the tiny staff of the Belarus embassy in Washington, D.C., seems to use Russian as their primary tongue.

ECONOMIC POLICY

Belarus has been remarkably slow in adapting to the market economy. However, the progressive deterioration of the Russian market and the inflationary pressures within the CIS ruble zone are forcing Minsk to rethink its policies. As the economic situation deteriorated in early 1992, the government moved to impose "transit taxes" on pipelines carrying gas and oil from Russia to Europe.[20]

The Russian market continues to be the key to Belarus's survival. The country remains totally dependent on Russian supplies of fuel and raw materials. In April 1993, when Russia increased tariffs and made Belorussian goods even less competitive, the country was confronted with the prospects of a severe economic crisis. Rather than seeking to diversify its markets, Minsk opted to rely on political rapprochement with Russia. The idea of an economic union with Russia, introduced by Prime Minister Kebich and strongly supported by the former communist deputies in the parliament and by the Belorussian military, includes a common currency, a common banking and credit system, the elimination of all trade barriers, and possibly a unified Belorussian-Russian state budget.[21]

The principle of maintaining close ties to Russia has been strongly supported by the managers of large state enterprises, which have faced a threat of bankruptcy without access to the Russian market. This is especially true about Belarus's defense industry, where the loss of Russian orders threatens to eliminate about 300,000 jobs. According to Supreme Soviet chairman Stanislau Shushkevich, half of the republic's industrial production is defense related.[22]

Belarus's industry remains vitally dependent on Russia not only for markets but also for the majority of its raw materials. According to the U.S. Department of Commerce, Belarus gets 70 percent of its raw materials from Russia. Even more important is the republic's reliance on Russia for 90 percent of its primary energy needs. The International Monetary Fund estimated that in 1991 net energy imports cost Belorussia the equivalent of $5 billion.[23] Hence, the drastic reduction in both Russian markets and the supply level of Russian raw materials has dealt a blow to Belarus's economy. According to the European Bank for Reconstruction and Development, real GDP declined by 15 percent in 1992, after dropping about 6 percent over the previous two years.[24]

So far, economic reform in Belarus has been limited in scope. In January 1992 the government announced a price reform, which freed prices of some 80 percent of wholesale goods and services. As of mid-1993, food and energy subsidies remained largely intact and amounted to about 20 percent of the state budget.[25] Likewise, privatization has made little progress, although on January 20, 1993, the Supreme Soviet passed a limited law on privatization. Still, the majority of the industry remains state-owned and land ownership is still prohibited, although peasants can lease land for up to ninety-nine years. Foreign investment is limited, with only some 150 joint ventures registered as of mid-1993. In 1993 large-scale privatization was put off and no references to land privatization were made.

Belorussian monetary policy has reinforced the country's continued dependence on Russia. Belarus has remained in the Russian ruble zone, with a limited introduction of the Belorussian coupon (Belorussian ruble), which, however, is used mainly in commercial transactions.

FOREIGN AND SECURITY POLICY

Since independence Belarus has steered a course closer to Russia than any other former Soviet republic. Historically, Russia considered Belarus its vital link to the West, more so even than Ukraine. The Belarus government sees the country's future in close relations with Russia, as demonstrated by the acceptance of a nonnuclear status and a number of cooperative agreements signed by the two countries. The prospects for an even closer relationship to Russia, including at some future date a confederation of the two, cannot be ruled out. The Belarus government has amply demonstrated that it wants the CIS formula to work.

Belarus made no effort to form a national army until March 1991, when the opposition Belorussian Social Democratic Party (BSDP) issued a call for the creation of a national army. In August of 1991, following an appeal by the BSDP, the Belorussian Association of Servicemen (*Belaruskae Zhurtavanne Vaiskoutsau*) was established and issued a call for the immediate creation of a national military force. On October 25, 1991, the creation of a Ministry of Defense and a national guard was proposed; the proposal to establish the ministry was approved in November.[26]

The new military doctrine accepted by the Supreme Soviet in November 1992 contains general statements on neutrality and focuses predominantly on the reorganization of the army. The critical aspect of the policy is Belarus's renunciation of nuclear weapons. In addition, in February 1993, the Belorussian Supreme Soviet ratified the START-1 Treaty, the Lisbon Protocol, and the Nuclear Nonproliferation Treaty, as well as two agreements with Russia governing the procedures for controlling the remaining nuclear weapons in Belarus prior to their transfer to Russia.[27] Considering the virtual absence of parliamentary opposition to the denuclearization policy, the future national armed forces of Belarus are likely to be solely conventional.

On January 28, 1992, Petr Chaus, former chief of staff of the Baltic Military District, was selected to head the newly created Belarus Ministry of Defense.[28] Chaus then proceeded to organize the skeleton of the new army based on the former Belorussian Military District.

Chaus was replaced in April 1993 by Pavel Kazlouski. The new Belarus national army as envisioned by Defense Minister Kazlouski would number approximately 90,000. In the new force structure, airborne, air-defense assault units would replace the Soviet tank formations. The new law setting up the Belarus Ministry of Defense and approving the text of the new oath to be administered to the military personnel was approved by the parliament on January 11, 1992. The same session of the parliament approved the transfer of control over all former Soviet troops stationed in Belarus.[29]

Belorussian defense policy appears to be increasingly driven by a commitment to good relations with neighboring countries, especially Russia. This is not surprising considering that during the Soviet period Belarus provided the Soviet military with more officers than any other republic except Russia itself.[30] In contrast to the position taken by neighboring Ukraine, Belarus early on expressed its commitment to becoming a nonnuclear state. On January 26, 1992, the deputy chairman of the security committee of the Belarus parliament, Leonid Privalau, announced the shipment of the first batch of Belorussian nuclear weapons to Russia for dismantling. Privalau indicated that Belarus expected to be free of all nuclear weapons no later than 1996 or 1997. Belorussian Foreign Minister Petr Krauchenka declared his country's security policy goal to become the first nonnuclear member of the CIS.[31] In the interim, all nuclear weapons still on Belorussian territory are firmly under Russian control. The excellent working relationship between the Russian and Belorussian military was recognized by General Yevgeniy Shaposhnikov, the CIS commander-in-chief. It is striking that only on December 31, 1992, over a year since the creation of independent Belarus, was the military finally administered an oath of allegiance to the new state. The oath did not stipulate that the soldier had to be a citizen of Belarus.

The military seems to play an increasingly important role in Belorussian domestic politics. The second draft of the Belorussian constitution, currently under review, explicitly identifies the minister of defense as the highest military commander in the republic. In effect, the minister of defense holds a much more powerful political position than at any time during the Soviet period.[32] Attempts to assert complete national control over security policy and military forces have been sporadic and have come largely from the civilian side. For example, in February 1992, the chairman of the Belorussian Commission on National Security, Mechislau Hrib, rejected the notion of creating unified CIS military forces, arguing that such a solution would be inappropriate because no unified state existed.[33]

The new national defense doctrine approved by the Belorussian Supreme Soviet identifies the potential for conflict involving territorial disputes along the republic's periphery. However, in addition to strong ties to Russia, Belarus's relations with Poland, which prior to World War II had controlled western Belorussian territory, are good following the April 1993 technical military cooperation agreement between the two countries. Likewise, relations with Lithuania, where potential for a territorial dispute over the Vilnius region exists, are good. The Popular Front opposition in the Supreme Soviet considers potential instability in Russia as the greatest threat to the security of Belarus and to the country's continued independent status.

Nothing is more indicative of the direction of Belarus's security policy than the April 9, 1993, vote by the Belorussian Supreme Soviet approving the state's inclusion in a 1992 Commonwealth of Independent States' collective security agreement. The agreement, put forth by Prime Minister Vyacheslau Kebich as part of his CIS economic integration program, was strongly supported by the military, while the Supreme Soviet chairman, Stanislau Shushkevich, and the Popular Front deputies denounced it as undermining the nation's pledge of neutrality and nonparticipation in military blocs.[34] In the aftermath of the vote, Shushkevich called for a national referendum in a month's time to gauge if the Belorussian voters supported the CIS security pact, but the referendum proposal was rejected by the parliament's communist majority.

The proposal to restore Belarus's security ties to Russia was strongly supported by the People's Movement of Belarus, a bloc that includes communist groups, the Union of Afghanistan Veterans, the Union of Officers of Belarus, and pan-Slavic organizations such as White Rus and Slavic Assembly.[35] The old-time communists scored an important victory in February 1993 when the ban on the activities of the Belorussian Communist Party was lifted.

It appears that in the long run Belarus may not be able to abide by its declaration of neutrality on security matters. Even though Belarus's adherence to the Tashkent security pact with Russia is conditional on Belorussian forces not being used outside the country's territory, and on the provision that the pact will automatically expire once Russian troops and nuclear weapons have been withdrawn from Belarus, the alliance has been a significant step in the direction of renewed alignment with Russia. In 1993, continued security cooperation with Russia was supported by both Prime Minister Kebich and Defense Minister Kazlouski, while Supreme Soviet chairman Shushkevich opposed continued ties to Russia as disadvantageous to the country's continued political independence.

BELARUS OR BELORUSSIA?

One has to keep in mind that the formative period of the Belorussian state administration was in the context of the Soviet Union, with the economy and the administration controlled directly from Moscow. In light of centuries of uninterrupted foreign domination by Lithuania, Poland, and Russia, Belarus lacks but the most tenuous historical attributes of independent statehood. Historically, western Belorussia was dominated by the Polish cultural ethos; eastern Belorussia was dominated by the Russian culture. In addition to the staggering cost of German occupation, which accounted for 2.2 million Belorussian lives, Belorussia was also an area where Soviet genocide took place. The mass graves at Kuropaty hold some 300,000 bodies. Finally, Belorussia was especially singled out for Russification, becoming a showcase of the alleged "merging together" of the Soviet nations. It took Gorbachev's *perestroika* to bring about nationalist reawakening in Belorussia, with the 1986 demands for reintroducing Belorussian as the official language of the republic. Still, the official reaction to the pressure for the republic's greater independence was virtually nil. Even in the aftermath of the Chernobyl nuclear plant disaster, which brought about devastation exceeding that in Ukraine, the Belorussian authorities reportedly followed orders from Moscow to confiscate all geiger counters.[36]

The prospects for the country's continued independence are questionable in light of the overwhelming odds against it. The history of Russian domination and the nature of Belorussian political elites suggest that statehood will not translate into complete independence from Russia; rather, Belarus will continue to follow Moscow's lead on key economic policy, foreign policy, and security issues. The agreements between Moscow and Minsk to extend the Russian ruble zone to Belarus and to coordinate military planning and the forced resignation of Supreme Soviet chairman Stanislau Shushkevich in January 1994 suggest that the process of bringing Belarus back into Russia's orbit may have already started.

NOTES

1. Nicholas P. Vakar, *Belorussia: The Making of a Nation* (Cambridge, Mass.: Harvard University Press, 1956), pp. 1–2.

2. Ibid., p. 74.

3. Ibid., p. 91.

4. *Karotki aglyad gistoryi Belarusi* (Tallinn: Belaruskaye Kulturnaye Tavarystva "Grunvald," 1990), p. 73.

5. Vakar, *Belorussia*, p. 108.

6. Ibid., pp. 105–106.

7. Ibid., p. 145.

8. Ibid., p. 146.

9. Ibid., p. 202.

10. Kathleen Mihalisko, "Belorussia: Setting Sail without a Compass," *RFE/RL Research Report*, January 3, 1992, p. 39.

11. Ibid., p. 40.

12. Ibid., p. 41.

13. Alexander Lukashuk, "Belorussian Draft Constitution: A Controversial Step Forward," *RFE/RL Research Report*, October 30, 1992, p. 43.

14. Ibid., p. 45.

15. Ibid., p. 46.

16. Each page of the petition was to be signed by the chairman of the group organizing the petition drive; however, instead of actually signing each page the chairman stamped his name. *Report of the IFES Delegation Examining the Evolution of the Election Process in Belarus, March 20–24, 1992* (Washington, D.C.: International Foundation for Electoral Systems, 1992), p. 11.

17. Igor Sinyakevich, "Stanislau Shushkevich ne khochet referenduma," *Nezavisimaya Gazeta*, October 3, 1992, p. 3.

18. "Belorussian Opposition Predicts Victory by This Fall," *RFE/RL Daily Report*, February 5, 1992.

19. *Report of the IFES Delegation*, p.15.

20. "Belarus Eyes Pipelines as Source of Income," *RFE/RL Daily Report*, February 5, 1992.

21. Kathleen Mihalisko, "Belarus: Neutrality Gives Way to 'Collective Security,' " *RFE/RL Research Report*, April 23, 1993, p. 26.

22. Ustina Markus, "Belarus Debates Security Pacts as a Cure for Military Woes," *RFE/RL Research Report*, June 18, 1993, p. 69.

23. *The Republic of Belarus Commercial Overview* (Washington, D.C.: BISNIS, U.S. Department of Commerce, 1993), p. 2.

24. Ibid.

25. Ibid., p. 3.

26. Markus, "Belarus Debates Security Pacts," p. 67.

27. Ibid., p, 69.

28. "Belarus Defense Minister Is Appointed," *RFE/RL Daily Report*, January 29, 1992.

29. "Belarus Takes Charge of Non-Strategic Forces," *RFE/RL Daily Report*, January 13, 1992.

30. *Report of the IFES Delegation*, p. 5.

31. "Belarus Wants to Be First Nuclear-Free State in CIS," *RFE/RL Daily Report*, January 27, 1992.

32. Lukashuk, "Belorussian Draft Constitution," p. 47.

33. "Belorussian Official Finds Most Military Proposals Unacceptable," *RFE/RL Daily Report*, February 12, 1992.

34. Mihalisko, "Belarus: Neutrality Gives Way," p. 24.

35. Ibid., p. 25.

36. *Report of the IFES Delegation*, p. 3.

11

UKRAINE

THE RISE OF THE UKRAINIAN NATION

Ukraine is the largest non-Russian successor state to the Soviet Union. The size of its territory of over 6,000 square kilometers makes it the second-largest country in Europe after Russia. Ukraine's population of approximately fifty-two million and its nuclear-power status make the country a vital part of the post–Cold War European order. At the same time, the newly established Ukrainian state has virtually no historical experience of statehood. It is a country where national identity developed under conditions of statelessness.[1]

The word *Ukraina* in both Russian and Ukrainian means literally "border-lands." It has been for centuries the cultural border between the East and the West. Ukraine lies on the threshold of Asia and along the fringes of the Mediterranean world. It is situated at what was once the border between the open steppe and the forests. Except for the Carpathian Mountains in the west and the small Crimean range in the south, Ukraine is 95 percent steppe cut by three major rivers flowing south to the Black Sea: the Dnieper (Dnipro), the Bug (Buh), and Dniester (Dnister). About two-thirds of Ukraine's territory is the exceptionally fertile *chernozem*, agriculturally rich black soil.

The Ukrainians trace their roots to the East Slavs inhabiting the right bank of the Dnieper River. They see the origin of their statehood in the experience of Kievan Rus in the Middle Ages and in the seventeenth-century Cossack state. The Ukrainian national experience has been molded by a history of outside domination, first by the Mongols after the collapse of the Kievan Rus in 1240, then by the Poles and Lithuanians until the decline of the Polish-Lithuanian

Commonwealth in the eighteenth century, by the Russians, by the Austrians (especially in the western parts of the country in Galicia), after the 1917 Bolshevik revolution by the Russians and, during the interwar period, by the Second Polish Republic. The period of Polish-Lithuanian domination brought Westernizing influences, especially Catholicism, to the predominantly Greek Orthodox Ukrainians. The result was the rise of Ukrainian and Belorussian Catholics known as the Uniates or Greek Catholics, who recognize the authority of the pope.

The experience of the Cossack state plays prominently in Ukrainian national consciousness. In 1648 the great Ukrainian uprising started by Bohdan Khmelnytsky led the Cossacks against Poland-Lithuania in a successful rebellion. The Cossacks, or "free men," first appeared in the Dnieper basin in the 1480s. They were predominantly runaway peasants, defrocked priests, burghers, bankrupt noblemen, and criminals running away from the courts to the vast steppes where Warsaw could never exercise effective control, despite the attempts to introduce the "register" of the Cossack units to serve under Polish command. The majority of the Cossacks lived outside the state authority with their own organization and raided the Turks and the Tatars, as well as the Russians and the Poles.

The independent Cossack state lasted less than a decade. In 1654 after protracted fighting with the Poles Khmelnytsky accepted Russian overlordship over Ukraine. From then on Ukraine became a prize in the war for its control between Poland and Russia, and by the end of the seventeenth century the Poles had reasserted their control over the right bank. However, the continued decline of the Polish-Lithuanian Commonwealth and Russian westward expansion in the eighteenth century brought about the complete destruction of the Cossack state. Ukraine became a province of the Russian empire.

The nationalist reawakening of the Ukrainian people has its roots in the growing interest of the Ukrainian intelligentsia beginning in the late eighteenth century in the Cossack tradition. Next came the interest in refining and uplifting the Ukrainian vernacular. The beginnings of written Ukrainian date back to 1780, with the publication of the first poem in Ukrainian.[2] However, the vernacular remained until the mid-nineteenth century largely confined to peasants and townsfolk, as the educated Ukrainian elite continued to speak Polish or Russian. Among the Ukrainian poets of the nineteenth century, Taras Shevchenko emerged as a master of the national language.

In the wake of Russia's defeat in World War I an attempt was made to create an independent Ukrainian state led by Symon Petliura, first independently and then in alliance with Poland. The infant Ukrainian state collapsed, however, in the face of concerted pressure from the Bolsheviks, the Romanians, the Hungarians, and the Poles, all of whom laid claim to various parts of Ukrainian territory. The Polish-Soviet war of 1919–1920, despite initial Polish successes, including the occupation of Kiev, ended in disaster for Ukrainian nationalists. The Red Army counteroffensive in 1920 overran all of Ukrainian territory and came close to destroying the nascent Polish state. Although the Poles managed to defeat the Russians at the gates of Warsaw and drive them out of their historical eastern territory, the fate of an independent Ukrainian state was sealed. The new border between Poland and the Soviet state left most of Ukrainian territory in the U.S.S.R.

During the interwar period Ukraine suffered terrible devastation under the communists. On Stalin's orders the great terror that accompanied collectiviza- tion fell the hardest on Ukraine, leading to a government-induced famine in 1932–1933.[3] Western Ukraine, which had been under Polish control until the outbreak of World War II, witnessed persistent tension between the Poles and the Ukrainians. In 1930 there were a number of attacks against Polish properties in western Ukraine, to which Warsaw responded with a "pacification campaign" by the Polish armed forces. A Ukrainian minority in Romania was also re- pressed; only in Slovakia did the conditions of a Ukrainian minority improve in the interwar period. It is not surprising then that in 1941, during the early stages of the German attack on the Soviet Union, the Ukrainians often wel- comed the entering Wehrmacht forces as their liberators.

The goal of Ukrainian independence remained the driving force of the Ukrainian emigre community. After 1929 the establishment of the Organization of Ukrainian Nationalists (OUN) in Vienna began a concerted campaign to establish an independent Ukrainian state.

During the war the Ukrainian Insurgent Army (*Ukrainska Povstanska Armiia*; UPA) became an active force in the Volhynia and other regions fighting the Germans, Soviets, and Poles alike. Led initially by Taras Bulba-Borovets, the UPA was about 40,000 strong and remained an effective force well into the late 1940s. It was finally destroyed during the so-called Vistula Operation, a coordinated campaign by Soviet and Polish forces in 1947, which included transferring entire Ukrainian villages to deprive the UPA guerrillas of their support base.

As late as the beginning of this century Ukraine was predominantly an agrarian society. It became industrialized in a particularly traumatic fashion and largely within the confines of Soviet economic planning. Ukraine modernized under Soviet domination, developing coal mining, iron-ore mining, and man- ganese mining, as well as machine-building, chemical, and defense industries and nuclear power. Ukraine remained the principal agricultural producer of the U.S.S.R., supplying the lion's share of the union's meat and grain. Indicative of the extent of Ukraine's transformation under Soviet control, when the Soviet Union was formally dissolved in 1991 Ukraine employed 41 percent of its labor force in industry and construction and only 19 percent in agriculture.[4]

The Ukrainian road to complete independence from Russia was driven by the rising tide of nationalist sentiment in the western and central regions of the republic. The organization that declared independence as its goal, *Rukh* (Movement), was created in 1989 and within two years reached 700,000 members. *Rukh* was largely a creation of anticommunists; its principal political rivals are former communistis.

Although the Communist Party itself had been disbanded after the 1991 August putsch, the Socialist Party of Ukraine (*Sotsialisticheskaya Partiya Ukrainy*; SPU) assumed its mantle. While *Rukh* had most of its constituents in western and central regions of the republic, the SPU was the strongest in the eastern regions.

Ukraine declared sovereignty in July 1990 and complete independence in August 1991 on the heels of the failed August putsch.

DOMESTIC POLITICS SINCE 1991

Ukraine became formally independent on December 1, 1991, when 90 percent of the population voted for independence. On the same day the country elected its first democratically chosen president. Former Communist Party leader Leonid Kravchuk became the first president, with over 61 percent of the vote.[5] The republic's decision to refuse participation in the Union Treaty promoted by Gorbachev accelerated the disintegration of the U.S.S.R. The results of the referendum were remarkable in that eleven million of Ukraine's fifty-two million people are Russian. They constitute a majority in the country's eastern parts, especially in the Donets (Donbas) Basin industrial region as well as a substantial group in the Crimea. According to the 1989 census, 72.7 percent of Ukraine's population was ethnically Ukrainian, with ethnic Russians accounting for 21.1 percent of the population.[6] Although Ukraine has a number of ethnic groups other than Russians, such as Jews, Poles, and Hungarians, Russian ethnics are the largest and the most important minority group.

In October 1989 Ukraine passed a law that made Ukrainian the sole official language in state offices and schools. After independence, the country moved to create an independent national army and independent currency. The law on the official language has created considerable controversy in Donbas and in the Crimea, with the Crimean parliament and the Donetsk-based Civic Congress of Ukraine calling in late 1992 for legislation that would make Russian the second official language in Ukraine.[7]

In addition to the former communists, the principal political organizations in Ukraine include *Rukh*, the Congress of National Democratic Forces (KNDS), and the center-left New Ukraine. In 1992 the political landscape was changed by the resurgence of Ukrainian communists. In the summer of 1992 the growing hard-line pressure from the communists to dissolve the parliament brought *Rukh* and the New Ukraine into a coalition called "For an Independent Ukraine—a New Parliament" (*Koalitsiya "Nezaleznii Ukraini–Novyi Parlament"*), which then launched an unsuccessful campaign for a new parliamentary election. At the same time, the Ukrainian Republican Party and the Democratic Party of Ukraine cooperated within the pro-Kravchuk KNDS.[8] In February 1993, when *Rukh* registered as a political party, the movement was led by Vyacheslav Chornovil. At the time it had 52,000 full members and over 100,000 associate members, thus constituting the largest mass political organization in the country.[9]

The Congress of National Democratic Forces (*Kongress Natsionalno-Demokraticheskikh Sil Ukrainy*; KNDS) was established on August 2, 1992, and led by Mykhailo Horyn, formerly a leader of *Rukh*. KNDS is committed to the building of an independent Ukraine as the best guarantee against a resurgence of Russian imperialism. The KNDS coalition has brought together the Democratic Party of Ukraine (*Demokraticheskaya Partiya Ukrainy*) and the Ukrainian Republican Party (*Ukrainskaya Respublikanskaya Partiya*), as well as a number of smaller right-of-center political parties, including the Ukrainian Peasant Democratic Party, the Ukrainian Christian Democratic Party, the Ukrainian National Conservative Party, and the Ukrainian Language Society *Prosvita*.[10]

KNDS is the strongest supporter of President Kravchuk; it is often informally described as the "presidential party." Although its platform calls for the resignation of the government and it supports early parliamentary elections, KNDS maintains that the president must be supported as the guarantor of stability in the country. The KNDS leadership has talked about the need to build a "presidential republic" with a strong executive presidency.[11] The KNDS considers the passage of a new Ukrainian constitution a necessary precondition of continued independence.

On economic policy, KNDS supports market reforms, privatization, and an end to discrimination against the companies favoring foreign investment. In foreign policy KNDS calls for Ukraine's complete and unequivocal secession from the CIS.

The center-left in Ukrainian politics today is represented by the New Ukraine (*Novaya Ukraina*), established in January 1992. It describes itself as a "liberal-democratic movement of politicians, lawyers, and entrepreneurs."[12] Led by Volodymyr Filenko, the New Ukraine is committed to close ties with the rest of the former Soviet Union as essential to Ukraine's economic recovery. The New Ukraine claims a membership of 30,000 and declares itself in opposition to the parliament, the president, and the government. In June 1992 it called for the government's resignation, new parliamentary elections, and the creation of a government of experts to oversee economic reform and privatization. The New Ukraine's stand on the question of a referendum on new parliamentary elections brought it closer to *Rukh*, and the latter's objectives were being defined by Chornovil.[13]

In January and February 1993, a grand coalition of all democratic forces in Ukraine, called the Anti-Communist and Anti-Imperialist Front of Ukraine (AAFU), was established in response to the rising strength of the former communists. The AAFU was established after the issue of lifting the ban on the Communist Party was placed before the Ukrainian Supreme Council. Ivan Drach, one of the founding fathers and the first head of *Rukh*, assumed the leadership of the AAFU coordinating council. The AAFU constitutes an umbrella organization bringing together *Rukh*, and the KNDS (the Ukrainian Republican Party, and the Democratic Party of Ukraine), which united in their opposition to the communist threat notwithstanding their political differences. The AAFU's primary objective is the continued opposition to the communists, the dissolution of the parliament, the creation of a constituent assembly, and the adoption of the new constitution, as well as rapid market reform, the strengthening of Ukraine's independence, and the complete dissolution of the CIS.[14]

The Ukrainian government was led by Vitold Fokin until September 1992, when he was replaced by Leonid Kuchma following a growing opposition in the parliament led by *Rukh* to Fokin's economic policies of continuing price controls and delaying economic reforms. The removal of Fokin was not tantamount to the replacement of his entire cabinet; rather, it was apparently a political expedient by President Kravchuk, who insisted on retaining the core of Fokin's cabinet. The ensuing confrontation between the president and the parliament led to the legislative action forcing the resignation of the entire cabinet and rejecting Kravchuk's first choice for the new prime minister.[15] On October 13, 1992, Kravchuk's nomination of Leonid Kuchma for prime minister was approved, and so were his new cabinet choices. Kuchma, a mechanical engineer and the former general director of the Dnipropetrovsk missile plant, was appointed with the expectation that he would pursue policies aimed at a gradual transition to a market economy. Upon taking office, Kuchma maintained that the privatization of Ukraine's economy was long overdue.[16] As the economy worsened, Kuchma was dismissed in 1993.

ECONOMIC POLICY

The Ukrainian economy is in disarray, with an inflation rate that, estimated in 1991 at an annual level of 83 percent, had by mid-1993 reached the level of hyperinflation, being rated consistently in 1993 at over 50 percent per month.[17] By 1993 the country's economic policy had become one of the points of contention in the power struggle among President Leonid Kravchuk, Prime Minister Leonid Kuchma, and the Ukrainian Supreme Council.

As a result of the different visions of economic policy, the structural transformation of Ukraine's economy has been slow. In March 1992 Kravchuk presented to a closed session of the Supreme Council his strategy for having Ukraine leave the common economic area of the CIS. The proposal was accepted by an overwhelming majority in the legislature, with only twenty-four votes opposed to the plan.[18] The plan was drafted by the Ukrainian State Council (*Gosudarstvennaya Duma Ukrainy*), established in February of 1992 to advise the president and headed by Kravchuk.

The "Foundations of the National Economic Policy of Ukraine," as the program was called, made control over economic policy the highest priority. It blamed Ukraine's continued economic problems on residual Russian influence in the areas of price, monetary, and fiscal policies and described continued economic dependence on Russia as a threat to Ukraine's sovereignty. The only solution to Ukraine's continued economic dependence on Russia was, according to the plan, the country's prompt departure from the Russian ruble zone. The program also called for the creation of new foreign markets for Ukrainian goods and full internal convertibility of the Ukrainian currency by the end of 1992.[19]

As of 1993, Ukraine had failed to develop a comprehensive privatization strategy. The Law on Foreign Investment effective as of April 1, 1992, was a positive signal to Western investors interested in exploring business opportunities in Ukraine, but its overall impact was hampered by the uncertainty about the country's monetary and privatization policies.[20] The complex monetary situation has contributed to the confusion. In January 1992 Ukraine introduced the *karbovanets*, the Ukrainian ruble, to replace the Russian ruble; by November of 1992, the Ukrainian ruble effectively dominated market transactions in Ukraine. On November 12, 1992, Ukraine formally left the Russian ruble zone, following charges by Moscow that the Ukrainian National Bank was destabilizing the Russian currency situation by issuing large credits in noncash rubles.[21] Since then all accounting and transactions in Ukraine have been conducted in the *karbovanets*. Transition to a national currency in Ukraine was accelerated following Russia's decision in the summer of 1993 to invalidate a number of ruble notes. Ukrainian Prime Minister Leonid Kuchma asserted at a press conference in Kiev on August 4 that the Russian Central Bank's currency reform would help stabilize the *karbovanets*, but it did not.[22]

The most important problem facing Ukraine's economy is the absence of fundamental structural changes that would transfer the collective farms and state enterprises to private owners. As of mid-1993 Kiev had failed to introduce a large-scale privatization program, while the occasional spontaneous efforts at privatization were insufficient to bring about a balance in the economy. From 1991 through 1993 Ukraine lagged behind Russia in terms of structural economic changes.

Another problem facing Ukraine's economy is conversion from military to civilian industries. During the Soviet period Ukraine was a major producer of weapons, including tanks, missiles, and military aircraft. According to President Leonid Kravchuk, as of 1993 there were 344 defense enterprises in Ukraine; also, Ukraine accounted for 37 percent of the Soviet shipbuilding industry. By 1993 Ukraine registered a 70 percent decline in military orders for its defense factories and thus faced the prospect of massive layoffs in the defense industry.

In 1993 the movement for economic reform continued to face resistance from the entrenched old-style *nomenklatura* opposed to change. In a stark admission of failure, President Kravchuk's chief economic advisor, Viktor Suslov, conceded that the economic policies of 1991 and 1992 had failed to arrest the country's decline and expressed hopes that "the country will fare better in 1993." Still, Suslov warned that the future of economic reform in Ukraine will be decided by the outcome of political infighting between the government and the old guard. "Power struggle," admitted Suslov, "will largely determine next year's development, with government-launched reforms running against opposition from old structures which fear losing a grip on the country's economy."[23]

DEFENSE POLICY

Independent Ukraine has inherited between 10 percent and 15 percent of the defense potential of the former Soviet Union. Today the Ukrainian army stands at about 700,000. In addition, the state has nuclear missiles and nuclear-capable long-range TU-95 strategic bombers stationed at two airfields.

During the fall and winter of 1992 the Ukrainian parliament devoted much attention to the creation of a national army. By February 1992 seventy new laws defining the procedures for building up a national force were adopted by the Ukrainian Supreme Council. The legislation included a new military oath of allegiance to Ukraine, which was administered to the troops and officers despite Russia's official protest and the defection of several Russian crews. By early 1993 a number of laws were enacted outlining the formation of Ukrainian national armed forces. In addition, a new military doctrine that emphasizes the defense of the national territory was drafted and presented for evaluation by the Ukrainian Supreme Council Commission for Questions of Defense and State Security.[24]

The issue of control over Ukraine's nuclear weapons has remained at the core of the problem.[25] During the CIS summit on December 21, 1991, in Alma Ata, Ukraine agreed to transfer the nuclear weapons to Russia, to sign the Nuclear Nonproliferation Treaty (NPT) and the START treaties, and to adhere to the NPT regime as a nonnuclear state. The December 30, 1991, CIS Minsk agreement made Ukraine one of the three key states to decide the use of nuclear weapons, while in return Ukraine agreed to place all the weapons on its territory specifically under the control of the CIS joint command. Furthermore, the Minsk agreement stipulated that the tactical nuclear weapons in Ukraine would be dismantled by July 1, 1992, while the remaining strategic weapons were to be dismantled by 1994.

Until March 1992 the transfer of tactical nuclear weapons from Ukraine to Russia proceeded smoothly, with over half of the 3,000 nuclear weapons in Ukraine moved to Russia. It was expected that the process would be completed by May 1992. However, in March 1992 Ukrainian President Leonid Kravchuk halted the withdrawal, charging that Ukraine had no adequate assurances from Russia that the weapons were being dismantled. Ukraine argued that, instead of being destroyed, these weapons were being added to the Russian arsenal and called for international monitoring of the process. In addition, Kravchuk asked that the dismantling and reprocessing plant be established in Ukraine, near Chernobyl, to ensure Russian compliance and to give Ukraine access to the reprocessed nuclear material to fuel its nuclear power plants.

Kravchuk's decision led to immediate Western pressure on Ukraine to comply with the previous agreements. Quiet Russian-Ukrainian negotiations followed, as well as talks during a March CIS meeting in Kiev, which led to an agreement on April 16 to complete the withdrawal of tactical nuclear weapons, but the Ukrainian side insisted that 70 percent of the uranium removed from the missiles be returned for use as nuclear fuel in Ukrainian reactors. Kravchuk also argued that Russia had been the first to move for complete military independence of the CIS structures, by setting up its defense ministry and the armed forces.[26]

Kravchuk moved to assuage Western fears during a June 17, 1992, visit to France, where he assured French President Mitterrand that Ukraine intended to ratify both START treaties.[27] Still, pressure in the Ukrainian Supreme Council to assert complete national control over the nuclear weapons stationed in Ukraine continued to mount. On November 12, 1992, the Ukrainian U.N. mission released a statement in which it claimed that all property on the territory of Ukraine when the U.S.S.R. was dissolved belonged unequivocally to Ukraine, including strategic nuclear forces. The declaration marked an effective reversal of Ukrainian policy on the residual Soviet military assets.

In response to the Ukrainian assertion of the right to the nuclear weapons on July 6, 1992, the CIS joint command was reorganized and the Russian Defense Ministry was created to take over a large portion of the CIS joint command responsibilities. Shortly thereafter, the Russian strategic rocket forces command was set up—a clear recognition that the CIS joint command was no longer effective, even though Russia did not assert that the Russian strategic rocket forces were independent of the CIS command. Ukraine insisted that it could dismantle the weapons itself, provided Russia would supply $1.5 billion to establish the requisite facility. In July 1992, Ukraine took another step toward creating an independent military posture when it announced that it would not join the CIS air defense system and that it would concentrate instead on developing its own antiaircraft defenses.[28]

The January 15, 1993, Kravchuk-Yeltsin summit in Moscow to address the issue failed to break the deadlock over nuclear weapons control. Yeltsin's offer of a security guarantee to Ukraine in exchange for the missiles and the ratification of SALT-1 was rejected by the Ukrainian Supreme Council as insufficient. On July 2 the Ukrainian parliament issued a statement declaring all nuclear weapons in Ukraine to be the property of Ukraine. Shortly thereafter Kiev asserted that Ukraine would hold on to its forty-six SS-24 nuclear missiles even after the ratification of START-1.

Russian-Ukrainian tension over the nuclear weapons issue continued into 1993. On August 4, 1993, Moscow released an official statement charging that Kiev's recent actions with respect to the disposition of strategic nuclear weapons on its territory were in violation of a number of international agreements. The statement charged that the Ukrainian decision "threatened world stability."[29] The nuclear issue would not be resolved until 1994.

FOREIGN POLICY

Since independence, relations with Russia remain the key issue of Ukrainian foreign policy. The tense relationship between the two largest Soviet successor states can be described as bordering on a new "cold war." Kiev has regarded all Russian initiatives to maintain ties among the former Soviet republics with utmost suspicion. Ukraine has been opposed to all initiatives aimed at strengthening the Commonwealth of Independent States; rather, it has maintained that the CIS ought to be little more than a formula for the complete emancipation of the former Soviet republics. Ukraine has consistently opposed the creation of interstate coordinating agencies, as they would give Russia a greater amount of control. In Ukrainian President Kravchuk's words, "The draft charter of the CIS goes against Ukraine's orientation to independence."[30] According to Ukraine's Foreign Minister Anatoliy Zlenko, Ukrainian foreign policy is driven by the need "to do everything to ensure the peaceful development of our state."[31] In short, the foreign policy of the newly independent Ukrainian state has been defined by a sense of uncertainty about its continued independence in the face of the Russian giant and the realization of its vulnerability to Russian pressure.

For Russia the existence of an independent Ukrainian state has raised the question for the first time in three hundred years about whether Russia will remain a European state not only in a geographic but also in a political sense. Continued Ukrainian independence will be tantamount to Moscow's decisive break with its imperial past and will make it possible for Russia to become a nation-state.

Disagreement over borders, especially over which country ought to control Crimea and Donbas, have kept tensions high. Crimea, which had been transferred to Ukraine in 1954 by Nikita Khrushchev to commemorate the 1654 merging of Ukraine with Russia, has been viewed by the Russians as rightfully a part of the Russian Federation. For its part, Ukraine has maintained that the territorial status quo as of 1991 was binding and that border revisions were unacceptable. In an address to the Ukrainian Supreme Council on June 1, 1993, Prime Minister Leonid Kuchma suggested that perhaps Ukraine could lease the port of Sevastopol to Russia, but the proposal was rejected by the Ukrainian Ministry of Defense as inimical to the country's national security.[32]

Crimea is pivotal to the balance between Russian and Ukrainian presence in the Black Sea area. A large Russian presence is viewed by Ukraine as a threat, while a dominant Ukrainian presence is regarded by Russia as tantamount to its exclusion from the region. The question of the future status of Crimea is further complicated by the rise of a Crimean independence movement, which has called for a Crimean state independent of both Russia and Ukraine. In addition to the territorial dispute, the question of the rights of ethnic Russians in Ukraine has remained high on the agenda.

Another area of intense disagreement between Ukraine and Russia since 1991 has been the question of control over the armed forces, specifically the Black Sea navy. In 1993 Russia offered the Ukrainians only 20 percent of the 300 Black Sea ships, while Ukraine insisted on the right to control over 90 percent of all ships and submarines within its territory. The problem of control is complicated by the fact that only 31 percent of Black Sea navy officers and 62 percent of its sailors are ethnic Ukrainians.

The most intractable problem, however, has been the argument over who has the authority to control the nuclear weapons stationed on Ukraine's territory. Although formally committed to a nonnuclear status, until 1994 Ukraine resisted both Western and Russian pressure to transfer its nuclear weapons to Russian control, regarding its control over the missiles as a prerequisite of independence from Russia. In early 1994, Ukraine finally agreed to the transfer.

At the heart of Kiev's mistrust of Moscow's intentions lies the conviction that the majority of Russians still find it difficult to accept the reality of Ukrainian independence. Ukraine has regarded growing difficulties in Russian-Ukrainian trade as Russia's attempts to bring about the collapse of independent Ukraine. Clearly, from the Russian point of view, the loss of Ukraine is a blow to its overall economic potential, if one considers that during the Soviet period Ukraine accounted for 25 percent of Soviet food production, 22 percent of the U.S.S.R.'s industrial output, and close to 30 percent of Soviet weapons production. In early 1992, as Ukraine's economy faltered, Russia charged that Ukraine may eventually engage in exports of nuclear material in order to earn hard currency.[33]

The security imperative to offset potential Russian pressure has driven Ukrainian policy to seek closer ties with Germany as a reassurance against Moscow's pressure. Another important potential partner for Ukraine is Poland, which shares Ukraine's interest of preventing the restoration of the Russian empire. Ukraine demonstrated on several occasions in 1992 and 1993 that it was interested in a military alliance with Poland as insurance against the resurgence of Russian imperialism. Conversely, Poland has been the strongest supporter in Central Europe of Ukrainian national aspirations and was the first to recognize Ukraine as an independent state in 1991.

Ukraine also strives for closer collaboration with the Visegrad Group states of Poland, the Czech Republic, Slovakia, and Hungary, both to improve its economic situation and as the best avenue for closer relations with NATO. Again, the primary concern driving Ukrainian rapprochement with the Visegrad Group is the singular preoccupation with Russia's intentions. Ukraine has also attempted to build better relations with Belarus to offset Russia's preponderant influence in that state. In late December 1992, Belarus's Prime Minister Vyacheslau Kebich paid an official visit to Ukraine during which a number of bilateral agreements, including a military technical cooperation protocol, were signed.[34]

Concern about resurgent Russian imperialism has also informed Kiev's efforts to bring about closer Ukrainian-Turkish cooperation, which would present a check on Russian influence in the Caucasus and weaken Russian influence in the Black Sea area. Still, the Ukrainian-German relationship remains the key to Ukraine's Western foreign policy, for it is directly tied to the pivotal Russian-German relationship, which will be decisive in the future of postcommunist Central Europe.

Ukraine's most significant security policy initiative in 1993 was President Leonid Kravchuk's call for the creation of an East Central European security zone to provide for security in the region. The proposal was first advanced by Kravchuk during his meeting with Hungarian President Arpad Goncz and Prime Minister Jozsef Antall in February of 1993.[35] As Kravchuk envisioned it, the new security zone would not exclude Russia, nor would it constitute a military bloc; rather, it would create a security structure within the framework of European security. Following a favorable Hungarian response, Ukraine then raised the issue at a CSCE meeting and in bilateral talks with Slovakia, Romania, and Poland. However, as the Russians were not consulted, it would appear that in reality Russia would be excluded from the Kravchuk security zone, the all-inclusive rhetoric notwithstanding.

CAN INDEPENDENT UKRAINE SURVIVE?

In early 1994 Ukraine found itself in a protracted economic and political crisis. The foundations of the state's economy were shattered, with Russia now in a position to use its energy policy to exact concessions from the increasingly desperate Ukrainian government. President Kravchuk's nationalist policy, with its insistence on seeking alliances in the West and standing up to the Russians, has left Ukraine with a powerful enemy in the East while earning it preciously few friends in the West. The dispute with Moscow over the control of nuclear weapons, which Kiev considered a matter of national sovereignty and the state's long-term survival, was regarded in the West as yet another case of Ukrainian obstructionism. Today, few in Western Europe seriously entertain prospects of including Ukraine in the existing Western security system.

In the domestic arena, the dismissal of Premier Kuchma by Kravchuk in late 1993 demonstrated an ever-greater chaos within the administration. The ultimately incompatible policies of an uncompromising position toward Russia, supported by the western parts of the state, and the more pro-Russian attitudes in Donbas and in central Ukraine may force the fragmentation of the state itself unless a formula is found for lowering tensions with Russia and rebuilding the economy.

NOTES

1. Orest Subtelny, an authority on Ukraine, considers the experience of statelessness one of the principal themes of Ukrainian history. See Orest Subtelny, *Ukraine: A History* (Toronto: University of Toronto Press, 1992).

2. Ibid., p. 230.

3. For the authoritative study of the famine, see Robert Conquest, *The Harvest of Sorrow: Soviet Collectivization and the Terror-Famine* (New York: Oxford University Press, 1986).

4. *The World Factbook 1992* (Washington, D.C.: Central Intelligence Agency, 1992), p. 352.

5. Ibid.

6. *Narodnoye obrazovaniye i kultura v SSSR: statisticheskiy sbornik* (Moscow: Finansy i Statistika, 1989), p. 88.

7. Roman Solchanyk, "The Politics of Language in Ukraine," *RFE/RL Research Report*, March 5, 1993, p. 1.

8. Roman Solchanyk and Taras Kuzio, "Democratic Political Blocs in Ukraine," *RFE/RL Research Report*, April 16, 1993, p. 14.

9. Ibid., p. 15.

10. Vitaliy Portnikov, "Kongress dlya prezidentskoy respubliki," *Nezavisimaya Gazeta*, August 4, 1992, p. 3.

11. Ibid.

12. V. B. Grinev, " 'Novaya Ukraine': ispol'zovat' shans," *Nezavisimost'*, March 13, 1992, p. 3.

13. Solchanyk and Kuzio, "Democratic Political Blocs," p. 16.

14. Ibid., p. 17.

15. Roman Solchanyk, "Ukraine: The Politics of Economic Reform," *RFE/RL Research Report*, November 20, 1992, p. 3.

16. Ibid., p. 5.

17. Simon Johnson and Oleg Ustnko, "Ukraine Slips into Hyperinflation," *RFE/RL Research Report*, June 25, 1993, p. 24.

18. "Doklad L. Kravchuka proizvel effekt razorvavheysya bomby," *Komsomolskaya Pravda*, March 26, 1992, p. 1.

19. Ibid., p. 2.

20. "Business Potential in Ukraine Exists, But Is Hampered by Slow Reforms," *Perspectives* (Washington, D.C.: International Freedom Foundation), September 30, 1992, p. 1.

21. Johnson and Ustnko, "Ukraine Slips into Hyperinflation," p. 25.

22. *RFE/RL Daily Report*, August 5, 1993.

23. "The President's Chief Economic Aide Viktor Suslov," *FBIS-SOV-93-002*, January 5, 1993, p. 42.

24. "Commission Chairman Views Military Policy," *FBIS-SOV-93-002*, January 5, 1993, p. 39.

25. For an extensive discussion of the nuclear issue, see John W. R. Lepingwell, "Ukraine, Russia, and the Control of Nuclear Weapons," *RFE/RL Research Report*, February 19, 1993, pp. 4–20.

26. A television interview with Ukrainian President Leonid Kravchuk, *TsT*, March 22, 1993, 11:40 AM, "Posle vstrechi v Kiyeve," as quoted in *Russia and CIS Today* (Washington, D.C.: RFE/RL), March 22, 1993, p. 4.

27. "Kravchuk Begins France Visit, Meets Mitterrand, Endorses Nuclear Arms Accords," *FBIS-SOV-92-118*, June 18, 1992, p. 52.

28. "Republic Not to Join CIS Air Defense System," *FBIS-SOV-92-131*, July 8, 1992.

29. "More Russian Criticism of Ukrainian Nuclear Weapons' Policy," *RFE/RL Daily Report*, August 5, 1993.

30. "Kravchuk on Membership in CIS, Ties with Russia," *FBIS-SOV-93-001*, January 4, 1993, p. 44.

31. "Foreign Minister Interviewed on START, U.S. Ties," *FBIS-SOV-93-002*, January 5, 1993, p. 36.

32. Roman Solchanyk, "The Ukrainian-Russian Summit: Problems and Prospects," *RFE/RL Research Report*, July 2, 1993, p. 29.

33. "Ukraine: yadernyye zaryady stanut tovarom," *Krasnaya Zvezda*, February 12, 1992, p. 3.

34. "Belarus' Kebich Discusses Cooperation with Kravchuk," *FBIS-SOV-92-245*, December 21, 1992, p. 49.

35. Roman Solchanyk, "Ukraine's Search for Security," *RFE/RL Research Report*, May 21, 1993, p. 5.

CONCLUSION:
POSTCOMMUNIST EUROPE
IN THE NEW EUROPEAN ORDER
Moving West or Drifting Apart?

NATO'S POOR COUSINS

After the half-century of communist stasis, the emerging states of postcommunist Europe are again being defined by cultural and historical factors that have shaped their national identities for centuries. Likewise, the enduring geopolitical question about the relative influence of Germany and Russia in central and eastern Europe has resurfaced with a new urgency. The host of economic and political problems facing the region, the prolonged economic recession in Western Europe, and the new assertiveness in Russian foreign policy have combined to cool off the West's early enthusiasm for integrating the former Soviet satellites into the existing political, economic, and security structures. Four years after the implosion of the Soviet empire, the states of postcommunist Europe are today the affluent West's poor relations, whose kinship no one can deny but whose outright inclusion in the family may be judged too costly. They have received encouragement from the West, and limited economic assistance, but they remain largely on their own in the grey zone of post–Cold War European politics. Three principal factors will define the region's future: the gradual closing off of the Western institutions to the broader membership of postcommunist states, the relative influence of Russia and Germany, and the surge of postcommunist nationalism.

The prospects for the region's successful transformation to democracy remain uneven, ranging from relatively good for Poland, the Czech Republic, Hungary, Slovenia, and the Baltic states to discouraging for the war-torn Balkans and the Soviet successor states. However, even in the ethnically homogeneous countries with a long history of statehood, such as Poland and Hungary, populist appeals may result in dramatic political realignments such as the 1993 election of the communist-dominated parliament in Poland and in the prospect of a similar development when the Hungarians go to the polls in 1994. In the Balkans populist leaders such as Ion Iliescu in Romania or Slobodan Milosevic in Yugoslavia continue to dominate the political arena. For all indications, in postcommunist Europe nationalism has replaced communist ideology as an organizing principle and an increasingly powerful force in the politics of the newly independent states. Whatever the final outcome of their domestic transformation, the former politically uniform "East" has been replaced by a diverse group of states struggling, with greater or lesser degrees of success, to reconstitute themselves as independent polities.

Four years of postcommunist transition have shown that traditional power and geopolitical constraints remain decisive in determining both the region's politics and the West's responses to the changing environment. Postcommunist Europe continues to exist in a security vacuum. For the lack of better alternatives, the question of the place of the postcommunist states in the new order to emerge in Europe is at its core a question about the future of NATO and of the European Union. The past four years have demonstrated both the relative political and economic weakness of the emerging democracies and the growing ambivalence in the West about the efficacy of extending its institutions eastward, for that might put it on a collision course with Russia.

For postcommunist Europe, NATO's willingness to open itself to new members has become the litmus test of the West's intentions behind the rhetoric of pan-Europeanism. By the end of 1993 the tragedy of Bosnia-Herzegovina and the threat that the Balkan war might engulf Kosovo and Macedonia had failed to galvanize NATO into action that would forge a new security system in Europe. In geopolitical terms, the Balkan war has become a tolerable war, notwithstanding the moral outrage it has generated in the West. The West's determination not to intervene directly in the war has laid foundations for a policy of containing the conflict along its periphery. This has served as a powerful reminder to the former Soviet clients that in the end the West may once more choose to stay out of the region. The alternative is the restoration of a Russian security zone, first in the "near-border" states of the former Soviet Union and then possibly in East Central Europe and the Balkans. The recreation of close ties between Russia and Belarus, as evidenced by the inclusion of the latter in the Russian ruble zone and the series of military agreements between Moscow and Minsk, suggest that the process may have already begun.

The January 10, 1994, summit meeting in Brussels demonstrated that NATO is not ready to offer the East Central Europeans a clear timetable for inclusion, preferring instead to rely on the Partnership for Peace formula, which permits cooperation with the former Warsaw Pact countries but extends no explicit security guarantees. In the words of U.S. Secretary of State Warren Christopher, the Partnership for Peace initiative "will be open to all members of the North Atlantic Cooperation Council—which includes the states of the former Warsaw Pact and the former Soviet Union—as well as to other European countries."[1] It remains to be seen whether the formula will indeed serve to narrow the gap between the West and the postcommunist states or whether it will prove to be another exercise in diplomatic futility. Whatever the final outcome, the Partnership for Peace is an implicit recognition of Russia's great power prerogative to reclaim influence along its western border rather than a new integrationist vision. Commenting on the Russian objection to extending NATO eastward, NATO Secretary General Manfred Woerner summarized the Western position, noting on the eve of the Brussels meeting that the opening of the alliance to new partners "will make sense only if it results in the enhancement of European security, not its deterioration."[2]

BETWEEN RUSSIA AND GERMANY: BIPOLARITY REVISITED?

In 1994 the prospects for the integration of postcommunist Europe with the West dimmed after the defeat of the reformist forces in Russia's parliamentary election in the fall of 1993, as best seen in the electoral victory of Vladimir Zhirinovsky's Liberal Democratic Party, and the emergence of a new consensus on Russian foreign policy. In 1994 Russia again pursued a policy reflecting imperial aspirations to a great-power position in Europe. As the economic conditions in Russia worsened, with the 20 percent monthly inflation in December 1993 threatening to escalate into hyperinflation,[3] President Boris Yeltsin apparently accepted the argument that Russia's passion for market reform was over. The resignations from his government of key Russian reformers, including his chief economic advisor, Yegor Gaidar, seem to bear this out. In response to the rising nationalist mood in Russia, Yeltsin adopted a hard-line foreign policy toward the former Soviet republics and the former satellite states. In the words of Yeltsin's spokesman Vyacheslav Kostikov, "The undisputed emphasis in [Russian] foreign policy will be given to the protection of Russia's national interests and the rights of Russians and Russian-speaking people . . . on the basis of pan-national solidarity."[4]

The resurgence of Moscow's influence along the Russian Federation's borders and, possibly, into East Central Europe and the Balkans in the future is remarkable in light of Russia's continued economic crisis and political instability. In large part, the rise of Russian influence in the region is a function of Western inaction. NATO's acceptance of Moscow's implicit right to veto the inclusion of the Visegrad Group in the alliance is a signal that the West may be willing to accept the restoration of a Russian sphere of influence.[5]

Germany is another key external factor in the politics of postcommunist Europe. While Russia appears poised to reclaim its power position in the region, the future role of Germany remains less clear. Since 1990 Germany has been preoccupied with the internal problems attendant to the reintegration of the five new *Länder* into the federal structure. At the same time, however, Bonn has already shown itself to be quite effective in defining West European policy on some regional issues. For instance, Germany was instrumental in bringing about the diplomatic recognition by the European Community of the successor Yugoslav republics. Likewise, the idea of extending NATO membership to selected postcommunist states has enjoyed strong German support from the start, although so far it has failed to win over the United States or France. For Germany, expanding NATO eastward is a matter of national interest, as expansion would stabilize the German periphery and help to insulate the country from possible shocks attendant to the reconstruction in the successor states to the Soviet Union. In the most rudimentary sense, for Bonn it is a decision on whether its security perimeter will end on the Oder-Neisse line or whether it will extend farther east to the Bug River along the eastern border of Poland. In 1993 the German Ministry of Defense in particular encouraged the East Central Europeans to view NATO membership as their ultimate security policy objective, and that position was also supported on several occasions by the German foreign minister, Klaus Kinkel. However, so far Germany has demonstrated a continued willingness to defer to the United States on NATO's strategy in the East, even though its national interests would dictate a more activist security policy in postcommunist Europe. It remains to be seen whether Bonn will continue to adhere to this principle in the future and, if not, in what form stronger German leadership within the alliance might be exercised.

In the United States support for the idea of extending NATO eastward has remained tenuous, although some in the U.S. Congress, for example, the powerful Senator Richard Lugar of Indiana, spoke in favor of such a policy. The Clinton administration has apparently accepted the Russian argument that the inclusion in NATO of selected postcommunist states would be destabilizing. In 1993 U.S. Secretary of State Warren Christopher, an early supporter of NATO's expansion, has shifted his position in favor of the Partnership for Peace formula and the effective postponement of the inclusion of the postcommunist states in the Western alliance. In the end, the issue of whether or not to bring new members into NATO is secondary to the broader question of NATO's future role. In 1993 the ongoing conflict in former Yugoslavia brought about some changes in the way NATO operates and a greater degree of cooperation between NATO and the postcommunist countries, but these fell short of transforming the alliance into a new security system in Europe. The alliance has engaged in "out-of-country" operations to assist the U.N. enforcement of sanctions against Serbia-Montenegro, while the peacekeeping forces in former Yugoslavia include not only NATO but also Polish, Czech, Slovak, and Ukrainian contingents, with Hungary allowing NATO planes to overfly its air space. Still, the changes have not yet gone far enough to remake the alliance from a Western defense organization into a broader European security system.

NATO's rejection of new members has had the ancillary but more immediate effect of further weakening the already strained regional cooperation in central and eastern Europe. Regional initiatives of the postcommunist states were originally defined as a step toward integration with the West. By 1994 these regional groups had all but faded from the scene. The Visegrad Group of Poland, the Czech Republic, Slovakia, and Hungary has continued to exist, but since the dissolution of the Czechoslovak federation there has been a visible lack of enthusiasm in Prague to continue the process. The Pentagonale/Hexagonal group of states in East Central Europe and the Danubian basin, including Italy, Austria, Slovenia, Croatia, the Czech Republic, Slovakia, Hungary, and Poland remained in 1994 largely on paper. Renamed the Central European Initiative, it put its plans for joint projects to improve the region's infrastructure on hold indefinitely because of the Balkan war. Overall, regional cooperation initiatives, with a possible exception of agreements among the Baltic states, have had a limited impact on the direction of postcommunist transformation. The course of change in the four years after the implosion of the Soviet bloc strongly suggests that, short of new initiatives by NATO and the European Union, the postcommunist economic and security order will be reconstituted through bilateral rather than regional agreements. Regionalism has receded into the background as the early optimism about a rapid integration of postcommunist states with the developed European democracies can no longer be sustained.

The prospect of a de facto bipolarity reemerging in Europe, with NATO countries counterbalanced by an increasingly assertive Russia, has raised anxiety in the region. Polish President Lech Walesa warned of the threat of resurgent neocommunism, facilitated by the West's acceptance of Russian influence in the East.[6] The mood of uncertainty in central and eastern Europe has been exacerbated by Yeltsin's 1994 promises to pursue a tougher foreign policy that would protect the rights of the Russian minorities living in the neighboring successor states, as well as to assert the rights of Russia to a strong position in the region.[7] The visible hardening of Moscow's foreign policy stance was underscored by a speech to Russian ambassadors to the CIS delivered by Foreign Minister Andrey Kozyrev on January 19, 1994, in which he asserted that Russia "should not withdraw from those regions which have been the sphere of Russian interests for centuries." In the speech Kozyrev also reportedly asserted that Russia would maintain its military presence in the former Soviet republics, including the Baltic states, to "prevent forces hostile to Russia from filling the security vacuum."[8] Although the inclusion of the Baltics in the Russian sphere of influence was subsequently denied by Kozyrev's aide, the overall thrust of the foreign minister's speech was in line with his earlier statements asserting Russia's intention to restore its domination over the areas conquered over the past centuries of imperial expansion.

The restoration of the traditional pattern of international relations in Europe seems more likely today than just a year ago. Still, even though Russia has been turning away from the path of democracy toward authoritarianism, Germany has remained firmly anchored in the West. This remains the basis for guarded optimism about the future direction of change in postcommunist Europe. Germany's role in the new Europe will ultimately determine whether the postcommunist states will move in the direction of stability and integration with the developed northwestern core of Europe or whether they will retain their peripheral status for years to come. Today, more than at any time since 1989, the question of Germany's new role is pivotal to the future transformation of the former Soviet clients into viable members of the European Union. Given the will to act, Germany has both the national interest and the resources—including its leadership position in Western Europe—needed to stabilize the region.

Reunified Germany is the premier European power today, with a third more population than France, Britain, or Italy and an economic base second to none, notwithstanding the current recession. If postcommunist Europe is to be integrated with the West, Germany will need to assume broader responsibilities for its reconstruction and stability. It has already done so to some degree through direct economic assistance, transfer of expertise, and German direct investment. Since 1989 Germany has contributed more than half of all the aid to the former Soviet bloc countries and, as a quintessential Central European power, it is uniquely positioned to play the leadership role. Although Germany must deal with the legacy of the Third Reich, it also has a historic experience of decentralized regional government, which preceded the Bismarckian reunification. In that sense, Germany may prove better suited than other Western European powers to navigate amid the regionalism and fragmentation of postcommunist Europe. The reunification of Germany, alongside the collapse of the Soviet Union, has been the truly revolutionary change in European politics. The success of the German reunification process will ultimately determine the relative success of reform in postcommunist Europe.

THE IMPACT OF POSTCOMMUNIST NATIONALISM

The West's decision to postpone if not downright reject the aspirations of the postcommunist states to join the existing European institutions is likely to have an impact beyond the immediate uncertainty about the security situation in the region. The decision to defer to Russian pressure to deny NATO membership to the Visegrad Group states, the West's assertions to the contrary notwithstanding, following on the heels of NATO's unwillingness to become decisively engaged in the Balkan war, has strengthened the nationalist forces in the region. There is a danger that resurgent nationalism in the East may yet prove paramount in shaping the political institutions of the new democracies.

In the aftermath of the Cold War nationalism has reemerged in the West as well as in the former Soviet bloc; however, nationalism in postcommunist Europe is fueled not only by the assertions of national separateness or the myth of a glorious past but more importantly by the sense of deprivation and defeat, especially strong when compared with the experience of the nations of Western Europe.[9] The resurgent nationalism in postcommunist Europe owes its vitality to the fact that many of the issues joined in 1914 have remained unresolved, notwithstanding the two interceding world wars and the Cold War. If anything, the outcome of World War II has infused ethnic passions in the East with a grievance against Soviet domination. Postcommunist nationalism is then also a reaction to the half-century of foreign occupation based on an explicitly antinationalist doctrine. In that light, the 1989 implosion of the Soviet bloc can be viewed as much a nationalist anti-Soviet revolt as an anticommunist revolution. The continued hold on power by the former communists in Romania and the return to power of former communists in Lithuania and Poland suggest that postcommunist nationalism could in the end prove dominant in postcommunist reconstruction over democratic and market reform.

The experience of former Yugoslavia and former Czechoslovakia shows that the centrifugal impact of postcommunist nationalism is likely to be felt most strongly in multiethnic states. The prospects of Russia returning as the principal force in postcommunist Europe as well as the closing off of Western Europe to new members are bound to raise nationalist passions in the postcommunist states. Although the postponement of the decision to expand NATO to the East is unlikely immediately to compromise the region's security, the delays in bringing the fragile postcommunist economies closer to the Western European economic system will have a strong negative impact. The West's unwillingness to open up its markets to products from central and eastern Europe will exacerbate the pains of economic reform, thereby aggravating national grievances and strengthening the postcommunist forces.

Over the four years since the collapse of communism, the grand national coalitions that brought about the implosion of the Soviet empire, such as the Polish Solidarity movement, the Czechoslovak Civic Forum, the Hungarian Democratic Forum (MDF), the National Salvation Front in Romania, or the Movement (*Rukh*) in Ukraine, have all fragmented into nascent political parties. The continued detachment from the West will weaken the liberal and centrist forces in eastern and central Europe and is bound to strengthen the postcommunist nationalist and chauvinist movements, thus undermining the prospects for democracy in the region. The demonstrated unwillingness on the part of the Western Europeans to include the aspiring postcommunist democracies in the existing economic and security institutions has already led to manifest disillusionment in postcommunist Europe with the Western European ability to lead.

THE RETURN OF HISTORY

The postcommunist transformation of the former Soviet clients has been traumatic and will no doubt impose additional strains on intra-European relations for years to come. Most of all, it will take much longer than originally anticipated for the fragile markets and nascent democratic institutions to become sufficiently stable to make the promise of the region's integration with Western Europe a realistic option. It may take much longer still for the volatile postcommunist nationalism to settle into a pattern of political compromise and collaboration. For now, with the possible exception of East Central Europe, the postcommunist states have few prospects for joining the West in the foreseeable future.

Judging from the experience of the past four years, and especially in light of the continued lack of a comprehensive Western strategy toward postcommunist states, it appears that the best hope they have lies not in the promise of future pan-European institutions but in the political realism of their own governments today. The lessons learned by the two successor states to the Czechoslovak federation are a case in point: The Czech Republic's consistency in pursuing economic reform has gone a long way toward making it a potentially attractive partner for the West; in contrast, Slovakia's reversal to populism at home and to nationalism in foreign policy have pushed the country further away from Europe than it had been at any time after 1989. Likewise, the war in the Balkans has solidified the new fault lines separating Europe's northwestern core from its southeastern periphery.

In the interim, the region remains volatile, with its southeastern periphery especially prone to destabilization. The ongoing war in former Yugoslavia, with NATO's attendant reluctance to become directly involved, and the reassertion of Russian influence in its "near-border" areas—especially the increasing Russian pressure on Ukraine—suggest that the West may opt for a new division of Europe based on economic rather than security considerations. Another danger is that the continued security vacuum may in the end reignite the rivalry between Germany and Russia.[10]

In the conditions of rising nationalism and the emergence of new nation-states, the problem of ethnic minority rights is bound to remain a powerful factor in the politics of postcommunist Europe. The war in former Yugoslavia, the breakup of the Czechoslovak federation, and the rising tensions between Hungary and Romania over the treatment of the Hungarian minority in Transylvania are clear reminders that, absent the mitigating influence of a supranational political and security organization, the ethnic minorities issue will shape postcommunist politics in the foreseeable future.

The early optimistic expectations of the rapid reintegration of the developed West with the postcommunist states have proven to be unfounded. Arguably, the most formidable challenge facing the region is the task of economic reconstruction. Considering the severity of the economic problems at hand, one can fully appreciate that open access to Europe is vital to the success of market reform in the eastern and central European countries. Membership in the European Union, and hence unimpeded access to the Western markets is the sine qua non of their continued movement toward democracy. The question of economic access, rather than the immediate security considerations that have informed the ongoing debate about extending NATO eastward, is at the heart of the problems confronting postcommunist Europe. Without access to Western markets, even the most successful postcommunist economies such as Poland and the Czech Republic will be saddled with double-digit structural unemployment, the attendant social dislocations, and vulnerability to the populist manipulation of the domestic political arena.

The pressures of change in eastern and central Europe are overwhelming. Still, the "return of history" in postcommunist Europe, notwithstanding the complexity and intractability of the current economic, political, and security dilemmas, holds a promise for the future. As the old grievances are revisited, these countries will have begun to address the complex problems bequeathed to them by the foreign domination by the great empires of the nineteenth and twentieth centuries. One should not be tempted to reminisce wistfully about the region's tranquility during the Soviet era; suffice it to remember that in the final analysis the calm was superficial at best.

The economic and political conditions in eastern and central Europe in early 1994 give one few reasons for optimism. Nevertheless, regardless of whether the postcommunist countries succeed or not in their effort to remake themselves into viable sovereign states, the opportunity to revisit history granted them by the ending of the Cold War has been a step on the road to their emancipation.

NOTES

1. Warren Christopher, "A Partnership for Peace Open to Former Warsaw Pact Members," *International Herald Tribune*, January 10, 1994, p. 6.

2. Manfred Woerner, "Kotwica Europy," *Wprost*, January 9, 1994, p. 48.

3. Peter Reddaway, "Russia Is in Trouble, and Outsiders Can't Provide Much Help," *International Herald Tribune*, January 10, 1994, p. 6.

4. Leyla Boulton, "Yeltsin Pledges Tough Foreign Policy to Please Right Wing," *Financial Times*, January 4, 1994, p. 1.

5. For an analysis of the new foreign policy consensus in Russia, see Suzanne Crow, "Russia Asserts Its Strategic Agenda," *RFE/RL Research Report*, December 17, 1993, pp. 1–8.

6. "Walesa Says NATO Risks New Communist Threat," *International Herald Tribune*, January 4, 1994, p. 1.

7. Boulton, "Yeltsin Pledges Tough Foreign Policy to Please Right Wing," p. 1.

8. "Kozyrev Statement and Denial on Baltics," *RFE/RL Daily Report*, January 19, 1994.

9. This cogent observation has been raised by the former Polish foreign minister Krzysztof Skubiszewski in "Nacjonalizm w dzisiejszej Europie," in the July–September 1993 issue of *Sprawy Miedzynarodowe* (Warsaw: PISM, 1993).

10. This has been the view taken by a group of senior analysts at the RAND Corporation. See Ronald D. Asmus, Richard L. Kugler, and F. Stephen Larrabee, "Building a New NATO," *Foreign Affairs*, September/October 1993, p. 30.

SELECTED BIBLIOGRAPHY

Antanaytis, Yustinas A. *Sotsyalisticheskoye sorevenovaniye i intensifikatsiya proizvodstva.* Moscow: Profizdat, 1987.

Armstrong, John A. *Ukrainian Nationalism*, 2d ed. New York and London: Columbia University Press, 1963.

Baltic States: A Reference Book. Tallinn, Riga, and Vilnius: Estonian Encyclopedia Publishers, Latvian Encyclopedia Publishers, and Lithuanian Encyclopedia Publishers, 1991.

Baltiyskaya Assambleya: Tallinn 13–14 Maya, 1989. Tallinn: Narodnyy Front Estonii, 1989.

"Baltic States" Collection, Hoover Institution Archives, Stanford, California.

Banac, Ivo. *The National Question in Yugoslavia: Origins, History, Politics.* Ithaca, N.Y.: Cornell University Press, 1984.

Banac, Ivo, ed. *Eastern Europe in Revolution.* Ithaca, N.Y.: Cornell University Press, 1992.

Batt, Judy. *East Central Europe from Reform to Transformation.* London: Pinter Publishers, 1991.

Beljo, Ante. *Yugoslavia Genocide: A Documented Analysis.* Sudbury, Ontario: Northern Tribune Publishing, 1985.

Beloff, Nora. *Tito's Flawed Legacy: Yugoslavia and the West: 1939–84.* London: Victor Gollancz, 1985.

Benkovic, Theodore. *The Tragedy of a Nation.* East European Collection, "Croatia" Collection, Hoover Institution Archives, Stanford, California.

Bilinsky, Yaroslav. *The Second Soviet Republic: The Ukraine after World War II.* New Brunswick, N.J.: Rutgers University Press, 1964.

Bilmanis, Alfred. *Baltic Essays.* Washington, D.C.: Latvian Legation, 1945.

Bonifacic, Antun F., and Clement S. Mihanovich. *The Croatian Nation in Its Struggle for Freedom and Independence.* Chicago: "Croatia" Cultural Publishing Center, 1955.

Borys, Jurij. *The Russian Communist Party and the Sovietization of Ukraine.* Stockholm: Kungl. Boktryckeriet P.A. Norstedt & Soner, 1960.

Bregy, Pierre, and Prince Serge Obolensky. *L'Ukraine: terre russe.* Paris: Gallimard, 1939.

Brown, J. F. *Eastern Europe and Communist Rule.* Durham, N.C.: Duke University Press, 1988.

Brzezinski, Zbigniew. *The Grand Failure: The Birth and Death of Communism in the Twentieth Century*. New York: Charles Scribner's Sons, 1989.

———. *The Soviet Bloc: Unity and Conflict*. New York: Frederick A. Praeger, 1961.

Butler, Ralph. *The New Eastern Europe*. London: Longmans, Green, and Co., 1919.

Chase, Thomas. *The Story of Lithuania*. New York: Stratford House, 1946.

Crampton, R. J. *A Short History of Modern Bulgaria*. Cambridge: Cambridge University Press, 1989.

The Creation and Changes of the Internal Borders of Yugoslavia. Belgrade: The Ministry of Information of the Republic of Serbia, 1991.

Croatia 1990. Zagreb: The Presidency of the Republic of Croatia, 1990.

Cronica insingerata a Bucurestului in revolutie. Bucharest: Tineretul liber, 1990.

Cvvic, Christopher. *Remaking the Balkans*. New York: Council on Foreign Relations, 1991.

Darski, Jozef. *Ukraina*. Warsaw: Instytut Polityczny, 1993.

Davis, Norman. *God's Playground: A History of Poland*, vols. 1 and 2. New York: Columbia University Press, 1984.

Djilas, Aleksa. *The Contested Country: Yugoslav Unity and Communist Revolution, 1919–1953*. Cambridge, Mass.: Harvard University Press, 1991.

Ecoglasnost-Plovdiska Oblast: Ustav na Nezavisimo Sdruzheniye s Nestopansk Tsel. Plovdiv: Ecoglasnost, 1989. East European Collection, "Bulgaria" Collection, Hoover Institution Archives, Stanford, California.

Economic Survey of the Baltic Republics: A study undertaken by an independent team of experts on the initiative of the Swedish Ministry for Foreign Affairs in collaboration with the government authorities of Estonia, Latvia, and Lithuania. Stockholm, June 1991, draft. Hoover Institution Library, Stanford, California.

Elections in the Baltic States and Soviet Republics: A Compendium of Reports on Parliamentary Elections Held in 1990. Washington, D.C.: Commission on Security and Cooperation in Europe, December 1990.

Fischer-Galati, Stephen. *Rumania in Transition*. Ruston, La.: American Foreign Policy Center, 1991.

Gerutis, Albertas, ed. *Lithuania: 700 Years*. New York: Manyland Books, 1969.

Griffith, William E. *Central and Eastern Europe: The Opening Curtain*. Boulder, Colo.: Westview Press, 1989.

Harrison, E. J. *Lithuania: Past and Present*. London: T. Fisher Unwin, 1922.

Hefer, Stjepan. *Croatian Struggle for Freedom and Statehood*. Croatian Liberation Movement, 1979. Place of publication in the United States not given; first published in Argentina.

Hint, Mati. *Balti Tee (The Baltic Way)*. Tallinn: Valgus, 1989.

Hryshko, Vasyl. *Experience with Russia*. New York: Ukrainian Congress Committee of America, 1956.

Jelavich, Barbara. *History of the Balkans*, vols. 1 and 2. Cambridge: Cambridge University Press, 1990.

Jelavich, Charles. *South Slav Nationalisms: Textbooks and Yugoslav Union before 1914*. Columbus, Ohio: Ohio State University Press, 1990.

Jelavich, Charles, and Barbara Jelavich, eds. *The Balkans in Transition*. Berkeley, Calif.: Archon Books, 1974.

Jurgela, Constantine R. *History of the Lithuanian Nation*. New York: Lithuanian Cultural Institute, 1948.

Kaluski, Marian. *Litwa: 600-lecie chrzescijanstwa 1387–1987*. London: Veritas Foundation Publication Centre, 1987.

Karotki aglyad gistoryi Belarusi. Tallinn: Belaruskaye Kulturnaye Tavarystva "Grunvald," 1990.

Kongress Estonii: Spetsyal'nyy vypusk glavnogo komiteta grazhdan estonskoy respubliki. Tallinn: GKGER, February 24, 1990.

Laird, Robbin F. *The Soviets, Germany, and the New Europe.* Boulder, Colo.: Westview Press, 1991.

Lampe, John R., and Marvin R. Jackson. *Balkan Economic History, 1550–1950.* Bloomington: Indiana University Press, 1982.

Legters, Lyman H. *Eastern Europe: Transformation and Revolution, 1945–1991.* Lexington, Mass.: D. C. Heath, 1992.

Lithuania Survey: A Businessman's Guide, 3d ed. Vilnius: Lithuanian Information Institute of the Government of the Republic of Lithuania, 1992.

Lithuanian Reform Movement Sajudis. Vilnius, 1989. "Baltic States" Collection, Hoover Institution Archives, Stanford, California.

Lithuanian Way 1. Vilnius: Lithuanian Reform Movement Sajudis, 1990. "Baltic States" Collection, Hoover Institution Archives, Stanford, California.

Marples, David R. *Ukraine under Perestroika: Ecology, Economics, and the Workers' Revolt.* New York: St. Martin's Press, 1991.

Maryanski, Andrzej. *Litwa, Lotwa, Estonia.* Warsaw: Wydawnictwo Naukowe PWN, 1993.

Materials of the 11th Extraordinary Congress of the Independent Bulgarian Trade Unions— Constituent Congress of the Confederation of Independent Syndicates in Bulgaria. Sofia: Sofia Press, 1990. East European Collection, "Bulgaria" Collection, Hoover Institution Archives, Stanford, California.

Mauclere, Jean. *La rayonnement de la France en Lithuanie.* Le Raincy: Les Editions Claires, 1946.

Meiksnis, Gregory. *The Baltic Riddle: Finland, Estonia, Latvia, Lithuania—Key-Points of European Peace.* New York: L. B. Fischer, 1943.

Michta, Andrew A. *East Central Europe after the Warsaw Pact: Security Dilemmas in the 1990s.* Westport, Conn.: Greenwood Press, 1992.

———. *Red Eagle: The Army in Polish Politics, 1944–1988.* Stanford, Calif.: Hoover Press, 1990.

1991 Military Forces in Transition. Washington, D.C.: U.S. Department of Defense, 1991.

Omrcanin, Ivo. *Dramatis Personae and Finis of the Independent State of Croatia in American and British Documents.* Bryn Mawr, Penn.: Dorrance & Company, 1983.

———. *Military History of Croatia.* Bryn Mawr, Penn.: Dorrance & Company, 1984.

Osnovni Dokumenti na Sindikalnite Tsentrali v Bylgariya: Sbornik ot Programi, Ustvi, Deklaratsii, Obr'shcheniya, Sporazumeniya. Sofia: Konfederatsiya na Nezavisimite Sindikati v Bylgariya, 1990. East European Collection, "Bulgaria" Collection, Hoover Institution Archives, Stanford, California.

Osnovnyye dokumenty vtorogo s'yezda Sayudisa. Vilnius: Sayudis Litvy, 1990.

Partie Polityczne w Polsce. Warsaw: Polska Agencja Informacyjna, 1991.

Pavlowitch, Stevan K. *The Improbable Survivor: Yugoslavia and Its Problems, 1918–1988.* London: C. Hurst and Company, 1988.

Petruitis, Jonas. *Lithuania under the Sickle and Hammer.* Cleveland, Ohio: The League for the Liberation of Lithuania, 1942.

Pick, F. W. *The Baltic Nations: Estonia, Latvia, and Lithuania.* London: Boreas Publishing Co., 1945.

Pilon, Juliana Geran. *The Bloody Flag: Post-Communist Nationalism in Eastern Europe, Spotlight on Romania.* New Brunswick, N.J.: Transaction Publishers, 1992.

Pinder, John. *The European Community and Eastern Europe.* London: Pinter Publishers, 1991.

Platforma Program a Frontului Salvarii Nationale din Romania. Bucharest: FSNR, 1990. East European Collection, "Romania" Collection, Hoover Institution Archives, Stanford, California.

Platform of the Confederation of Independent Syndicates in Bulgaria. Sofia: Sofia Press Publishers, 1990. East European Collection, "Bulgaria" Collection, Hoover Institution Archives, Stanford, California.

Political Parties in Eastern Europe. Munich: RFE/RL Research, February 1990.

Politicheski Partii i Dvizheniya v Republika Bylgariya. Sofia: Konfederatsiya na Nezavisimite Sindikati v Bylgariya, 1990. East European Collection, "Bulgaria" Collection, Hoover Institution Archives, Stanford, California.

Polska Akademia Nauk i Instytut Polsko-Radziecki. *Seja Naukowa w Trzechsetna Rocznice Zjednoczenia Ukrainy z Rosja, 1654–1954*. Warsaw: Panstwowe Wydawnictwo Naukowe, 1956.

Potichnyj, Peter J., ed. *Poland and Ukraine: Past and Present*. Edmonton and Toronto: The Canadian Institute of Ukrainian Studies, 1980.

Poulton, Hugh. *The Balkans: Minorities and States in Conflict*. London: Minority Rights Group Publications, 1991.

Ramzenko, Vsevolod. *Chomu mi za Ukrainsku samostiynu derzhavu*. Lvov: Atlas, 1991. "Ukrainian" Collection, Hoover Institution Archives, Stanford, California.

Ratesh, Nestor. *Romania: The Entangled Revolution*. New York and Westport, Conn.: Praeger, 1991.

Revolt against Silence: The State of Human Rights in Romania. Washington, D.C.: U.S. Commission on Security and Cooperation in Europe, 1989.

Roskin, Michael G. *The Rebirth of East Europe*. Englewood Cliffs, N.J.: Prentice Hall, 1994.

Rothschild, Joseph. *East Central Europe between the Two World Wars*. Seattle and London: University of Washington Press, 1992.

——— . *Return to Diversity: A Political History of East Central Europe since World War II*. New York and Oxford: Oxford University Press, 1993.

Rozauskas, E., ed. *Documents Accuse*. Vilnius: Gintaras, 1970.

Rudnitsky, Stephen. *Ukraine, The Land and Its People: An Introduction to Its Geography*. New York: Rand McNally and Co., 1918.

Rutter, Owen. *The New Baltic States and Their Future: An Account of Lithuania, Latvia, and Estonia*. London: Methuen and Co., 1925.

Sacks, A. A. *An Excursion to Lithuania*. New York: Hudson Bay Press, 1934.

Senn, Alfred Erich. *The Emergence of Modern Lithuania*. New York: Columbia University Press, 1959.

——— . *Lithuania Awakening*. Berkeley, Calif.: University of California Press, 1990.

Shafir, Michael. *Romania: Politics, Economics and Society*. London: Pinter Publishers, 1985.

Slyusarenko, A. G., and M. V. Tomenko. *Novi politichni partii Ukraini*. Kiev: Tovaristvo "Znannya" Ukrainskoi RSR, 1990.

Staar, Richard F. *Communist Regimes in Eastern Europe*. Stanford, Calif.: Hoover Press, 1988.

Staar, Richard F., ed. *Transition to Democracy in Poland*. New York: St. Martin's Press, 1993.

Statistisches Bundesamt, ed. *Country Reports: Central and Eastern Europe, 1991*. Luxemburg: Statistical Office of the European Communities EUROSTAT, 1991.

Stokes, Gale. *The Walls Came Tumbling Down: The Collapse of Communism in Eastern Europe*. New York and Oxford: Oxford University Press, 1993.

Subtelny, Orest. *Ukraine: A History*. Toronto: University of Toronto Press, 1992.

Sugar, Peter F., ed. *A History of Hungary*. Bloomington: Indiana University Press, 1990.

Szajkowski, Bogdan. *New Political Parties of Eastern Europe and the Soviet Union*. London: Longman Group, 1991.

Terry, Sarah Meiklejohn, ed. *Soviet Policy in Eastern Europe*. New Haven, Conn.: Yale University Press, 1984.

The Road to Negotiations with the USSR. Vol. 1, *May 1990–May 1991*, 2d rev. ed. Vilnius: State Publishing Centre, 1991.

Tonchev, Vasil, and Lidiya Yordanova. *Izbori 1991: Obshchestvenoto Meniniye v Bylgariya*. Sofia: Logis, 1991. East European Collection, "Bulgaria" Collection, Hoover Institution Archives, Stanford, California.

Tych, Feliks, ed. *Socjaldemokracja Krolestwa Polskiego i Litwy: Materialy i Dokumenty*, vols. 1–3. Warsaw: Ksiazka i Wiedza, 1962.

Ukraina, politicheskaya oppositsya. Moscow: Panorama, 1991.

Ustav na Zelenata Partiya v Bylgariya. Sofia: Zelenata Partiya, 1989. East European Collection, "Bulgaria" Collection, Hoover Institution Archives, Stanford, California.

Vakar, Nicholas P. *Belorussia: The Making of a Nation*. Cambridge, Mass.: Harvard University Press, 1956.

Wandycz, Piotr. *The Lands of Partitioned Poland, 1795–1918*. Seattle and London: University of Washington Press, 1993.

Wanklyn, H. G. *The Eastern Marshlands of Europe*. London: George Philip and Son, 1941.

War Crimes against Croatia. Zagreb: "Vecernji list," 1991.

Winnifrith, Tom, ed. *Perspectives on Albania*. New York: St. Martin's Press, 1992.

Wolchik, Sharon L. *Czechoslovakia in Transition: Politics, Economics and Society*. London: Pinter Publishers, 1991.

Yefremenko, A. P. *Agrarnyye preobrazovaniya i nachalo sotsialisticheskogo stroitel'stva w litovskoy derevnye v 1940–1941 godakh*. Vilnius: Akademiya Nauk Litovskoy SSR, 1972.

Zakon o yazyke. Tallinn: Olion, 1990.

Ziugzda, Robertas. *Lithuania and Western Powers, 1917–1940*. Vilnius: Mintis Publishers, 1987.

INDEX

About the Author

ANDREW A. MICHTA is Associate Professor and Mertie W. Buckman Chair of International Studies at Rhodes College, Memphis, Tennessee. A specialist in East and Central European politics and security issues, Professor Michta has published extensively, including *East Central Europe after the Warsaw Pact* (Greenwood, 1992).